The Best Flatwater Paddles in Oregon

MORE THAN 50 GREAT PLACES TO TAKE YOUR
STANDUP PADDLEBOARDS, KAYAK, OR CANOE

Christopher Heaps

Voyageur Media LLC
Portland, OR

Copyright © 2017 by Christopher Heaps.

All rights reserved. No part of this book may be reproduced in any written, electronic, recording, or photocopying without written permission of the publisher or author. The exception would be in the case of brief quotations embodied in articles or reviews and pages where permission is specifically granted by the publisher or author. All content, maps, and photography by the author.

Voyageur Media LLC
2224 N Willamette Blvd
Portland, OR 97217
www.oregonpaddles.com
Printed in USA

Although every precaution has been taken to verify the accuracy of the information contained herein, the author and publisher assume no responsibility for any errors or omissions. No liability is assumed for damages that may result from the use of information contained within.

Corrections or updates may be provided at the website above.

Cover: The author taking a break from paddling Hosmer Lake beneath South Sister

Back: Boulders at the bottom of Waldo Lake (top); my Salem watches sunset at Waldo Lake (bottom)

The Best Flatwater Paddles in Oregon/ Christopher Heaps -- 1st ed.

ISBN 978-0-9982148-2-5 Print Edition
ISBN 978-0-9982148-3-2 Ebook Edition

Library of Congress Control Number: 2017910716

Contents

Introduction 1

Paddling Tips 4

Dogs on the Board 8

Best-of Lists 10

The Best Flatwater Paddles in Oregon – Statewide Map 13

Map Key 14

I. The Coast and Coast Range

   1. Salmon River Estuary: Beautiful Cascade Head and a picnic-perfect beach 15

   2. Yaquina Bay: A historic coastal town with a bustling port, lots of marine life, and miles of wetlands 21

   3. Beaver Creek: Pristine coastal wetlands and beach access 28

   4. Alsea Bay and Drift Creek: A peaceful bay shared with fishers and crabbers and a secluded creek 33

   5. Lower Siuslaw River: Endless wetlands along a lightly-traveled river 37

   6. Siltcoos River: Six miles of serenity between the ocean and the lake 42

   7. Loon Lake: A beautiful and secluded, but well-shared, mountain lake 49

   8. Eel Lake: The dedicated paddler's paddle 54

   9. Other Good Places to Paddle – The Coast and Coast Range 58

II. The Lower Columbia and Greater Portland

10. Lewis and Clark National Wildlife Refuge: History and wilderness on the Mighty Columbia 61

11. Columbia River at St Helens: Island camping, beaches, an old lighthouse, and historic St Helens 65

12. Upper Gilbert River and Sturgeon Lake: Experience the other side of Portland's island 69

13. Lower Gilbert River (Sauvie Island): Quiet paddling on Portland's bayou 74

14. Scappoose Bay and Cunningham Slough: Outstanding solitude and wildlife viewing, just minutes from Portland.. 77

15. Scappoose Bay and Scappoose Creek: Another remote bayou paddle close to Portland 82

16. Willamette River at Portland: Paddle through the middle of America's best big city 86

17. Other Good Places to Paddle – The Lower Columbia and Greater Portland 95

III. Willamette Valley

18. Lower Luckiamute & Middle Willamette River: Wildlife and river camping on the Willamette 97

19. Middle Willamette River: Paddle through the heart of the valley 103

20. Coyote Creek and Fern Ridge Lake: Eugene's bayou . 108

21. Other Good Places to Paddle – The Willamette Valley 112

IV. Cascades – North

22. Lost Lake (Mt Hood): "Heart of the Mountains" 113

23. Timothy Lake: By far the best thing about Clackamas County 117

24. Olallie Lakes: A group of small but fantastically secluded mountain lakes 123

25. Other Good Places to Paddle – The Cascades – North 131

V. Cascades – Central

26. Leaburg Lake / McKenzie River: See one of Oregon's few remaining historic covered bridges and enjoy the McKenzie without the rapids 133

27. Blue River Lake: Paddle through an isolated conifer canyon 137

28. Clear Lake (McKenzie River): The best small lake paddle in Oregon 141

29. Big Lake: Great swimming, great views, and nice beaches, not particularly big 145

30. Other Good Places to Paddle – The Cascades – Central 148

VI. High Cascade Lakes

31. Sparks Lake: Lava fjords! 149

32. Hosmer Lake: The best wetland paddle in Oregon 154

33. Lava Lake, Little Lava Lake, and the Blue Pools: Paradise at the headwaters of the Deschutes River 158

34. Little Cultus Lake: A quiet lake, good for learning 163

35. Waldo Lake – North: The crown jewel of Oregon paddling 166

36. Waldo Lake – South: The crown jewel of Oregon paddling, Part II 170

37. Gold Lake: Yes, it really is golden! 173

38. Davis Lake: Solitude, wildlife, lava fjords, and electric green water 176

39. Crescent Lake: Beautiful sandy beaches waiting for you! 182

40. Summit Lake: The best paddle in the whole state!...... 185

41. Paulina Lake and East Lake: Paddle in the crater of a volcano, soak in hot springs.. 188

42. Other Good Places to Paddle – The High Cascade Lakes:194

VII. Southern Oregon

43. Squaw Lakes: A tiny, hidden beauty with sweet rope swings.. 197

44. Wood River: A challenging paddle on a crystal-clear, spring-fed creek 201

45. Upper Klamath Canoe Trail: Endless wetlands filled with wildlife... 205

46. Other Good Places to Paddle – Southern Oregon 209

VIII. Eastern Oregon

47. Wallowa Lake: A majestic lake in The Alps of Oregon 211

48. Hells Canyon Reservoir – Big Bar: Paddle through the deepest gorge in North America..................................... 216

49. Hells Canyon Reservoir – Oxbow Dam: Paddle through the deepest gorge in North America, Part II 220

50. Powder River / Brownlee Reservoir: A remote desert canyon at The Crappie Capital of the Northwest................... 224

51. Owyhee Reservoir: The most isolated flatwater paddle in Oregon 227

Bibliography 231

To my B, for believing in me, and for inspiring me every day;

To Jason and Alice, for making this project financially viable, and for sharing a great summer with me;

And to my Salem, the best paddling buddy anyone could ever ask for.

Introduction

"One touch of nature makes the whole world kin."
-Shakespeare

"Not what we have, but what we enjoy, constitutes our abundance." -Epicurus

I tried standup paddleboarding on the high Cascade Lakes, in central Oregon, in the summer of 2014 with my wife, and I fell in love with it. The following summer, we paddled several more places, and by 2016 I decided I wanted to paddle all of the best places in Oregon and catalogue them for people like me who would want to explore new places to paddle. So, I paddled at nearly 70 places around the state, and scouted several more.

This book really started with the pure joy of standup paddling and the desire to share that with others. But then I realized that helping connect people to the natural world is a very important and powerful thing. It's only when people see the beauty and appreciate the connectedness of humans and the natural world that they are willing to stand up for clean water, sustainable development, and sensible climate change policies. So, whether you've got (or want to get) a standup paddleboard (SUP), kayak, or canoe, my hope is that this book will help you enjoy Oregon's waters and, in that way, help ensure they remain protected and open to public use.

The paddles in this book are generally described as "*flatwater*," meaning that there is no whitewater (big waves) involved. Most of the paddles are on lakes, where there is no current or surf. Others are on smaller rivers or creeks in places where the current is minimal. But some of the paddles stretch the definition of flatwater a little bit. For example, the Columbia River at St Helens paddle is done on one of the biggest rivers on the continent, with a strong current, occasionally big waves, and other challenges.

The idea in selecting the paddles was to include all the best places to enjoy a day on the water. That can mean different things to different people, of course. Fortunately, there is enough diversity in Oregon's waters that I have been able to include a broad range of experiences, from places where beginners will feel comfortable learning to paddle, to hardcore adventures on the board, and everything in between. I have highly valued places where paddlers can see the state's outstanding wildlife and scenery, experience wilderness and near-wilderness places from the water, and avoid close interactions with motorboats.

I have written descriptions of each of the best paddles and created accompanying maps. The maps focus on important details of the paddle, and are not suitable as a navigation aid. I have exaggerated the size of certain features, such as beaches, to better show their relative position. And I have left out other details, such as minor or irrelevant roads or buildings.

I have included detailed information about the difficulty and distance of all the best paddles as well. For riverine paddles, I have included river mile markers where that information was available. Please treat the distance figures as approximate. In most cases, I measured the distances with my GPS. But sometimes I take little side excursions, and other times I have not used a GPS but simply measured distances using my physical maps. Like all the other information in this book, I believe the distances are accurate. But like R-2, I have been known to make mistakes, from time to time. If you find a mistake in this book, please let me know.

I have also included directions on how to find the launch and return points for each paddle, as well as nearby places to rent a board or boat, nearby campgrounds, and occasionally fun things to do in the area. I've tried to include details such as whether drinking water is available at a site, how much (if anything) it costs to park, and whether there are toilets. This information may change, of course, so you will need to do your own fact-finding before planning your trip. The idea is simply to let you know what's available, so that you can call ahead and make camping reservations, for example.

Where the paddle description refers to a "primitive" launch, it means an area where you can hand-carry a board or boat to and from the shoreline, and where it refers to a "formal" launch, it means a boat ramp accessible by vehicle. Where the description refers to "river left" and "river right" it is referring to the right and left side of the river, respectively, when looking downstream.

Paddling Tips

I have done a lot of paddling in the past few years, and I have learned a good deal about how to minimize the hassles and maximize the fun of paddling. Since this book is all about having the best paddling experiences, I want to share some of the more important things I have learned. If you are interested in a book about the basics of paddling, including paddling techniques, how to pick the best gear, and how to paddle safely, I recommend *The Art of Stand Up Paddling*, which fits the bill nicely and also does a good job of covering the history, people, and culture of stand up paddlboarding as well.

It should be obvious to even the dullest of people that there are risks to activities like paddling, and you can even die doing it. Understanding the nature and extent of the risks you face is key to avoiding problems. As they say on *South Park*, if you go paddling unprepared, *you're gonna have a bad time*. There are three important sources of considerations in any outdoor adventure: the environment, your gear, and your capabilities.

Conditions: Weather, Current, Wind, and Tide. Start by understanding the predicted whether and what weather is possible in the area at that time of year. You don't just need to know basics such as the low temperature and the chance of rain. For paddling, you will also want to know the predicted wind speed and direction throughout the day. If you are paddling anywhere along the Coast, the lower Columbia River, Sauvie Island, or the Portland area, you will also need to know the times and sizes of the high and low tides for the day. If you are paddling in a river, you will want to know the direction and strength of the current. If you want to try paddling at night, you will want to know moonrise and moonset times.

The average speed for a reasonably fit paddler will be between two and four miles per hour. This can vary quite a bit based on the current, wind, and tide. Knowing your likely speed will allow you to know how long it will likely take you to paddle a set distance. These three factors – current, wind, and tide (current and tide when applicable, of course) – should be vetted in detail before paddling. At a minimum, these variables will affect your paddling speed. And for the best paddling experience, they can be managed to minimize your effort.

Where river current is a factor, for example, it makes sense to paddle upriver – against the current – first, so that your are assisted by the current on the return trip when you are more tired. If the water is tidal, picking a time when the tide is flowing opposite the current will minimize the current's effects. For low-volume rivers, the effect of the tide can be stronger than that of the current.

Paddling at high tide will minimize one of the most important hazards for paddleboards, the risk of snagging the fin(s) on an object hidden in the water. Anything within a foot of the surface could stop your board cold and send you hurtling forward. Always keep an eye on the water directly in front of you, and be especially vigilant in murky water. The most common snag hazards are stumps and tree limbs – they are literally everywhere near shorelines in Oregon (and sometimes not so near as well).

And then there is the wind. Wind is the single most important weather-related variable for a paddler to consider.

A headwind can slow your pace considerably and a sufficiently strong wind can totally stop forward progress for even strong paddlers. You don't want to find yourself pinned down several miles from your return point. Fortunately, it's easy to both avoid the wind and minimize its detrimental effects.

Each day in Oregon under normal conditions, the wind speed varies in a sine wave. The windiest time of the day is around sunset, and the calmest time of the day is around sunrise. Thus, the best time of the day to paddle is in the morning because it is the least windy. If you are able to launch by 8 or 9 am, the wind will be increasing throughout the paddle, but you should be able to enjoy at least a few hours of paddling with low winds. To facilitate getting on the water early, I typically camp at or near the launch point the night before.

But, as they say, wind happens. For some paddles, such as circling around a lake, you can't do much planning to avoid the wind. But for paddles that have a clear ordinal direction, plan to go against the wind at the beginning of the paddle if possible so that you will be paddling with the wind on your return, when you are more tired.

And when you find yourself struggling to paddle into a wind, sit down. Paddling from your knees negates most of the wind drag and will allow you to make good progress even in a strong wind. It takes some getting used to paddling with the longer SUP paddle from a kneeling position, but it can actually be more effective because the strokes are shorter and therefore quicker.

The best daily wind forecasts I have found are on the Weather Underground website (wunderground.com). Tide charts are available online at tidesandcurrents.noaa.gov.

<u>Suggested and Required Gear.</u> Once you know what conditions to expect, you can make a decision about whether to paddle, as well as what gear to choose. One piece of gear I always use, except perhaps on very hot days, is a wet suit. I get a great deal of confidence on the board from knowing that I will be warm enough to continue paddling even if I get soaked.

Another key piece of gear is my navigation equipment. I run a GPS-based navigation app on my phone whenever I am in a new place or could possibly get lost. To support it, I carry an extra phone battery and connection cord, all in a dry bag. And of course I'm not going to let my phone end up on the bottom of the lake, so I also ensure I have the gear to strap it securely to myself or my board. I recommend you use the same setup. With the technology available now, there really is very little excuse for getting lost any more.

There is also some gear you are legally required to choose and carry, specifically a personal flotation device (PFD)/life vest, a whistle, and an Invasive Species Permit. It is possible to get a citation from a boat cop for not having these things onboard. You can purchase the permit online for $7 at the Oregon State Marine Board website.

You can be well-prepared, but it won't matter if you forget something. If you're as absentminded as I am, it is not out of the question that you might leave home without something as important as your paddle, only to realize where it is as you unload your board after a two-hour drive. That has not actually happened to me so far because I use a pre-paddle checklist that ensures I don't leave anything important behind, and I recommend you do the same.

<u>Your Capabilities.</u> Lastly, as Harry Callahan once famously said, a man's got to know his limitations. So does a woman. Paddling is a lot like riding a bike in that it is a repetitive exercise isolating one set of limbs and the core. Will your shoulders be sore after six miles of paddling? Will you have enough endurance to paddle back upriver against the current after paddling three miles downriver? Understanding your own capabilities is the final piece of the puzzle in selecting the right place to paddle.

Have fun out there!

Dogs on the Board

I love taking my dog on the board with me. When we first started paddling together, she dumped me into the water more than a few times by getting a little too excited and leaping from the board (like that time she saw some deer on the shore). I've learned a thing or two about keeping dogs still and happy on the board, so here are a few considerations that might make things go more smoothly for you too.

First, consider the weight rating of your board. Only longer boards will be big enough to safely carry both of you if you or your dog is on the heavier side. Second, make sure your dog has a "traction" area on the board so she doesn't slide around or fall off. Just like you, your dog's feet will have no traction on the smooth enamel parts of the board, only on the softer decking pad. You can buy decking pads to stick to your board if the existing area is not adequate for the dog.

Second, spend some time working on the "sit" and "stay" commands before your first paddle. Get your dog familiar with the board in shallow water first. Give the commands and a reward while you are both sitting on the board. Emphasize the "stay" command and then try paddling a little. At this point, you will know whether you can start a longer paddle, need to do some more training work, or perhaps it is better to paddle solo. If it does work out, I also recommend adding a "release" command. For example, when we are coming into land my dog knows to stay put until I say "OK," at which point it is ok for her to jump off the board.

Once you're up and paddling, there are a few other things you can do to keep things gliding along smoothly. I recommend getting your dog a "float coat," which is basically a doggie life vest. Not only is this essential safety equipment for your dog-friend, but the buoyancy also allows them to swim with less effort. Best of all, it comes with a handle on the back, which is very handy for lifting your dog back onto the board.

If you don't have a float coat and your dog needs to get back on the board, when she puts her front paws on the board, put your open hand on the back of her head and push her head toward the middle of the board. She will naturally push against your hand, and this will allow her to use your hand as leverage to pull herself up.

Best-of Lists
(in no particular order)

Best Places for Beginners
Beaver Creek
Loon Lake
Upper Gilbert River and Sturgeon Lake (Sauvie Island)
Lost Lake (Mt Hood)
Timothy Lake
Olallie Lakes (Monon and Horseshoe only)
Big Lake
Sparks Lake
Hosmer Lake
Lava Lake and Little Lava Lake
Little Cultus Lake
Waldo Lake
Crescent Lake
Squaw Lakes
Wallowa Lake

Best On-Site Rentals
Siltcoos River
Loon Lake
Scappoose Bay and Cunningham Slough (Sauvie Island)
Scappoose Bay and Scappoose Creek
Lost Lake (Mt Hood)
Lava Lake
Crescent Lake
Paulina and East Lake
Wallowa Lake

Best Places to See Wildlife
Salmon River Estuary
Yaquina Bay
Siltcoos River
Columbia River at the Lewis and Clark National Wildlife Refuge
Upper Gilbert River and Sturgeon Lake
Scappoose Bay and Cunningham Slough
Lower Luckiamute and Middle Willamette River
Hosmer Lake
Davis Lake
Upper Klamath Canoe Trail

Best Beaches
Salmon River Estuary
Beaver Creek
Siltcoos River (with restrictions)
Crescent Lake

Best Paddles for Solitude
Salmon River
Beaver Creek
Lower Siuslaw River
Eel Lake
Scappoose Bay and Cunningham Slough
Olallie Lakes
Blue River Lake
Waldo Lake
Davis Lake
Summit Lake
Lower Powder River / Brownlee Reservoir
Owyhee Reservoir

Best Adventure Paddles (some combination of long-distance, back-country camping, and solitude)
Lower Siuslaw River
Lower Luckiamute and Middle Willamette River
Middle Willamette River
Blue River Lake
Waldo Lake
Summit Lake
Upper Klamath Canoe Trail
Hells Canyon Reservoir – Big Bar
Lower Powder River / Brownlee Reservoir
Owyhee Reservoir

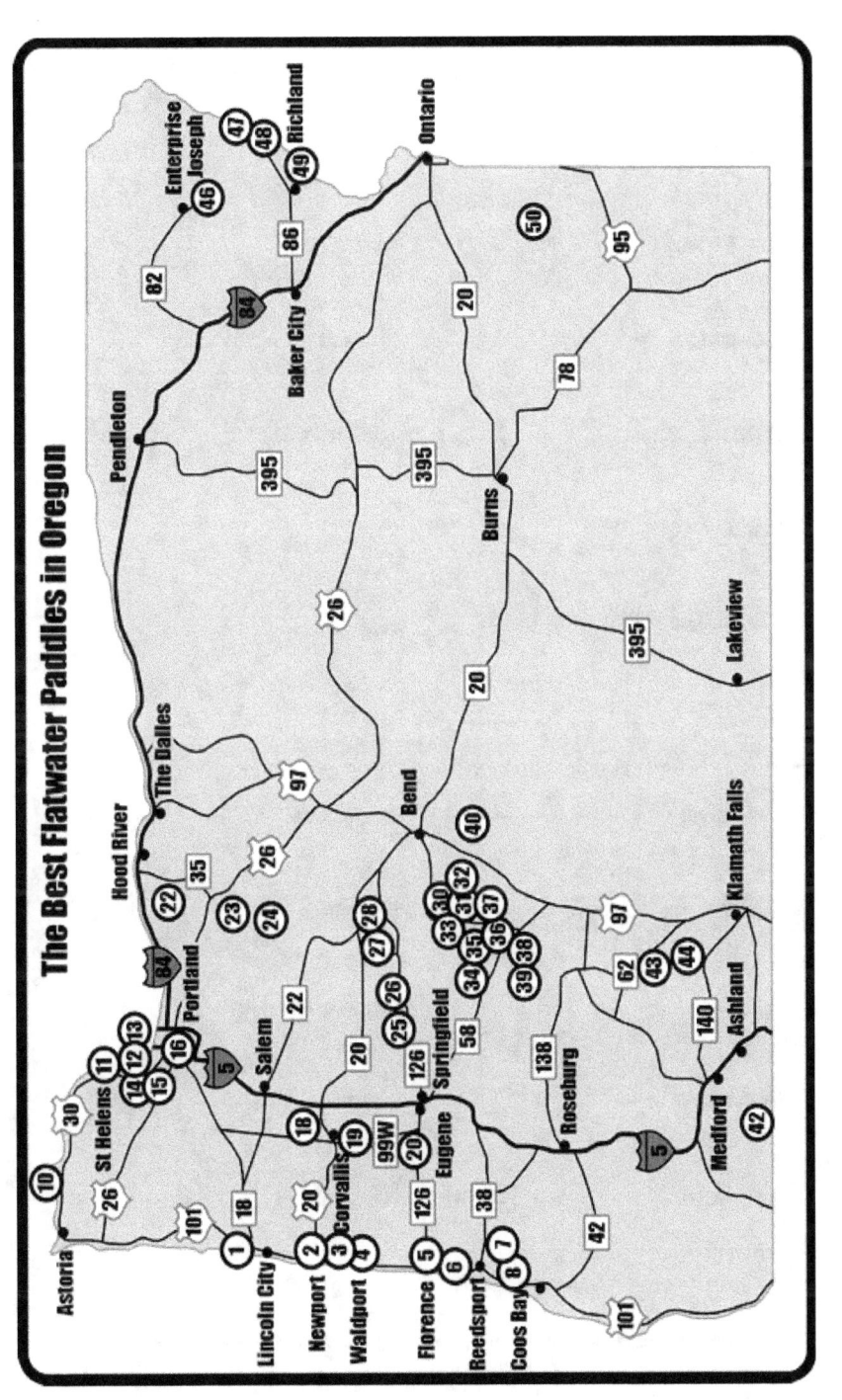

Map Key

Launch/Return Point	◇	Forest	🌲
Scale Bar (miles)	[12 miles 1]	Sage/Scrub	🌿
Compass Rose	✦	Wetlands	⊥⊥⊥
Direction of Current	↑	Tidal Wetlands	⊥⊥
River Mile	135	Sand	(dotted)
Water Obstruction	(ripples)	Mud	(speckled)
Highway	▬▬	Lava Rock	(textured)
Road (paved)	───	Rock Outcrop	●
Road (dirt)	-----	City or Town	(grid)
Trail	- - - -	Cultivated/Deforested	(light)
Day Use Area*	🎪	Industrial	(dark)
Campground*	⛺	Powerline	┄┄┄
Point of Interest	◎		

*Campground or day use icons may not be shown in some locations due to space limitations

I. The Coast and Coast Range

1. Salmon River Estuary: Beautiful Cascade Head and a picnic-perfect beach

The Salmon River is a relatively small and short river for the Oregon Coast, with a typical flow of just 339 cubic feet per second (cfs) and a length of only 26 miles. Compare these numbers to the nearby Nehalem River, with an average flow of 2,660 cfs and a length of 128 miles. The paddle described here is relatively short too, set in the three-plus miles of the estuary (though see below for a longer option). But what the paddle lacks in length, it more than makes up for in scenic beauty and solitude.

The mouth of the Salmon flows past the base of Cascade Head, a spectacular headland named for the waterfalls cascading off its cliffs into the Pacific. This is literally where a mountain meets the sea, and Cascade Head is the highest such mountain on the Oregon coast. The paddle takes you past high meadows, steep forested hills, and rocky cliffs to the mouth of the Salmon, to beautiful beaches and ocean views. On your way downriver, look for elk and deer in the meadows above on Cascade Head.

Beneath the cliffs of Cascade Head, at low tide you will find a narrow sandy beach strewn with boulders. This is a fun place to explore among the rocks and crevices, but don't get trapped by the tide! And always keep your eye on the sea to avoid being surprised by a sneaker wave. Just offshore, beyond the surf, sits Three Rocks, an aptly named rock formation whose triple spires guard the mouth of the Salmon River like sentinels.

The wide, flat sand beach on the south shore of the Salmon (river left) is more suitable for a longer stay. This area is also isolated, over a mile from the nearest accessible public road. The only folks nearby are at Westwind, a nonprofit camp dedicated to providing outdoor experiences for youth and families. During the summer, you may see their campers on the river or on the beach. During the fall, fishers will congregate on the river to catch Chinook and coho.

From the launch/return point at Knight County Park, it is approximately 0.8 miles downriver to the mouth. To visit the beaches on either side of the river, take out just before reaching the surf. Do not attempt to cross the bar unless you are experienced at paddling in the open ocean.

Seals and sea lions frequent these beaches. I recommend bringing binoculars for enjoying any sightings, because it is dangerous (and illegal) to approach them. The sign at Knight County Park states that people must remain at least 50 yards away. The mouth of the river and the surrounding seas are part of the Cascade Head Marine Reserve and Marine Protected Areas, which impose restrictions on taking fish and other marine life.

The shoreline at the launch/return area is muddy and choked with mushy seaweed, so it is not ideal for launching a non-motorized craft. The river's flow peaks in the autumn, but the tide is strong enough in the estuary that it effectively counters the current. Because of this, it is best to paddle with the tide, especially when going against the current (see Paddling Tips). This would mean going downriver just before or around low tide, then returning and/or paddling further upriver on an incoming tide or around high tide. Perhaps enjoy lunch on the beach while the tide changes.

At low tide, the river can get very shallow between the launch/return point and the mouth. This ensures that this portion of your paddle will not involve any motorized accompaniment, but it is also so shallow that it presents a fin-drag hazard in places. The best navigation strategy is to follow the river channel (the deepest part of the river). Fortunately, the water is clear, offering good views of hazards, as well as fish and crabs hanging out in the sandy shallows.

Upriver from the launch/return point, the water is deeper and the shores are marshy. Between the launch/return point and the Highway 101 bridge – a length of nearly two miles – there are a few bigger side channels that you can explore, especially on the south side of the river. This area is best paddled at higher tide and/or in times of higher flow (spring or autumn). You are more likely to encounter motorized boats in this area, especially in the autumn when people will be fishing for Chinook and coho.

It is possible to extend the paddle by going upriver past the Highway 101 bridge for another mile or so, but I have not paddled that far. It is also possible to get some spectacular "aerial" views of your paddle route by hiking Cascade Head from the trailhead at the launch/return point.

Difficulty: Easy.

Distance: 2.4 to 6.5+ miles.

Directions: Highway 18 runs west to the coast from Salem, joining Highway 101, the Oregon Coast Highway, just a few miles north of Lincoln City. Approximately 1 mile north of the 18-101 junction, turn west onto Three Rocks Rd. Three Rocks Rd road runs down the Salmon River for approximately 2.3 miles before making a sharp bend to the left where Savage Rd joins from the right. Just around the bend is Knight County Park. This is also the parking lot for the South Trailhead of the Cascade Head Trail.

Launch/Return: Knight County Park. Toilets, parking, boat launch. No water. No day use fee.

Nearby Rental/Tours: Safari Town Surf, in Lincoln City, offers two-person, two-hour or three-hour guided kayak tours of the Salmon River estuary (safaritownsurf.com).

Nearby Camping: None, really. The closest campground is at Cape Lookout State Park, 30 miles north on Highway 101.

Nearby Fun: One of my favorite day trips on the Oregon coast is a visit to Pacific City and Cape Kiwanda, which is a little over 20 miles north of this paddle. After a few hours of exploring the tidepools, dunes, and fantastic vistas of Cape Kiwanda, I like to sit on the beachside patio of the Pelican Pub and Brewery and watch the beachcombers, surfers, and doryboats as the sun sets behind Haystack Rock and Cape Kiwanda.

There are also several great hikes along this part of the coast, most notably Cape Lookout, and the Valley of the Giants, as well as Hart's Cove and the other trails on Cascade Head. Note that the Nature Conservancy, whose board controls access to the Cascade Head Preserve, does not allow dogs on the trails.

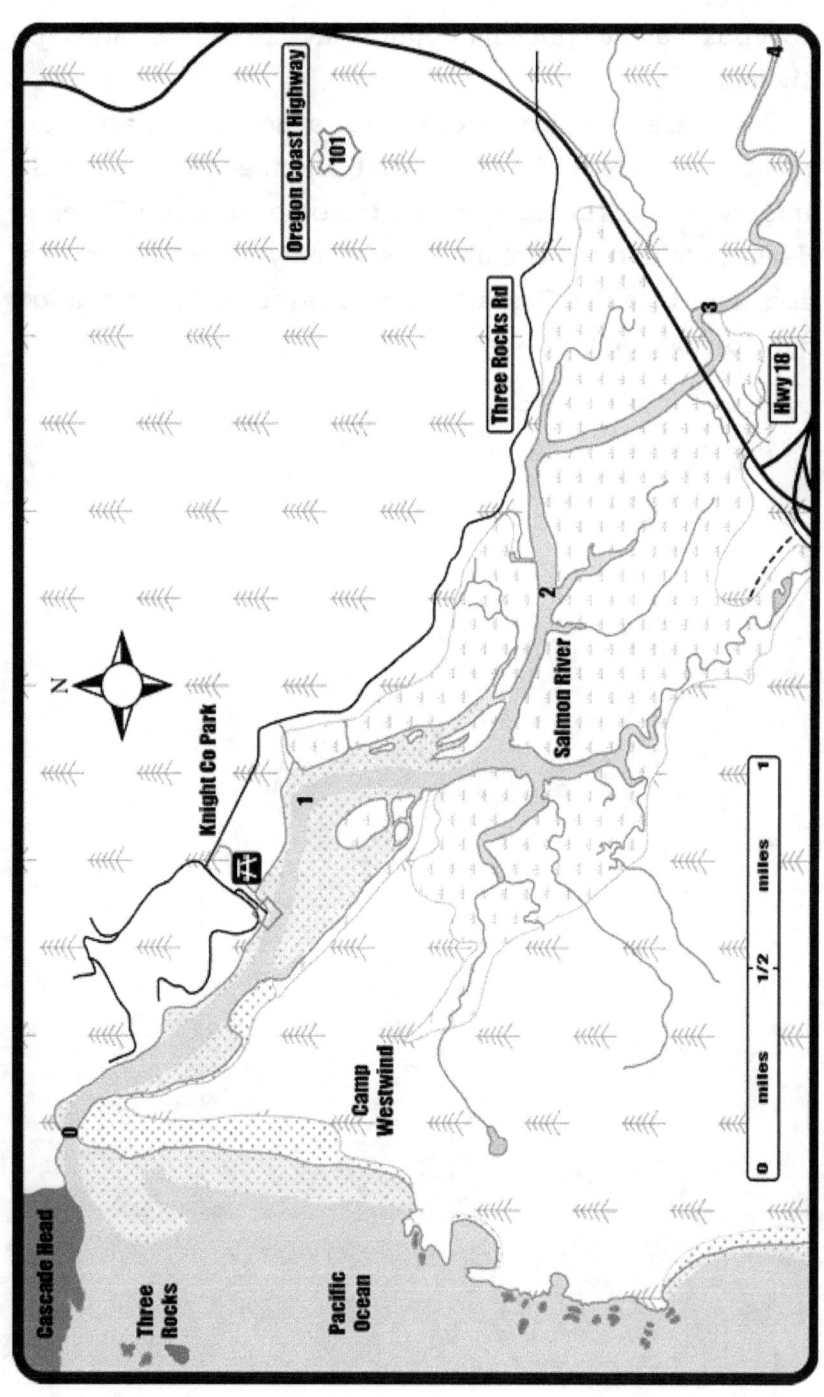

2. Yaquina Bay:
A historic coastal town with a bustling port, lots of marine life, and miles of wetlands

There are many places worth visiting on the Oregon Coast, and visitors can find unique scenic beauty virtually anywhere along the 363 miles of the coast. But if people have time to visit only one place on the coast, I always recommend Newport. That's because it has several excellent attractions, a historic downtown area, lots of oceanfront hotel rooms, and good access to beaches.

At the heart of Newport is Yaquina Bay. On the north shore is Newport's quaint downtown Bayfront area, which is part working fishing port and part old-school tourist-y promenade, complete with cotton candy vendors and a wax museum. On the south shore is Oregon State University's eminent marine laboratory, the Hatfield Marine Science Center, as well as the Oregon Coast Aquarium. Joining the two shores 246 feet above the bay is the gracefully arching Yaquina Bay Bridge.

Paddling Yaquina Bay is yet another great reason to visit Newport, one that is perhaps overlooked. This paddle offers a close-up look at a bustling ocean port and outstanding views. In one direction, the bay bridge towers over the Pacific Ocean, and in the other the low green mountains of the Coast Range frame the bay. You can also find extensive freshwater wetlands to paddle around if you venture a little further upriver.

Head westward/downriver from the launch/return point to reach the Bayfront. Large, ocean-going research ships are frequently docked at the National Oceanic and Atmospheric

Administration (NOAA) facility here. These ships are really neat to see in the water, but be sure to keep a safe and respectful distance.

The area just west of NOAA near the Newport Bayfront features views of the bay bridge towering overhead. This semi-arch bridge is distinctive and somewhat eccentric, with six below-deck arches on the south side of the main arch and just one such arch on the north side. The bridge was built in the mid-1930s, of steel and concrete, and combines elements of Art Deco, Art Moderne, and Gothic architecture. It was placed on the National Register of Historic Places in 2005.

There is not much to see downriver of the bridge, and the current becomes stronger in this area, so it is best avoided. Turning north/upriver, along the north shore of the bay you will see the Newport Bayfront. Paddling along the Bayfront can be quite entertaining, as you become a point of interest for both humans and sea lions. You will get a very different perspective on the town while paddling past the bay-view restaurants and shops, deep sea fishing tour boats, commercial fishing operations, canneries, and the public pier. The pier is where you are most likely to see sea lions. Be sure steer clear of the wildlife and wave to everyone watching you from the shore.

Paddling further upriver along the north shore will give you a little bit of a break from waves and wakes, as the marina area sits behind a breakwater. East of the marina lies a peninsula that contains Newport's industrial port terminal. Above the terminal is Sallys Bend, an area out of the main river channel lined with rural residential development that offers a few more miles of relatively calm paddling.

Along the south shore, between the launch/return point and Idaho Point, lies an unnamed bay out of the main river channel. Here, you will see the Hatfield Marine Science Center and the Oregon Coast Aquarium, as well as some commercial and residential areas along the shore.

On the other side of Idaho Point lies King Slough, another area out of the main river channel. Development along the shoreline is much lighter here, with the shores almost entirely forested. The quiet of this area makes a nice contrast to the busier and more developed areas closer to Newport and also offers a few more miles of relatively calm paddling.

Upriver of King Slough and Sally's Bend, the river narrows and flows northward for about a mile before making a 90-degree turn (not shown on the map). Where the river begins flowing west, there are two major sloughs along the south shore around McCaffrey Island and Oysterville, offering many more miles of wetland paddling out of the main river channel.

Yaquina Bay has a relatively strong current in the main river channel and strong tides. It also features heavy water traffic, with everything from speedboats and small fishing boats to large commercial fishing boats and ocean-going ships. The bay is not protected from the ocean winds, and usually becomes quite windy and wavy in the afternoons.

Because of these factors, the best time to do this paddle is when the wind is lower than normal. Launching around a high tide will help with the current and, if you want to explore the more natural areas upriver, will allow a return on an outgoing tide flowing in concert with the current.

It is also worth noting that the bay is home to three significant federal facilities. In addition to NOAA, there is a Department of Homeland Security facility on the north shore between the bridge and the Newport Bayfront and a US Customs and Border Protection facility at the marina on the north shore. For your own safety, it is best to stay clear of these places.

Difficulty: Advanced.

Distance: 2 to 20+ miles.

Directions: Highway 20 runs between Corvallis and Newport. At Newport, Highway 20 joins Highway 101, the Oregon Coast Highway, just north of the Yaquina Bay Bridge. At the south end of the bridge, turn west on SE Marine Science Drive. In one-half mile, you will reach a roundabout. Turn right at the roundabout and park in the parking lot.

Launch/Return: The primitive launch/return is from a small beach on the north side of the unnamed parking lot. No toilets. No water. No day use fee.

Nearby Rental: Ossie's Surf Shop, at Agate Beach on the north side of Newport, offers kayak rentals for paddling around the Newport Bayfront (ossiessurfshop.com).

If you're coming through Corvallis, you can rent SUPs, kayaks, and canoes at Peak Sports in Corvallis (peaksportscorvallis.com/index.cfm).

Nearby Camping: South Beach State Park is about two miles south of the launch/return point on Highway 101. Beverly Beach State park is about 9 miles north of the launch/return point on Highway 101.

Nearby Fun: As mentioned above, there are several excellent attractions around Newport. The first is the shops, galleries, and restaurants of the charming Newport Bayfront. Be sure to check out the mural about Mohava Niemi, the locally-famous founder of Mo's Restaurants, a small Oregon chain of seafood restaurants.

The Yaquina Head Lighthouse, at the north end of town, is the tallest lighthouse in Oregon at 93 feet and is still active. The area around the lighthouse features tidepools full of interesting creatures. You can learn about the lighthouse and the marine life in the tidepools at the associated Interpretive Center. You can also reserve a spot on a lighthouse tour there, available on a first-come, first-served basis.

The Oregon Coast Aquarium has several great exhibits, including glass tunnels beneath huge tanks filled with many kinds of fish. One of the highlights of my entire life, though, occurred here when my wife and I paid extra to get up-close and personal with a live Pacific octopus. Even after reading the latest science demonstrating the intelligence of these animals, I was stunned by how closely she observed the people around her and how eager she was to interact with us. If you decide to meet an octopus here too, don't be surprised if she douses you with cold seawater, because that is just something octopuses like to do to people sometimes.

Rogue Ales was founded in Ashland, but their Bayfront Brewpub has been an institution in Newport since 1989. The old pub is a great place to meet some crusty locals and enjoy a pint of classic Oregon microbrew. Rogue also has a massive brewery on the south shore of the bay (Brewer's on the Bay) deliciously close to the launch/return point of this paddle. The brewery includes a restaurant and pub with an extensive tap list, expansive views of the bay, and daily brewery tours.

Newport's Nye Beach neighborhood, to the northwest of the Bayfront area, also features some good restaurants and galleries, as well as some nice beachfront hotels. One of the better deals on the coast is the Hallmark Resort, which offers oceanview rooms at reasonable prices. In addition to easy beach access, the Hallmark has first-floor, dog-friendly rooms with the potty right out the sliding glass doors.

For other good area beaches, check out the South Beach State Park, on the south shore of the bay, the Yaquina Bay State Recreation Site, on the north shore of the bay, and the Agate Beach State Recreation Site, on the north side of town.

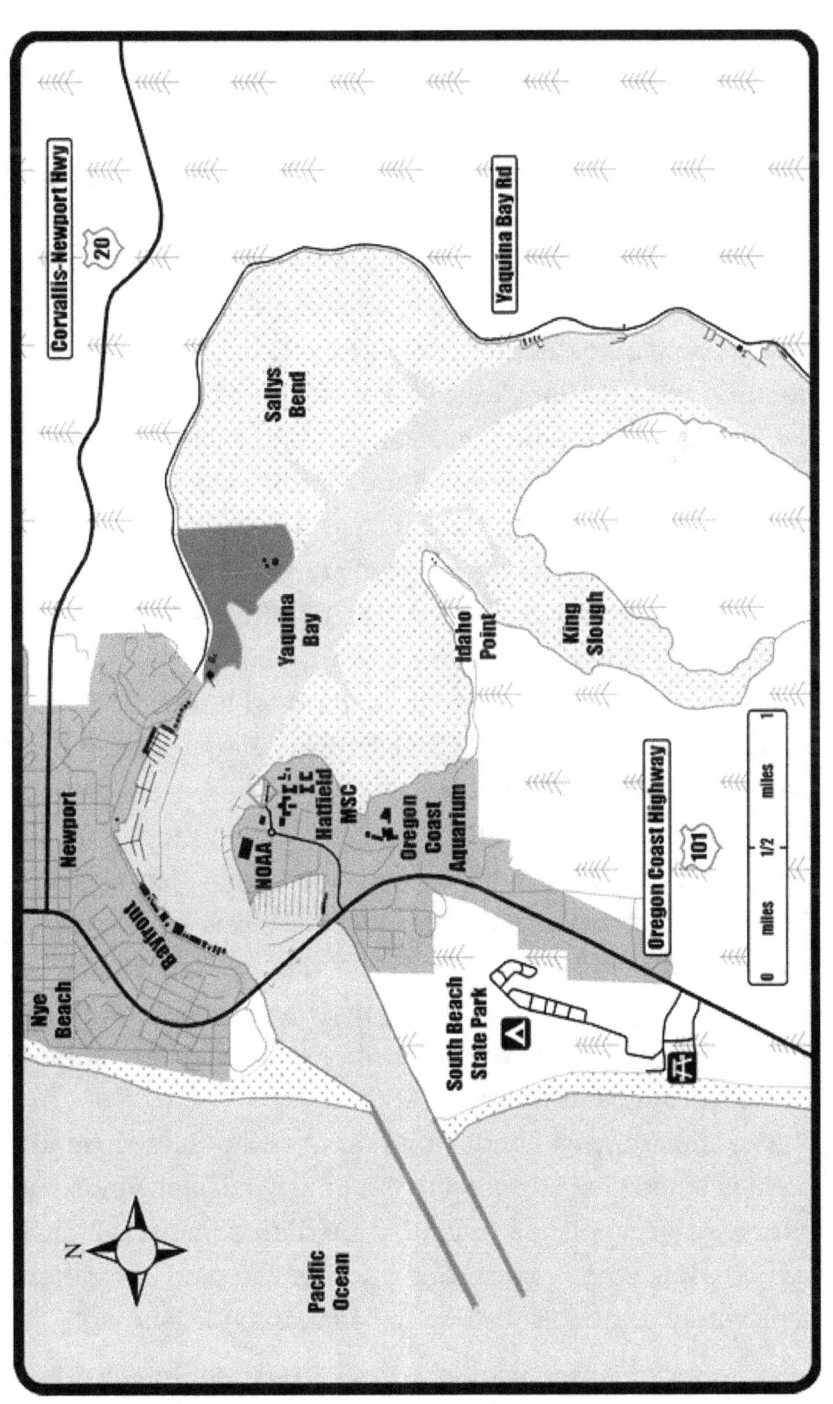

3. Beaver Creek:
Quiet coastal wetlands and beach access

Beaver Creek is a meandering little waterway surrounded by pristine freshwater wetlands and coastal forest. The creek is too shallow for all but the smallest motorized boats, and the current is slack, allowing easy padding both up and downriver, subject only to the tides, which are also gentle due to the large bar at the mouth of the river. Near the launch/return point, there are several shady, creek-side picnic tables at Brian Booth State Park. At the mouth of the creek is Ona Beach, a wide, flat stretch of lovely white sand.

The launch/return area is heavily forested, with brush and tree limbs hanging over the water. Within the first quarter-mile upriver, the creek makes a sharp 180-degree turn and the forest gives way to wetlands filled with aquatic plants, wildflowers, and birds such as osprey, marsh wrens, bald eagles, blue herons, and egrets.

You may see deer or Roosevelt elk grazing in the meadows along the creek. Of course, there are also beavers, though you're more likely to see the signs of beavers – gnawed logs and beaver lodges – than an actual beaver. They are very secretive, even in their namesake creek. The few fishers who visit will be hoping to catch coho salmon, cutthroat trout, and winter steelhead.

The meadow-wetlands area above the launch/return point is somewhat exposed to the hearty coastal winds and offers very few places to land, providing some small challenge to this otherwise serene paddle. The land along here is privately owned as well, so not available for landing.

At the 1.5 mile mark above the launch/return is a private dock with a sign labeled "Bobby's Cove." There are also some snags in the river in this area. When I visited, there was a snag lying across nearly the entire width of the river, followed by a submerged log in the center of the channel that would catch a fin even at high tide.

The South Beaver Creek Road bridge is 1.7 miles above the launch/return. The shoreline area above the bridge is part of the state park, but there are still no good places to land. At 1.9 miles, near the power lines, the creek splits into multiple channels and some side bayous that can be explored. At this point, navigation becomes difficult, but is easier with a high tide.

Downriver from the launch/return point, the creek makes a big bend through the forest and passes under the park's pedestrian bridge. After this, the water becomes shallow and the forest gives way to the beach. At high tide, I was able to paddle for nearly another mile past curious onlookers at the beach before the braided stream became too shallow to navigate. It would be very difficult to accidentally cross the bar here, but you should not attempt to do so unless you are experienced at open-ocean paddling.

If the small parking lot adjacent to the boat launch is full, a common occurrence on summer weekends, there are some primitive places to launch in the picnic area across the highway (on the west side), as well as a larger parking lot.

Another nice feature of this paddle is that the Brian Booth State Park rangers offer regularly-scheduled, guided kayak tours for just $20 per person. All the necessary equipment is included, from your PFD to flat-bottomed kayaks suitable for beginners. So bring your friends who don't have boards and share one of the best flatwater paddles in Oregon with them. The tours are offered from mid-July through Labor Day weekend on Thursdays, Fridays, Saturdays, Sundays, and Mondays and start at the Beaver Creek Welcome Center. Reservations are accepted beginning June 1. For more information or to make a reservation, call 541-563-6313.

The Welcome Center at Brian Booth State Park is open 7 days a week from noon to 4pm, and from 10am to 4pm during June, July, and August. There is also a network of trails upriver from the paddle area, some of which go through old growth Sitka spruce. Maps and additional information are available at the Welcome Center.

Difficulty: Easy; suitable for beginners.

Distance: 6 miles. 4 miles round-trip going upriver and another 2 miles round-trip going downriver.

Directions: On Highway 101, the Oregon Coast Highway, seven miles north of Waldport and eight miles south of Newport, there is a big bend in the highway to accommodate the estuary of Beaver Creek. Turn east onto North Beaver Creek Road, then immediately turn right for the main boat launch and smaller parking lot. Or turn west off of Highway 101 for the picnic area and larger parking lot with primitive launch areas. To reach the Welcome Center, go another mile east on North Beaver Creek Road. Note that Brian Booth State Park was formerly known as Ona Beach and still appears with that name on some maps.

Launch/Return: Brian Booth State Park. Toilets, parking, boat launch. No water. No camping. No day use fee.

Nearby Rentals: Ossie's Surf Shop, at Agate Beach on the north side of Newport, also offers kayak rentals for paddling around Beaver Creek (ossiessurfshop.com). And see above for details on the State Park's tours.

Nearby Camping: South Beach State Park is six miles north at Newport. Beachside State Recreation Site is about 18 miles south and is open from March 15 to November 1. Tillicum Beach Campground is about 19 miles south.

Nearby Fun: See the "Nearby Fun" entry for Paddle 2, Yaquina Bay.

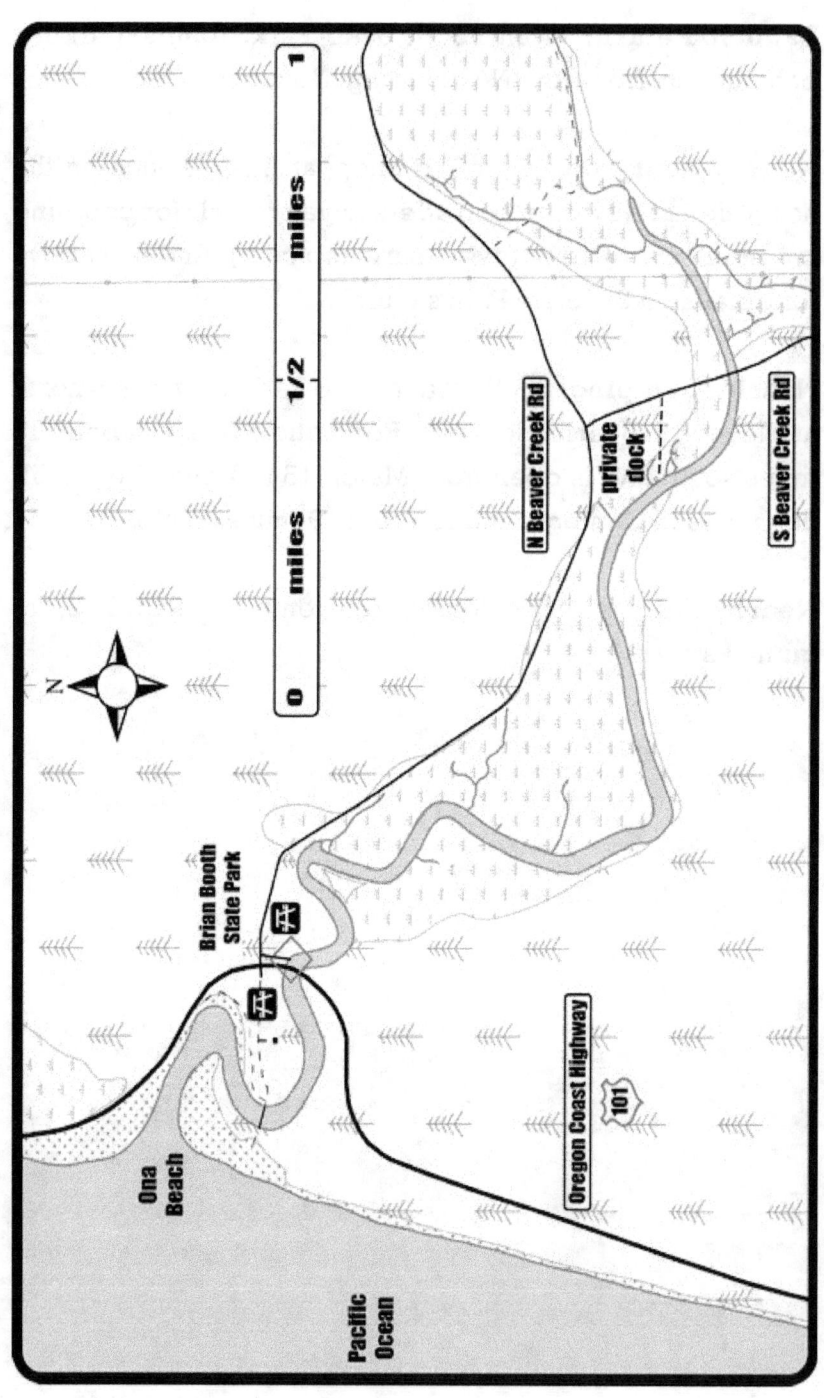

4. Alsea Bay and Drift Creek:
A peaceful bay shared with fishers and crabbers and a secluded creek

Waldport is a pleasant little town with nice beaches and a sleek, modern bridge crossing Alsea Bay. The name for Alsea Bay comes from the Native American word "alsi," meaning "peace." This paddle is similar in character to the paddle described in Yaquina Bay, but calmer due to the smaller town, smaller river, and lack of an ocean port. The main attractions here are the wetlands along Lint Slough, the northern shore of the bay, and the Alsea River above the bay, as well as the quiet paddling along secluded Drift Creek.

The bay is known for its excellent crabbing, clamming, and salmon fishing. Anglers come for Chinook and coho salmon, steelhead, and coastal cutthroat trout. Small fishing boats make up most of the water traffic around the area. Paddling along the side channel on the north side of the bay affords a close look at the wetland areas, as well as a more mellow current. About 3.8 miles upriver from the launch/return point, the mouth of Drift Creek appears. From the river, it can be difficult to distinguish the mouth of Drift Creek from some of the side channels of the Alsea, so note that, when paddling upriver, Drift Creek is the final side channel on the north side of the river in this area.

From its mouth, you can paddle at least three and a half miles up Drift Creek, depending on the tide and time of year, with river flows peaking in the spring and late autumn. The creek narrows a few miles in, and there are some snag hazards in this area.

Alsea Bay has a strong current in the main river channel and strong tides. The bay often gets windy and wavy in the afternoons. Because of these factors, the best time to do this paddle is when the wind is lower than normal. Launching around a high tide will help with the current and will allow a return on an outgoing tide flowing in concert with the current. It will also open a lot of areas out of the main river channel to navigation. Conditions can be dangerous near the mouth of the river, so it is best not to venture west of the Highway 101 bridge.

The area described in this paddle is part of the Alsea River Water Trail, which is a designation made by the Oregon Parks and Recreation Department for waterways "that have been mapped out with the intent to create an educational, scenic, and rewarding experience for recreational canoeists and kayakers." Additional information on the trail can be found online at hikebikepaddle.org and portofalsea.com.

Difficulty: Moderate to advanced, depending on distance.

Distance: 3 miles round-trip to reach the wetlands on the northeastern side of the bay. 7.6 miles round-trip to reach the mouth of Drift Creek. 13.6 miles round-trip if you paddle three miles up Drift Creek.

Directions: Highway 34 takes a twisting path from Philomath, just west of Corvallis, to Waldport. In Waldport, on Highway 34 0.4 miles east of Highway 101, turn north onto NE Broadway St. Robinson Park/Port of Alsea is at the end of Broadway, in another 0.4 miles.

Lunch/Return: Robinson Park/Port of Alsea. Picnic tables, beach access, toilets. No water. **$7 day use fee.**

Nearby Rental: The Waldport Kayak Shack may offer guided tours of Alsea Bay as well as kayak rentals. At press time, their website says they are reorganizing and "hope to" open during summer 2017.

Nearby Camping: Beachside State Recreation Site is 4.4 miles south on Highway 101. Tillicum Beach Campground is 5.5 miles south on Highway 101.

Nearby Fun: About 9 miles south of Waldport is Yachats, one of the more interesting and less touristy towns on the coast. There you will find my favorite breakfast place on the coast, The Green Salmon.

About 10 miles south of Waldport is Cape Perpetua, one of the more dramatic headlands on the coast. The trails at Cape Perpetua feature old-growth forests, extensive tidepools, and the legendary blowhole known as Devil's Churn.

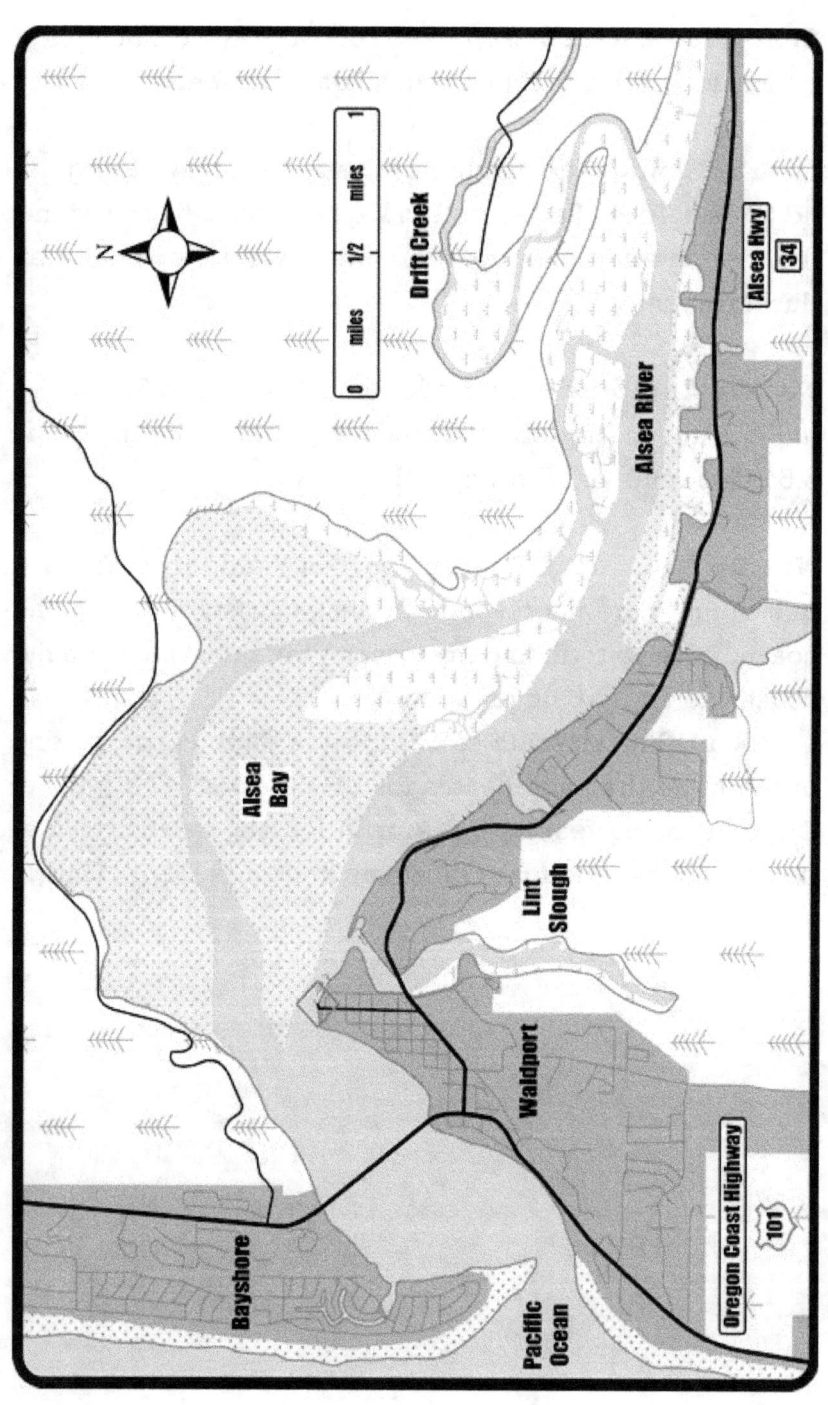

5. Lower Siuslaw River:
Endless wetlands along a lightly-traveled river

To encourage ... well, the same thing this book seeks to encourage – connection to the natural world through water recreation – the State of Oregon, specifically the Parks and Recreation Department, has designated a series of, at last count, nine "water trails" around the state. One of the best one for flatwater paddling is, in this writer's humble opinion, the Siuslaw Water Trail.

First things first, this Native American word is pronounced "sy-yew-slaw." The Siuslaw were people who lived along the river until 1860, when they were forcibly removed to a reservation on the coast at Yachats. The river is not particularly long at 109 miles, but with an average flow of 2,285 cfs, it is the 18th largest in Oregon.

The lower reach of the river between Florence and Tiernan, and the North Fork Siuslaw River above Florence, are home to extensive wetlands that attract significant numbers of migratory birds, as well as the usual suspects such as otters and blue herons. The richness of the wetlands is due in no small part to the fact that none of the major forks of the Siuslaw have been dammed, a rarity in western Oregon.

Unfortunately, the upper reaches of the river, mostly under federal ownership, have been extensively logged. Most of the remaining old-growth forest in the Siuslaw watershed was destroyed in the 1980s. Habitat loss caused by logging devastated the coho run, which declined from over 100,000 fish per year to just 1,700 in the early 2000s. Restoration of the area began in the mid-1990s and continues. The river also hosts populations of cutthroat, Chinook, and winter steelhead.

Traffic on the river is almost exclusively small fishing boats. There is some development along the lower stretch of the river, mostly associated with Highway 126, which runs along the north shore. But long stretches of the river feel isolated, and are isolated, especially in the side channels running through the wetlands south of the main river channel, and in the North Fork.

The Siuslaw Watershed Council has published a brochure for the Siuslaw River Water Trail. The brochure includes a good, detailed map complete with some excellent suggested itineraries. You can download the brochure at siuslawwatertrail.com or siuslaw.org. Because of this resource, this is the only featured paddle for which I have not created a custom map.

The longest suggested route is a 17.4-mile stretch between Farnham Landing, a small park 2 miles above Mapleton, and Florence. This stretch makes for a great down-river, day-trip float for experienced paddlers who can organize a shuttle. When floating this route, be sure to enter the unnamed side channel on river left just below Tiernan to enjoy several miles of paddling closer to wetlands and outside of the main river channel.

Further downriver, after re-joining the main channel, another side channel on river left allows you to go around Cox Island and get outside of the main river channel again. From here, you can also explore Duncan Inlet and South Inlet, both "dead ends" deep in the wetlands of the Siuslaw estuary.

Finally, along the north shore between the mouth of the North Fork Siuslaw River and Florence, there is an unnamed bay where you can also paddle out of the main river channel again before landing in Florence.

This route also has a shorter option. Put in at Tiernan (where you would enter the side river channel almost right away) and the float to Florence is just 9.75 miles. This shorter option allows you to do most of your paddling outside of the main river channel, by taking the side channels as explained above.

The river trail brochure includes two other suggested routes. The first is a 4.9-mile stretch of the North Fork Siuslaw River, which joins the main river just above Florence, between Bender Landing (another small park) and Florence. This could be done as a short float down (shuttle), a good option for inexperienced paddlers given the slower current and lighter traffic on the North Fork, or as an up and back from Florence, which is a more substantial 9.8-mile paddle. The North Fork also includes a navigable side-channel around Bull Island, as well as several dead-end bayous that can be explored.

The final suggested route in the brochure is called the "Old Town Sunset Loop." It sounds nice, doesn't it? The route starts in Florence and goes upriver along the south shore of the river and Cox Island to explore the wetlands around the island and Duncan Inlet and South Inlet. The map identifies the route length as 3.06 miles but a loop into this area, depending on how far you explore, is probably closer to 4-6 miles.

When floating down and landing at the Port of Siuslaw in Florence, look for the narrow boat launch between the piers of the marina before reaching the Siuslaw River Bridge.

Difficulty: Moderate to advanced.

Distance: Many options, from an approximately 5-mile up-and-back above Florence to a 17.4 mile float down the river.

Directions: Highway 126 runs between Eugene and Florence, where it intersects with Highway 101, the Oregon Coast Highway. In the area around these paddles, Highway 126 runs along the north side of the Siuslaw.

Port of Siuslaw: One-half mile south of the 126-101 junction on Highway 101, turn east onto 2nd St. Go four blocks and turn right on Harbor St. The boat launch is straight ahead, and the parking lot and campground are on the left.

Farnham Landing: From the Highway 126-36 junction in Mapleton, Farnham Landing County Park is 1.8 miles north on Highway 36 on the right.

Tiernan: From the Highway 126-101 junction in Florence, Tiernan is 9.1 miles east on Highway 126 on the south side of the highway. Look for the mile marker signs.

Bender Landing: From Highway 126, turn north onto North Fork Rd. North Fork Rd is one mile east of the Highway 126-101 junction in Florence, on the western shore of the North Fork Siuslaw River. Go 2.7 miles on North Fork Rd. Bender landing is on the right.

Launch/Return:
Port of Siuslaw: Parking, toilets. Water available at the campground. **$2 day use fee.**

Farnham Landing: Toilets, parking. No water. **$4 day use fee or $40 Lane County Parks Annual Pass.**

Tiernan: No facilities. **$4 day use fee or $40 Lane County Parks Annual Pass.**

Bender Landing: Toilets, parking. No water. **$4 day use fee or $40 Lane County Parks Annual Pass.**

Nearby Rental: None.

Nearby Camping: The Port of Siuslaw Campground is adjacent to the Port of Siuslaw launch/return point. Jessie M Honeyman Memorial State Park is 3.8 miles south of Florence. Harbor Vista County Park is essentially in Florence on the northern shore of the Siuslaw at the mouth of the river. Sutton Campground is about 6 miles north of Florence on Vista Road off Highway 101. Alder Dune Campground is 7 miles north of Florence on Highway 101.

6. Siltcoos River:
Six miles of serenity between the ocean and the lake

The Oregon dunes are one of our state's most unique geological features. Stretching approximately 40 miles along the coast between Florence and Coos Bay, these white sand dunes reach up to 500 feet high and comprise the largest expanse of coastal sand dunes in the United States. As if this weren't cool enough, this vast sea of sand served as part of the inspiration for Frank Herbert's legendary science fiction novel Dune. If you visit, you will understand why.

And now you can paddle through the dunes too! The Siltcoos River slices right through them, draining Siltcoos Lake into the Pacific. The river runs approximately 6 miles and is quite small at just 278 cfs. The entire length except for the beach is heavily forested with alders, waxmyrtle, and pines. The branches reach out over the river and often enclose the river in their canopy, creating shade and a tunnel-like feel and blunting the worst of the coastal winds. The water is smooth and glassy throughout, with negligible current and tidal influence.

The main difficulty in this paddle comes from the numerous snags in the river. The snags were so prolific when I paddled the Siltcoos that I counted five places where timber had nearly completely blocked the channel, and there were at least three places where I had to kneel down to get clear of overhanging branches. One spot even involved a tree that was still in the process of falling in the river, which I could hear creaking and groaning as I passed underneath. Not for the faint of heart! Think of this as your chance to practice some yoga on the board.

Although this paddle is otherwise quite easy, it is best done after you have a mastery of the board-handling skills required to do tight maneuvers around obstacles. To minimize these fin-drag hazards, and to negate the negligible current, this paddle is best done at or near high tide, especially when paddling upriver from the mouth.

This paddle also involves a very brief takeout and portage (approximately 15 feet) on the north side of the river (river right) around a weir approximately one mile upriver from Waxmyrtle Campground. Above the weir, launch and land at a concrete ledge. Below the weir, launch and land at a ramp that you must carry your board or boat up or down. The ramp includes a handrail on the northern side, so position yourself to use the rail with one hand and carry your board in the other. The water immediately above the weir is somewhat stagnant and not a good place to go for a swim (either accidentally or intentionally).

This paddle can be roughly divided into three parts. The top mile or so, near Siltcoos Lake, features deeper water and a northern shoreline dotted with houses and docks. From here, you can paddle out into the lake and enjoy several more miles of paddling on Siltcoos Lake, Oregon's largest coastal lake. The lake tends to be windy though, and there are no restrictions on motors.

The larger, middle portion of this paddle goes through the dunes. It features sandy cliffs with occasional views of the dunes, along with the sounds of ATVs farting along trails on the northern shore. This is where the snags present their challenge, and where you stand the best chance of seeing a river otter. There are also big mats of aquatic plants with tiny white flowers that bloom both below and above the surface of the water. These create a drag hazard in places.

The last part of this paddle is around the mouth of the river, where the forest gives way to beautiful beaches and expansive views up and down the coast. As serene as the rest of the paddle is, this may be the prettiest part of the paddle. At high tide, it is possible to paddle more than a mile downriver from the Waxmyrtle Campground. Keep your eye out for seals on the beach, but don't approach them – it is both dangerous and illegal. Stay at least 50 yards away.

If you can find a high tide near sunset, you may have one of the most sublime experiences of your life paddling through the golden sands while the sun turns the sky red, orange, and purple. But do not cross the bar unless you are experienced at paddling in the open ocean.

For most of the year, the beaches here are totally deserted. That's because the area is the habitat of the Western Snowy Plover, a small brown-and-white shorebird threatened with extinction. Plovers lay their eggs in the sand and their nests are easily trampled by humans or preyed upon by small mammals and larger birds. Additionally, the best sandy nest sites are disappearing thanks to the encroachment of invasive European beach grass, something that is also destroying the dunes relatively quickly in geologic time.

The birds are easily frightened as well, and will sometimes abandon nests if they are disturbed. As a result, the beaches on both shores are closed to all human entry from March 15 through September 15, when the birds are nesting. This makes for a very isolated paddle, but it also means that paddlers may not go ashore in this area during the restricted time period. If you must land in this area during the nesting period, stick to the wet sand.

Difficulty: Easy to moderate – easy it you're comfortable navigating snag hazards.

Distance: Approximately 6 miles round-trip between Siltcoos Lake and the mouth of Siltcoos River at the Pacific Ocean.

Directions: The road leading to the Lodgpole Picnic Area and the Waxmyrtle Campground is apparently unnamed. Turn west off Highway 101, the Oregon Coast Highway, 7.8 miles south of the Highway 101-126 junction in Florence or 13.8 miles north of the Highway 101-38 junction in Reedsport. The turnoff is not well-marked, but look for the sign that says "Siltcoos Campgrounds Beach Access." From the turnoff, it is 0.5 miles to Lodgepole and 0.9 miles to Waxmyrtle.
Tyee Campground is right off Highway 101 on the east side. It is 6.6 miles south of the Highway 101-126 junction in Florence and 14.8 miles north of the Highway 101-38 junction in Reedsport.
To reach Westlake Boat Landing, from Highway 101, turn west onto Pacific Ave and go 0.3 miles. Pacific Ave is is 6.5 miles south of the Highway 101-126 junction in Florence and 14.7 miles north of the Highway 101-38 junction in Reedsport.

Launch/Return: There are four separate places to launch along the Siltcoos.

Waxmyrtle or Tyee Campground: There is nothing like being able to launch directly from your campsite, and both Waxmyrtle and Tyee Campgrounds offer primitive launch sites from individual campsites or other areas around the campground. Tyee has a formal boat launch. But there are no day use areas at these campgrounds, so parking and launching here requires paying the $22 nightly camping fee. Both have toilets and water available.

Lodgepole Picnic Area: Primitive launch site. Toilets, no water. $5 day use fee or Northwest Forest Pass.

Westlake Boat Landing: Lane County's Westlake Boat Landing, in the town of Westlake, is a formal boat launch with toilets. $4 day use fee or no additional charge with purchase of a $40 Lane County Parks Annual Pass.

Nearby Rental/Tours: Westlake Resort (westlakeresort.net) and Siltcoos River Kayak Rentals (siltcoosriver.com) rent kayaks in Westlake on sites adjacent to the river. Central Coast Watersports (541-997-1812) rents kayaks and Bill's Rentals (541-999-2372) rents kayaks and canoes. Both are in Florence and will deliver and pick-up boats to your launch/return site (e.g., Lodgepole Picnic Area). Central Coast Watersports and Bill's Rentals do not have dedicated websites, but both have good reviews online.

Nearby Camping: There are numerous campgrounds, mostly federal, around the Siltcoos River. In addition to the ones mentioned above, Driftwood, Driftwood II and Lagoon Campgrounds are very close to this paddle. Jessie M Honeyman Memorial State Park is just about 4 miles north of Westlake on Highway 101.

More Info: The Oregon Dunes NRA Visitor Center website has information about current conditions, trail maps, and lots of other information. On Youtube, by searching "Siltcoos River" you can find a video (featuring river otters and seals!) of people paddling the Siltcoos River in kayaks, as well as an entire episode of the intrepid Oregon Field Guide dedicated to the Oregon Dunes.

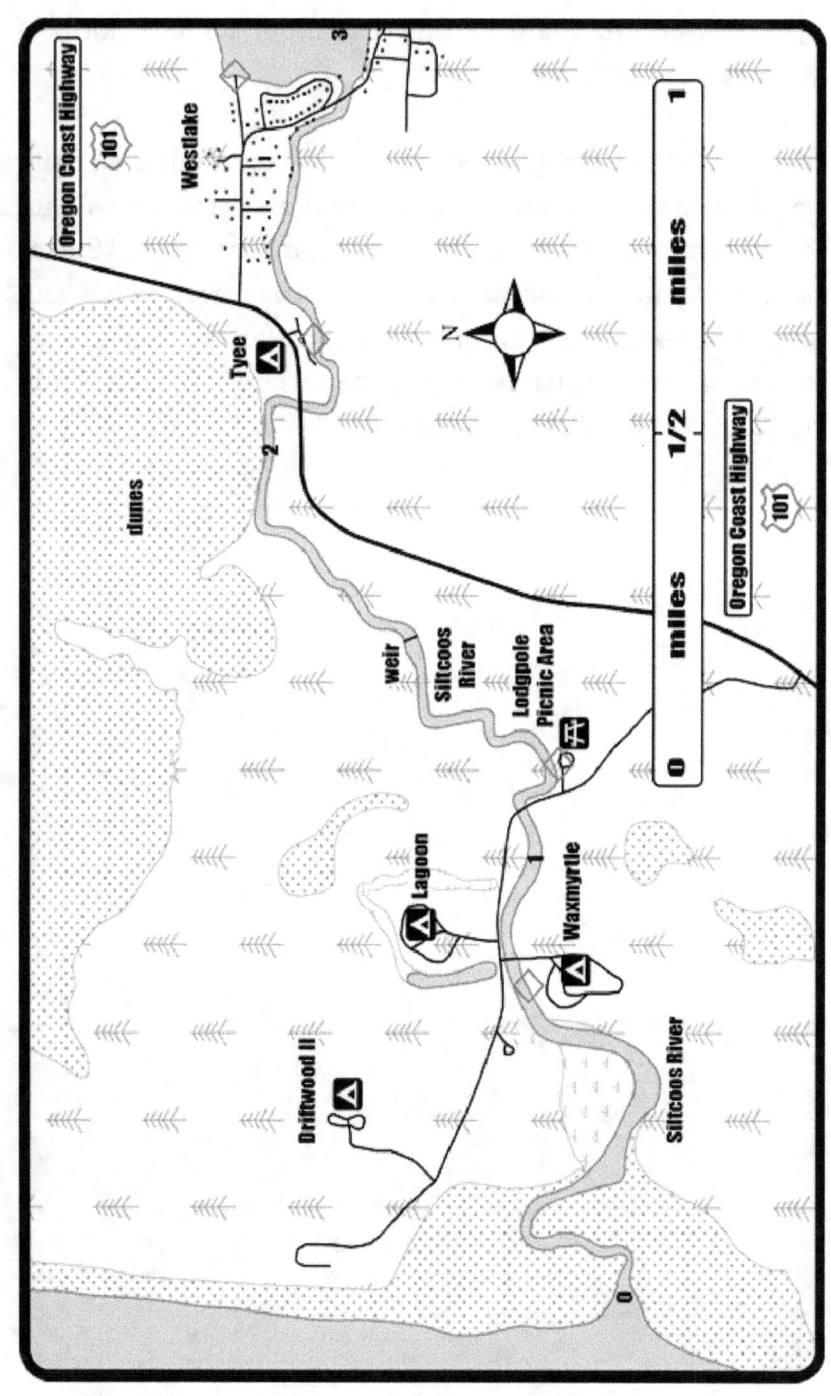

7. Loon Lake:
A beautiful and secluded, but well-shared, mountain lake

In a deep valley of the Coast Range, over a thousand years ago, an epic landslide cascaded down from the mountaintops, blocking a creek that flowed into the Umpqua River. The creek backed up behind the landslide, and the result is the zig-zag-shaped, 190-feet deep Loon Lake, named by European settlers for the birds that no longer visit the lake.

Loon Lake is tucked away in a classic Coast Range valley, steep-sided and heavily forested with Douglas fir, western hemlock, and red cedar. Morning mists shroud the surrounding peaks. The water is clear and filled with fish; it's stocked annually with bass, rainbow trout, bluegill, and crappie. There is a lovely sandy beach and swimming area at the bottom of the lake (the Bureau of Land Management's Loon Lake Rec Site) where fish and rough-skinned newts can be seen swimming around in the shallows.

Beehive Rock, a large, rounded rock spire, rises above the northeastern shore. The marshy area at the top of the lake is a good place to watch osprey and bald eagles do their fishing. It's also pretty, featuring wildflowers and lily pads. Elsewhere in the lake, there are mats of aquatic plants with tiny white flowers blooming both above and below the surface. Perhaps best of all, the lake's steep sides shield it from the coastal winds.

All these wonderful attributes make Loon Lake a popular place. It has been a favorite getaway for Oregon families since the early 1960s, after it stopped being used to float logs down to market, and now the Loon Lake Recreation Site alone gets 150,000 visitors a year. The southwestern shore is covered with mostly modest vacation homes. And there is a "Lodge and RV Resort" on the eastern shore where you can rent jet skiis, motorboats and waterskiis, and even houseboats. You can also rent a canoe, kayak, or paddleboard.

Though there is ostensibly a lake-wide 10 MPH speed limit, it does not seem to be widely observed and zooming waterskiiers and big wakes are common. A further annoyance is the fact that your dog is not allowed to hang out with you on the beach at the bottom of the lake or anywhere else in the day use area at the Loon Lake Recreation Site, for reasons that would be stupid even if the BLM bothered to tell us what they were.

Despite the crowds (and the lack of loons), Loon Lake is a joy to paddle, thanks to its beauty and the secluded feel that comes from being surrounded by steep mountains, tall trees, and clear water. The total lack of AT&T phone coverage also helps. And to further enhance or assist in creating that secluded feeling, I suggest going at a time of year when the kids are in school, or on a weekday, or perhaps both.

I have listed it as a good place for beginners because there are board rentals and shallows where new paddlers can avoid the worst of the big motorhead waves. There is a small "no wake" area from the resort to the northern end of the lake that allows new paddlers to enjoy the wetland area in peace. Loon Lake is also a good place to practice dealing with wakes, an essential skill for getting the most out of your board, since the water is relatively warm and clean.

The lake can be circumnavigated in approximately 5.6 miles, a nicely manageable distance for a day on the board. Because the shores are so steep or privately owned, there are few places to land along the shoreline. But the beach, the marshy area, and the less crowded East Shore Recreation Site are all good places for an extended stay to enjoy a snack and contemplate the lake.

Difficulty: Easy or moderate; good for beginners.

Distance: 5.6 miles to circle the lake.

Directions: Highway 38 runs along the Umpqua River from I-5 near Cottage Grove to Reedsport. From Highway 38 near the coast, turn south onto Loon Lake Road between mileposts 13 and 14. From there, the lake is approximately 7 miles. Loon Lake Road is narrow, steep, twisty, and frequented by large logging trucks.

Launch/Return: There are three separate places to launch, with the Lodge and RV resort having two sites.

Loon Lake Recreation Site: Toilets, parking, boat ramp, picnic area (for humans only), camping (walk-up and reserved sites; $18-36 + $7 for extra vehicles). No water. Day use fee of $5 or Northwest Forest Pass. Campground is open from the Thursday before Memorial Day weekend through the end of September. Information: 541-599-2254 or online at recreation.gov.

East Shore Loon Lake Recreation Site: Toilets, parking, primitive launch requiring a short port across the road, camping. No water. Day use fee of $5 or NWFP.

Loon Lake Lodge and RV Resort: Hotel, yurts, RV park, camping, deli, store, gas, boat launch and boat rental, ice, water, firewood. Day use fee of $7.

Nearby Rental: Loon Lake Lodge and RV Resort. Board rental fees: $20/1 hour, $60/4 hours, $100/8 hours. Kayak rental fees: $14/1 hour, $42/4 hours, $70/8 hours. Canoe rental fees (seats 2-3 people): $15/1 hour, $45/4 hours, $75/8 hours. Paddle Boat rental fees (seats 4 people): $18/1 hour, $54/4 hours, $90/8 hours. For other rates and additional information online at loonlakerv.com. Or call 541-599.2244.

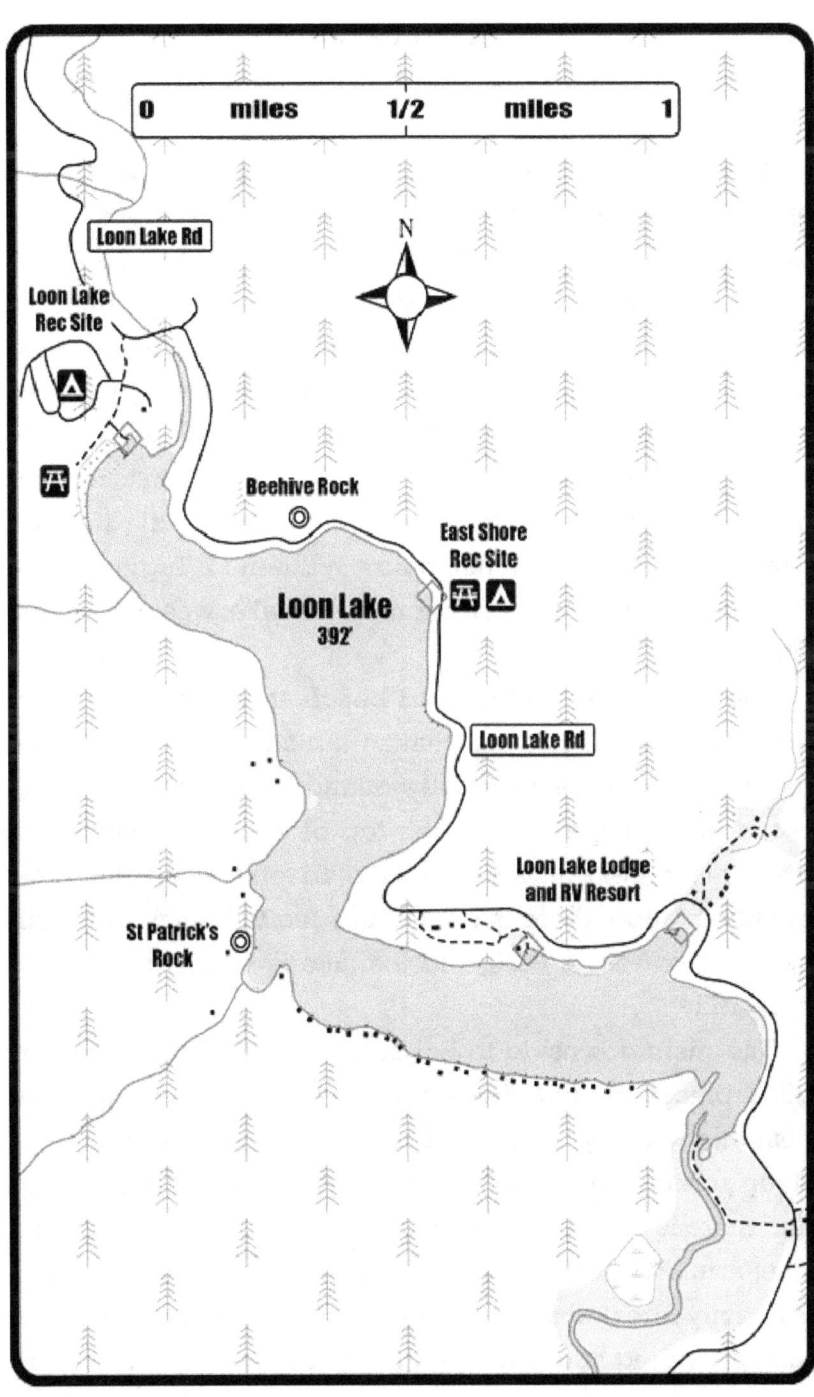

8. Eel Lake:
The dedicated paddler's paddle

There is nothing spectacular about Eel Lake, but it is a really nice place to paddle thanks to its general lack of motorized traffic and its unpopulated, heavily forested shores.

What is now Eel Lake was once the bed of two unnamed creeks flowing into the Pacific. To the west, coastal sand dunes grew until they impounded the creeks and produced a unique, V-shaped lake. The lake was used for log storage for decades, and the pilings of an old dock remain at the end of the near/west arm, which you can now paddle through like a slalom course. What is now William M. Tugman State Park, on the southwestern shore of the lake, was once a mill site.

There is a tiny golden sand beach at the delta of the inflowing Clear Creek that makes a nice place to stop and hangout. And there are small wetland areas scattered in the lake's inlets, especially at the top of each arm where the main inlet creeks flow into the lake. To top it all off, the water quality is good, there is no day use fee to launch from William Tugman State Park, and the lake is usually is not very crowded.

The main downside to Eel Lake is that it only has a few good places to land. Aside from the beach, there is a reddish clay outcrop at the end of a peninsula that features a steep scramble up to a wooden bench overlooking the lake, and there is an in-water dock in one of the inlets of the near/west arm. And that's about it; the remainder of the shoreline is heavily forested or swampy. Unfortunately, all of these potential landing spots are within a mile of the launch/return point. Also, the lake can get windy even though it's separated from the sea by two miles of dunes. So paddling around the whole lake requires some stamina on the board. You could say it's a paddle for those who really enjoy paddling.

The launch/return point is on the west side of the lake, close to the base of the V. You can reach the top of the near/west arm in approximately 1.5 miles, and you can reach the top of the far/east arm in approximately 2.5 miles. To go up both arms and around the lake, you will paddle approximately 8.5 miles.

The lake is primarily used by fishers, but is also frequented by paddlers and swimmers. It is stocked with rainbow trout and has populations of largemouth bass, crappie, steelhead, and Coho salmon. The Coho must be released. As the state park's website states, "[t]he brush-lined shore, steep drop-off and underwater structure makes it the perfect lake for ... bass fishing."

There are many snags that have fallen into the water and created near-shore hazards, but these can easily be avoided thanks to the steep shoreline. Unfortunately, paddlers will not be able to avoid views of the huge clearcuts that mar the areas outside the park on the eastern slopes of the lakebed, or the sounds of logging trucks engine-braking their way along nearby Highway 101.

Another big upside to Eel Lake is William M. Tugman State Park, which is open year-round and has lots of amenities, including ample day-use parking, a fully-accessible fishing pier, hot showers, flush toilets, tons of RV and tent camping sites, and 16 yurts. Two of the campsites and 11 of the yurts are accessible for folks with disabilities. Eight of the yurts even allow pets.

Difficulty: Easy or moderate.

Distance: 1.5 to 8.5 miles.

Directions: William M. Tugman State Park is right off Highway 101, the Oregon Coast Highway, on the east side. It is 9.8 miles south of the Highway 38-101 junction in Reedsport, and 17.3 miles north of Coos Bay.

Launch/Return: William M. Tugman State Park (see above). Camping, toilets, parking. No day use fee.

Nearby Camping: William M. Tugman State park (see above). Reservations can be made online at oregonstateparks.org or by phone at 800-452-5687.

Nearby Fun: Just a mile or so south of Eel Lake is the John Dellenbeck Dunes Trail. This is like no other hike in the state, as the trail traverses the 2.7 miles of sand dunes between the highway and the ocean shore. For most of the trail, there is no marked route. Instead, as the Siuslaw National Forest says, "hikers are advised to climb the tallest dune to get their bearings." See the Siuslaw NF website for more information.

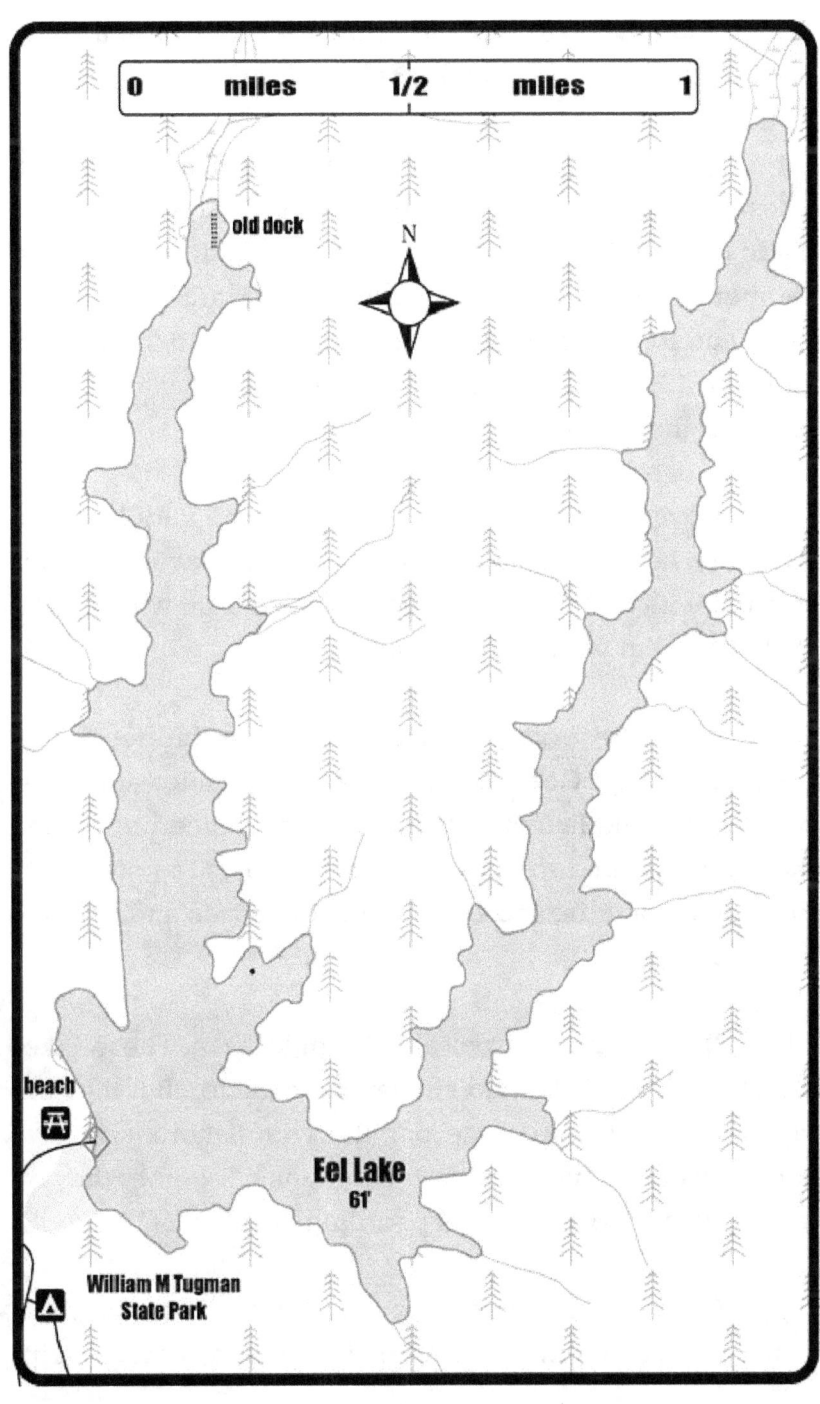

9. Other Good Places to Paddle – The Coast and Coast Range

(a) <u>Tillamook County Water Trail</u>: The Tillamook Estuaries Partnership has published a set of brochures that include lots of interesting information and great maps on four segments of the Tillamook County Water Trail: (1) Nehalem River and Bay; (2) Sand Lake, Nestucca Bay, and the Nestucca River; (3) Netarts Bay; and (4) Tillamook Bay. Find them online at tbnep.org.

(b) <u>Devils Lake</u>: Devils Lake is right in the middle of Lincoln City. Its shorelines are almost entirely developed, it is popular with motorboaters, and it can get a bit windy, but it is also popular with recreational paddlers.

(c) <u>Olalla Reservoir</u>: Olalla Reservoir is hidden in the green hills of the Coast Range just about 10 miles northwest of Newport. The launch/return point has a nice beach, and the shores are undeveloped and forested It is big enough to find some solitude, and there are many coves and inlets to explore.

(d) <u>North Tenmile Lake and Tenmile Lake</u>: These lakes are close to Eel Lake and similar in character. But they are larger than Eel Lake, more popular with fishers, and have some development along their shorelines. Together they offer many miles of additional paddling close to Eel Lake.

(e) <u>Coos Bay Estuary Water Trail</u>: The Coos Regional Trail Partnership published a set of maps and short descriptions of eight paddles around the Coos Bay area. Some, such as the Charleston Slough paddle, are quite scenic. Find them online at coostrails.com/water-trails.html. Note that the guides are fairly dated now, so it is likely that some conditions have changed.

(f) <u>New River and Floras Lake</u>: The New River is one of the oddest geological features of Oregon. First of all, it actually is new, at least in geological terms. In 1890, floodwaters rushed down Floras Creek and created a new river channel, earning the river its name. Second, the New River grows noticeably in length each year, with the mouth inching slowly northward. In 2003, the New River was approximately 10 miles long. But the truly odd thing about the New River is that it flows parallel to the coastline for several miles just a few hundred feet from the sea. This makes for a unique paddle with beautiful, secluded ocean beaches on one shore and coastal forests, marshes, and ranchland on the other. Unfortunately, the area tends to be very windy and there are restrictions on landing on the beaches. Still, there is lots of paddling here. You can access the New River at its north end at Croft Lake Rd (off Hwy 101 south of Coos Bay), which allows a visit to the BLM's New River Nature Center along the way (call ahead for details on paddling restrictions). Or you can access the new river at its south end via Floras Lake (also off Hwy 101). Floras Lake is small but a nice paddle. It's so close to the ocean that the western shore is also an ocean beach.

II. The Lower Columbia and Greater Portland

10. Columbia River at the Lewis and Clark National Wildlife Refuge:
History and wilderness on the Mighty Columbia

In the estuary of the mighty Columbia River, just upriver from Astoria, there are a group of large marshy islands, sand bars, mud flats, and tidal marshes on the Oregon side of the river. Lewis and Clark were the first Europeans to see the islands, referring to them as the "Seal Islands" when they came upon them in November 1805. The Lewis and Clark National Wildlife Refuge was established in 1972 to protect the estuarine ecosystem of the islands. It stretches over 27 miles and includes about 20 islands.

The area hosts thousands of migratory tundra swans, geese, and ducks, among others, with populations swelling in the winter months. It is also critical habitat for juvenile salmon. They pause here to fatten up and become acclimated to salt water before making the final dash to the Pacific. Seals, harbor seals, and California sea lions are frequently seen on the sand bars and mud flats. They fish alongside raptors such as bald eagles and northern harrier. On the islands, there are strong populations of beaver, coyote, raccoon, white-tailed deer, weasel, mink, muskrat, and river otter.

The islands are only accessible by boat, and there is endless paddling in the channels and bayous of the Seal Islands. The area is open to motors, and is populated mostly by fishers. This is not a paddle for beginners, as the Columbia River features strong current and wind, large tides, remote areas, and huge ships (and wakes) in the main channel of the river (to the north of Fitzpatrick Island). Still, there are a lot of protected areas for paddling where these hazards are minimized. And the diversity of wildlife is unmatched elsewhere in Oregon.

Deep channels separate the islands during high tides. During low tides, some areas may not be navigable, but many areas also become too shallow for motors. Snag hazards exist nearly everywhere outside of the main channels, and of course become more common at low tide. Some of the islands have "dry land" where you can stop, and there are some really nice beaches. For great views of Mt St Helens and the shipping traffic on the river, venture out to beaches on the northern shore of Grassy Island and Woody Island, or a much larger beach on the northeastern shore of Welch Island. And keep an eye out for hunters during hunting season.

As mentioned, the area offers limitless paddling options. Camping is not permitted in the refuge, so be sure to organize your adventure into a day trip. The map shows areas within several miles of the Aldrich Point launch/return site, but there is a second launch site known as John Day (not shown on the map), within reach of even more islands, further west off Highway 30.

For a basic yet substantial paddle, launch at John Day and paddle approximately six miles around Lois Island. Or launch at Aldrich Point and paddle approximately 3.5 miles around Tronson Island. You can download a map of the entire refuge, as well as an informative brochure, at the Refuge's website (fws.gov/lc/).

Difficulty: Moderate to advanced.

Distance: 3.5 to 20 miles.

Directions: Ziak-Gnat Creek Rd is about 17 miles east of Astoria on Highway 30, the Columbia River Highway, and about 50 miles northwest of St Helens. Turn north off Highway 30 onto Ziak-Gnat Creek Rd. Go 1.0 miles and turn right onto Aldrich Point Rd. Aldrich Point Boat Ramp is 4.3 miles ahead on the right.

Launch/Return: Aldrich Point Boat Ramp. No facilities. No parking fee.

Nearby Rental: None.

Nearby Camping: None.

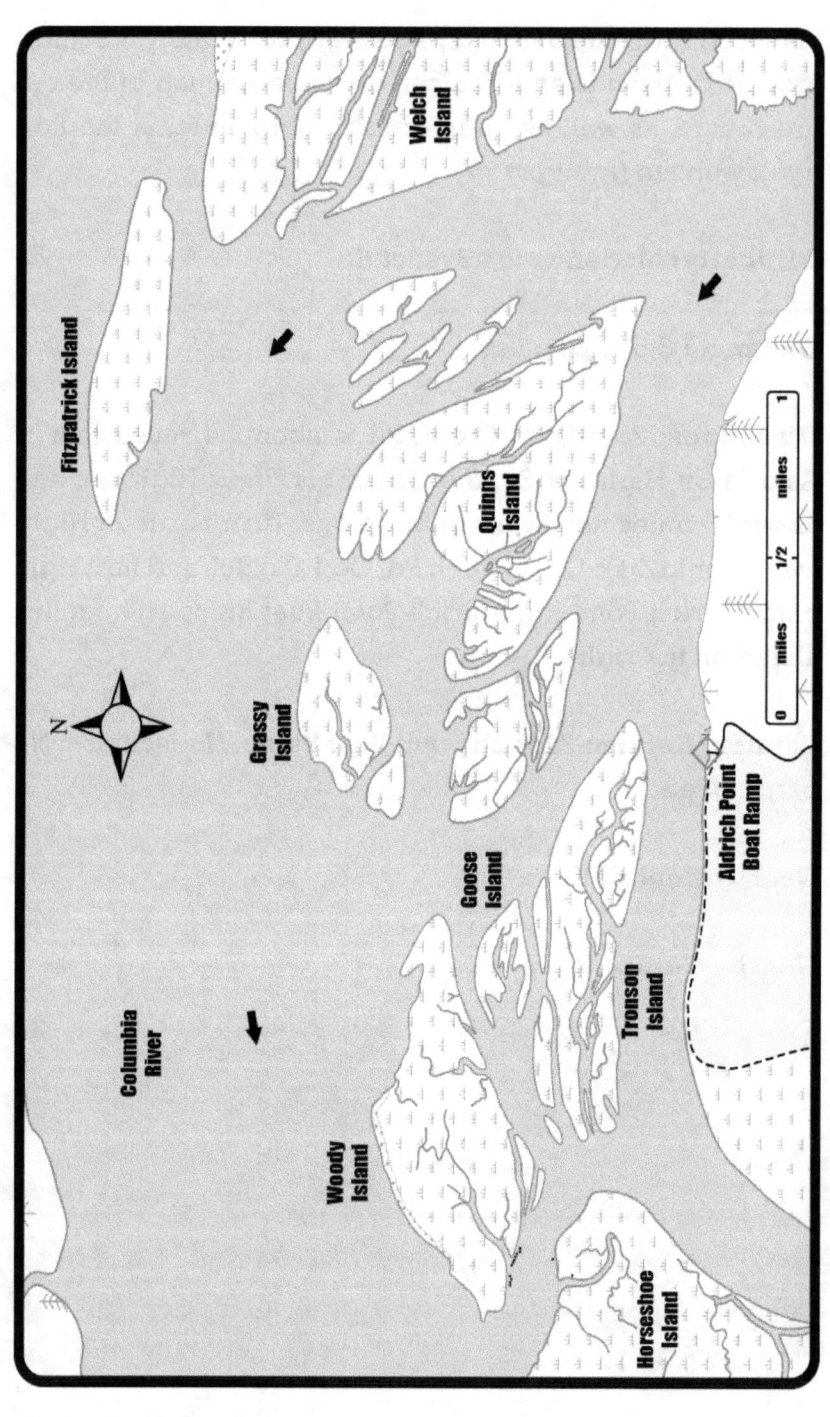

11. Columbia River at St Helens:
Island camping, beaches, an old light house, and historic St Helens

A paddle on the Columbia River definitely stretches the definition of "flatwater" a bit. The Columbia is truly a great river. It is the largest North American river draining into the Pacific, and the fourth-largest river in the US. It carries over eight times more water than the Willamette. Paddling hazards include strong current, cold water, heavy traffic, huge wakes from ocean-going ships, in-water objects, strong winds, and large waves.

As with every entry in this book, the paddle described here is well worth the trouble. This route has nice views of Mt St Helens and Mt Hood, good beaches, island camping opportunities, and some historic sites. It will also give you a close-up look at immense freighters carrying hundreds of cargo containers from Asia, tugs pushing barges full of logs downriver, and the stately riverfront homes and docks of Columbia City and St Helens.

You will be able to get close to eagle nests, which sit atop many of the in-water pilings along the route. Of particular note along the way is the historic Columbia County Courthouse, which sits near the water just upriver from the St Helens Marina. It's a two-mile paddle upriver from the launch/return point at Pixie Park in Columbia City. And if you paddle far enough, you will reach the Warrior Rock Lighthouse, Oregon's smallest lighthouse and the only one not located on the coast. The lighthouse is about 3.4 miles upriver from Pixie Park, and about 1.5 miles upriver from Grey Cliffs Waterfront Park in St Helens.

Sand Island makes a nice stop along the way. The entire island is a park with bathrooms as well as several boat-in campsites hidden in the forest. White sand beaches wrap around much of the island, with the widest areas at the northern and southern ends. The island also shelters paddlers from wakes in the main river channel.

The area around Warrior Point, the northernmost point of Sauvie Island, is strewn with rotting pilings from an old dock that no longer exists. The pilings offer a slalom course for practicing paddling skills, and submerged structures pose a hazard in this area.

Visiting the lighthouse requires paddling nearly a mile past Warrior Point along the edge of the main river channel. This stretch of Sauvie Island is lined with a wide sandy beach that is virtually deserted since this part of the island is a three-mile hike from the nearest road. Most rivergoers spend their time enjoying the more accessible beaches on nearby Sand Island.

To mitigate the influence of the current, this paddle is an up-and-back. A shorter paddle can easily be done here by returning home after checking out Sand Island, or by launching from Grey Cliffs Waterfront Park in St Helens. Note that the area near Grey Cliffs Waterfront Park is sheltered from the main river channel by Sand Island.

Difficulty: Moderate to advanced.

Distance: Less than a mile to 6.8 miles.

Directions:
Pixie Park: From Highway 30, the Columbia River Highway, in the town of Columbia City, turn eastward onto I St. Go six blocks and the park is straight ahead.

Grey Cliffs Waterfront Park: From Highway 30, the Columbia River Highway, in the town of St Helens, turn eastward onto Columbia Blvd. Go 1.1 miles and turn right onto S 4th St. Go one block and turn left on St Helens St/Old Portland Rd. Go four blocks and turn left on River St. The park is straight ahead about two blocks.

Launch/Return:
Pixie Park: Pixie Park is a tiny park consisting of about eight parking spots and a 40-feet wide beach in tiny Columbia City. Launch from the beach. No facilities. No parking fee.

Grey Cliffs Waterfront Park: Grey Cliffs Waterfront Park is also essentially just a parking lot and a boat ramp. No facilities. No parking fee.

Nearby Rental: Oregon River Rentals, in Clackamas, rents inflatable kayaks and SUPs. SUPortland, in the Jantzen Beach neighborhood of Portland, rents SUPs.

Nearby Camping: None.

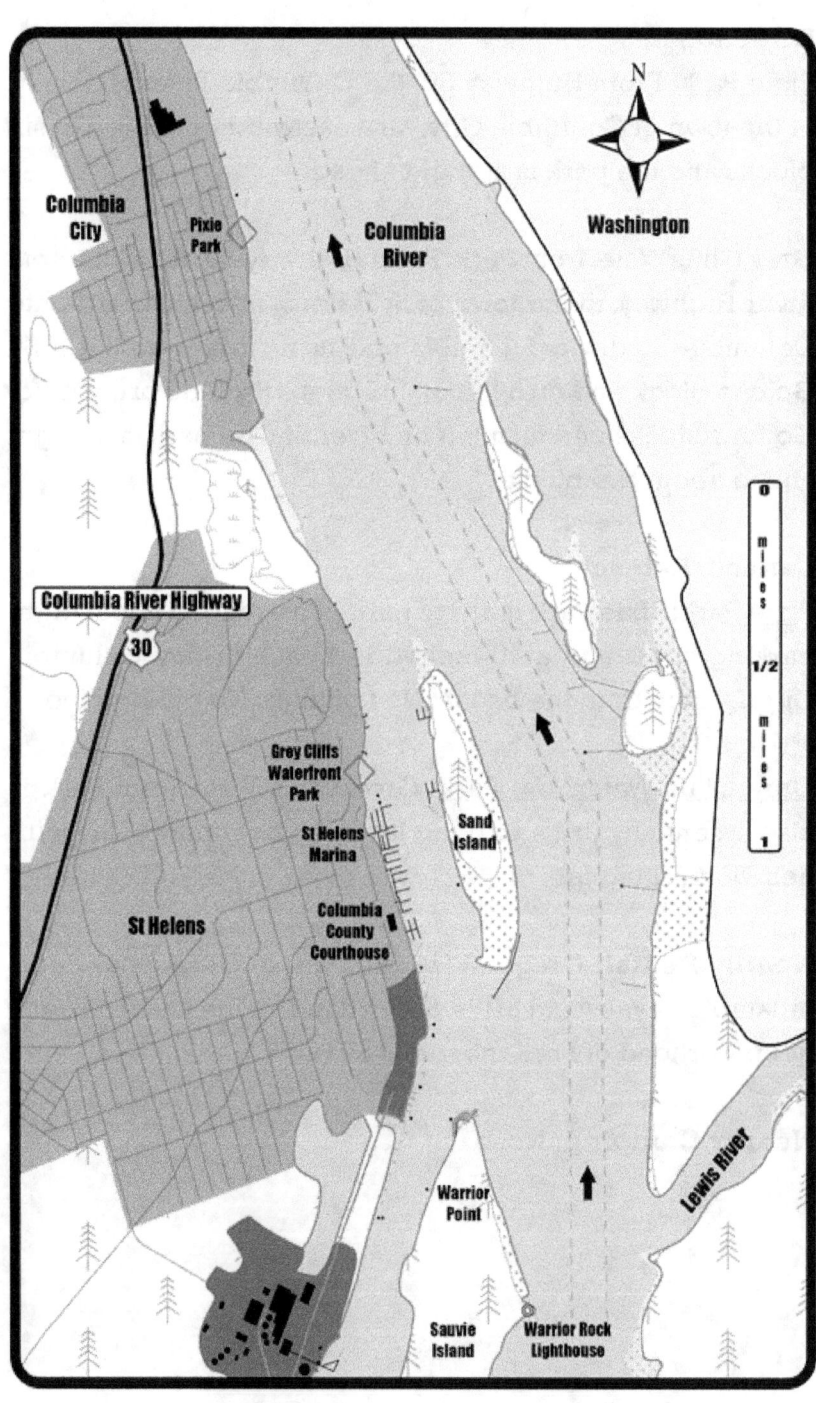

12. Upper Gilbert River and Sturgeon Lake (Sauvie Island):

Experience the other side of Portland's Island

Have you ever been on an island in a lake on an island in a river? You can be if you paddle Sturgeon Lake.

Sauvie Island, and especially the Gilbert River, reminds me of where I grew up, on the bayous of southern Mississippi. The muddy water, the thick, green vegetation, and the narrow, twisting, plant-choked channels are all so evocative of a southern swamp that I found myself keeping an eye out for gators on this paddle just out of instinct. There are none of those, but other wildlife abounds here. This is an absolutely fantastic paddle through a very isolated part of "Portland's island."

The Gilbert River is a curious thing. For now, it is a river channel with well-defined banks, but the banks themselves are only a fraction of a mile wide – they are simply long narrow peninsulas or islands. On the far side of the banks is Sturgeon Lake. So the Gilbert is a river somehow flowing through, or between, a lake. This may soon change, as officials are planning to let more water into the Sauvie Island wetlands.

After bisecting Sturgeon Lake, Sauvie Island's largest lake, the Gilbert River continues northerly downstream through the island until it converges with the Multnomah Channel, the major waterway separating Sauvie Island from the rest of Oregon, near the island's northern end.

To the west of Sturgeon Lake is a channel that connects to a series of smaller, interconnected lakes, including Steelman Lake, West Arm, Wagonwheel Hole, and Mud Lake.

There are a few side river channels in this area that can be explored as well. The same is true on the northern side of Sturgeon Lake. Throughout the area, there are also isolated lakes and river channels.

The Gilbert River channel offers the best paddling of all these areas. The biggest advantage is that the channel is protected from the winds that can make paddling on the open lakes quite challenging. I encountered near whitecap-level waves in Sturgeon Lake in only a 10mph sustained wind due to the shallowness of the water.

In addition to the wind, in low water conditions the lakes are unpredictably shallow. In fact, I was occasionally dragging my fin in certain places even near the center of Sturgeon Lake. In lower water conditions, most or all of the lakes can be impassable. By contrast, the Gilbert River channel is quite well defined and sufficiently deep. And the northern-flowing current is slight. The shores of the channel also offer some secluded places to take out.

The shallowness of the water, even in the Gilbert River, conveys the key advantage of making the water largely impassible for motorboats, though lower parts of the River are passable for smaller motorboats in higher water. This in turn conveys the key advantage of solitude, as the river and lake shorelines are almost totally undeveloped. The sound of airliners overhead and the faint rumble of the city in the background are reminders that civilization is not far away. However, the feel of the immediate environment is one of wilderness. It isn't often you can say a place so close to a major city is teeming with wildlife, but the Sauvie Island wetlands certainly are.

Note that this area is closed for a portion of the year, usually from October 1 to April 16 or May 1. Access also becomes impossible sometimes during the spring due to high water levels. Check the Oregon Department of Fish and Wildlife's Sauvie Island Wildlife Refuge webpage for detailed information and current conditions. The best time for finding high water conditions is in the spring.

Difficulty: Easy or moderate or advanced, depending on desired length. Suitable for beginners.

Distance: 2 to 20 miles.

Directions: Sauvie Island is accessed from Highway 30, 3.9 miles north of the St Johns Bridge in Portland, and 9.8 miles south of Scappoose. Turn east onto NW Sauvie Island Rd. Stay on NW Sauvie Island Rd for 10.2 miles (Stay left at the stop sign at NW Reeder Rd) and then turn right onto an unnamed dirt road. The primitive launch area is 0.4 miles from the turn.

For the more northerly launch area, continue another 0.7 miles on NW Sauvie Island Rd before making a sharp turn to the right. Continue for another 0.7 miles to the primitive launch area.

Launch/Return: Both launch/return areas are primitive with no water and possibly a portable toilet. Parking fee is $10/day or $30 for an annual pass. Parking passes should be purchased at the store next to the Sauvie Island Bridge.

Nearby Rental: Next Adventure, in SE Portland, rents SUPs and kayaks. Oregon River Rentals, in Clackamas, rents inflatable kayaks and SUPs. SUPortland, in the Jantzen Beach neighborhood of Portland, rents SUPs.

Nearby Camping: None.

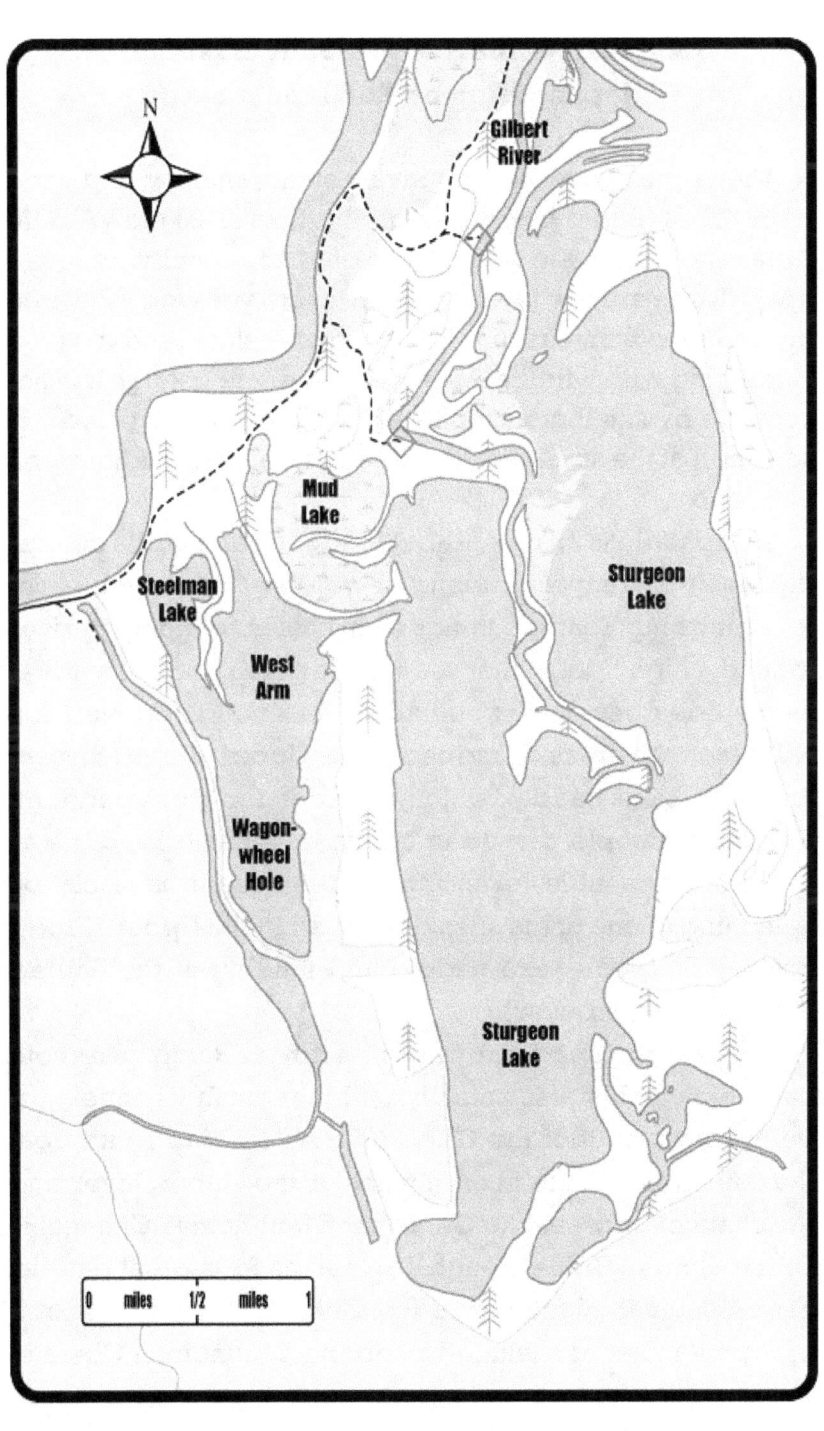

13. Lower Gilbert River (Sauvie Island): Quiet paddling on Portland's bayou

The Gilbert River is a relatively small, shallow, and wide river channel that flows through the Sauvie Island Wildlife Area. The banks are heavily forested and totally undeveloped. There are few places to land where you won't sink into mud when coming ashore. The current is slack, and the area is teeming with wildlife. Most folks here are fishing. It is accessible by small motorboats only. For a more detailed description of the area, see the Upper Gilbert River & Sturgeon Lake entry.

This paddle is an up-and-back, so you can paddle against the weak current for as long as you feel comfortable before returning. To make things even easier, try going upriver around a high tide, so that you will be going back downriver as the tide goes out. If you paddle far enough upriver, you will reach the areas described in the Upper Gilbert River & Sturgeon Lake paddle, which provides for more paddling than most people can do in a day. It can also be done as a downriver shuttle (even though the current is slack) by launching at one of the sites described in the Upper Gilbert River & Sturgeon Lake paddle and landing at the Gilbert Boat Ramp (see below).

When launching from the Gilbert Boat Ramp, take note that the launch site is actually on Multnomah Channel, just below the mouth of the Gilbert. When looking south from the launch site, the leftmost channel is the Gilbert River, and the channel between the Gilbert and Multnomah Channel is Crane Slough. Crane Slough also makes for a great paddle, very similar in character to the Gilbert, and offers another 3-plus miles of secluded paddling. Multnomah Channel can also be paddled from here, but has some development along its shores, stronger current, and larger boat traffic.

Note that this area is closed for a portion of the year, usually from October 1 to April 16 or May 1. Check the Oregon Department of Fish and Wildlife's Sauvie Island Wildlife Refuge webpage for detailed information and current conditions.

Difficulty: Easy or moderate or advanced, depending on desired length.

Distance: 2 to 20 miles.

Directions: Sauvie Island is accessed from Highway 30, 3.9 miles north of the St Johns Bridge in Portland, and 9.8 miles south of Scappoose. Turn east onto NW Sauvie Island Rd. In 1.9 miles, turn right onto NW Reeder Rd. Go another 11.5 miles on Reeder Rd (stay left at stop sign at NW Gillihan Rd) and turn left onto an unnamed dirt road. Look for the sign that says "Gilbert River Boat Ramp ½ Mile." The boat ramp is on the right. Note that the road continues past the boat ramp but dead-ends soon thereafter.

Launch/Return: Gilbert Boat Ramp. Toilets, parking. No water. Parking fee is $10/day or $30 for an annual pass. Parking passes should be purchased at the store next to the Sauvie Island Bridge.

Nearby Rental: Next Adventure, in SE Portland, rents SUPs and kayaks. Oregon River Rentals, in Clackamas, rents inflatable kayaks and SUPs. SUPortland, in the Jantzen Beach neighborhood of Portland, rents SUPs.

Nearby Camping: None.

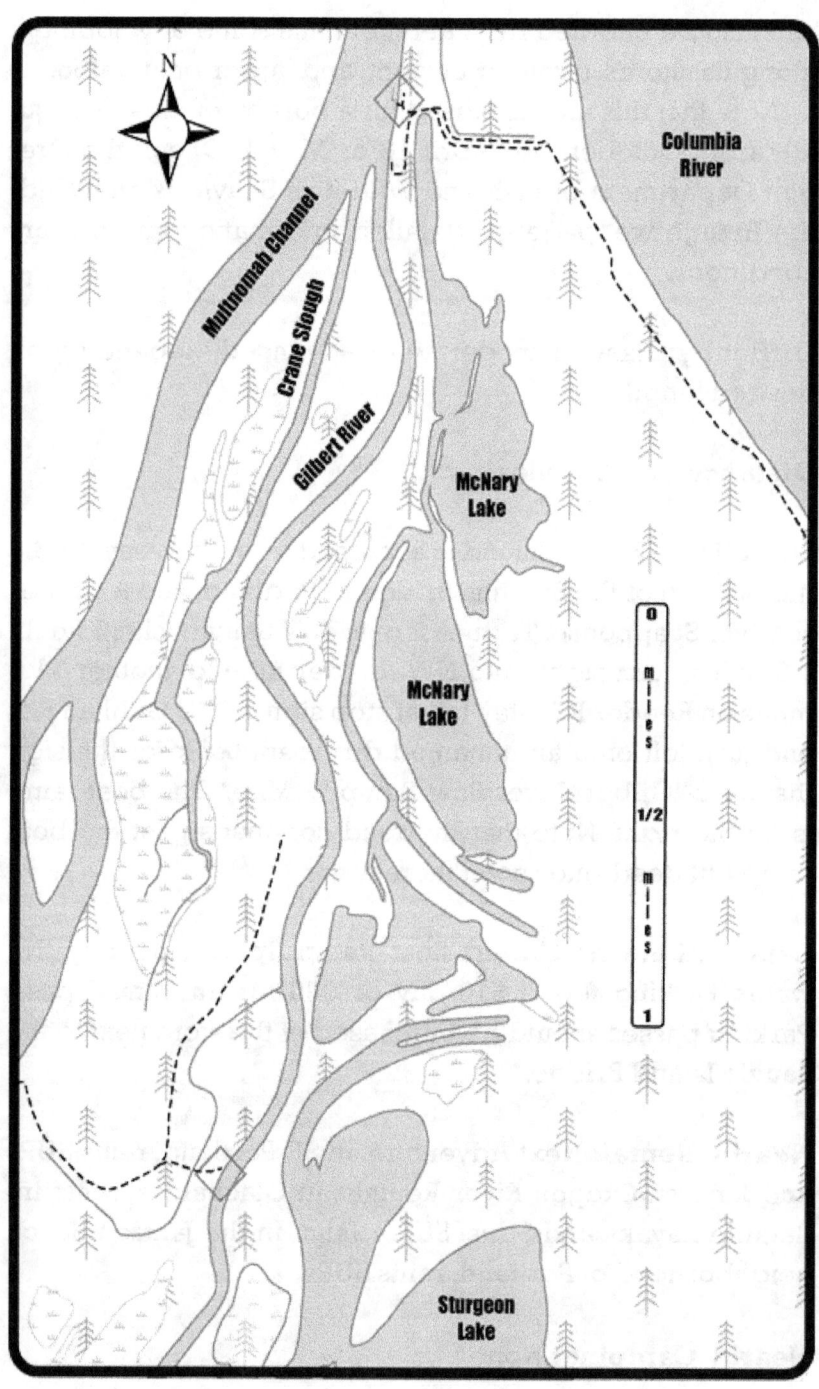

14. Scappoose Bay and Cunningham Slough (Sauvie Island):

Outstanding solitude and wildlife viewing, just minutes from Portland!

My paddle through Cunningham Slough really blew me away. I saw more wildlife here than on any other paddle in the entire state, and the launch point is only about 27 miles from downtown Portland. I saw coyote pups playing outside of their riverside den, and I even got close-up views of beavers, which are notoriously reclusive. Both the coyotes and the beavers seemed pretty curious about the human standing on the water with a dog sitting at his feet.

On my paddle, there were no other humans around for miles. Most of the slough is more than a mile away from the nearest public road, and there are no trails in the area either. So it was just me and my first mate gliding through a pristine temperate bayou ecosystem, a veritable paddling paradise, with eagles and herons perched in the overhanging trees. This is not the only paddle in this book on Sauvie Island, of course, but it made me realize what an asset this area is for metro-area folks. Did I mention it's less than 30 miles from downtown Portland?

The wonderful isolation of the slough contrasts with Scappoose Bay, which has industrial development along its shores and motorboat traffic, mostly fishers. But the bay is also quite charming, with its houseboats, decaying docks, and clear views of Mt St Helens on the paddle toward the slough. The bay also has some sheltered wetland areas to explore, and lots of birds.

This paddle presents some challenges too, making it one that is not appropriate for beginners. The first challenge is crossing Multnomah Channel, twice. The channel has a significant current, can get wavy and windy at times, and features larger marine traffic, including commercial ships and large pleasure craft. These vessels create correspondingly large wakes, so I recommend surveying the channel from either end before crossing, and timing the crossing to avoid any large wakes, if possible.

The second challenge is finding the mouth of Cunningham Slough. From the paddler's perspective at Cathlacom Point, the mouth is hidden behind Louse Island. After spotting the island, it is tempting go around the south end of the island, as that appears to be the shortest route to the mouth. However, the island has a huge tidal sandbar on its southern end. At low tide, going to the south of the island will require paddling an additional mile farther to get around the bar. If you do this paddle at low tide (not recommended), it is shorter to go around the north end of Louse Island.

The third challenge is the distance. It is nearly three miles – one way – from the launch/return point to the mouth of the slough. From there, you can go almost four more miles along the slough in lower water conditions. If you go all the way along the slough, you will have paddled 12 to 14 miles by the time you reach the return point.

And as if that weren't enough of a challenge, the banks throughout this paddle are muddy and marshy, and the mud is thick and deep. There are very few suitable places to land.

Lastly, the slough itself is a small, muddy channel with numerous snag hazards in the form of in-water vegetation, mostly dead tree limbs. Fortunately, the surrounding forest shelters the slough from higher winds. At the 3.7-mile mark (from the launch), there is a side channel connecting to Millionaire Lake. This "lake" is a bayou during low water conditions, and an approximately mile-around lake dotted with tree islands during higher water conditions. Note that I have drawn the map to reflect the more common, and more challenging, low water conditions.

At the 6-mile mark, the forest opens up to meadow. This is Cunningham Lake, also a bayou during low water conditions and a lake during higher water conditions. During lower water conditions, the bayou splits at mile 6.2. Both forks peter out soon thereafter.

The entire slough area is easier to navigate during the rainy season, and also affords a longer paddle, due to higher water. But the area is only open from April 16 to October 1, so spring is the best time to visit for higher water conditions. In the early summer, a high tide is the best time to paddle. Later in the summer or early autumn, water conditions may be too low to paddle parts of the slough, but the paddling is still great.

Around a high tide, paddlers can also explore a sheltered part of the bay along its eastern shore near Cathlacom Point. This part of the bay is separated from the rest by a series of islands.

Difficulty: Advanced.

Distance: 6 to 14 miles.

Directions: The Scappoose Bay Marina is accessed from Highway 30, the Columbia River Highway. From Highway 30 about 3 miles south of St Helens and 5 miles north of Scappoose, turn southeast onto Bennett Rd and make an immediate left onto Old Portland Rd. The marina is 0.5 miles ahead on the right. The address is 57420 Old Portland Rd, Warren, OR 97053.

Launch/Return: Scappoose Bay Marina. Parking, toilets, and advice on conditions at the Scappoose Bay Paddle Center, in the marina building. $3 parking fee.

Nearby Rental/Tours: The Scappoose Bay Paddle Center rents SUPs, kayaks, and canoes, as well as offering paddling tours and classes.

Nearby Camping: The Bayport RV Park and Campground is adjacent to the Scappoose Bay Marina. Showers, wifi.

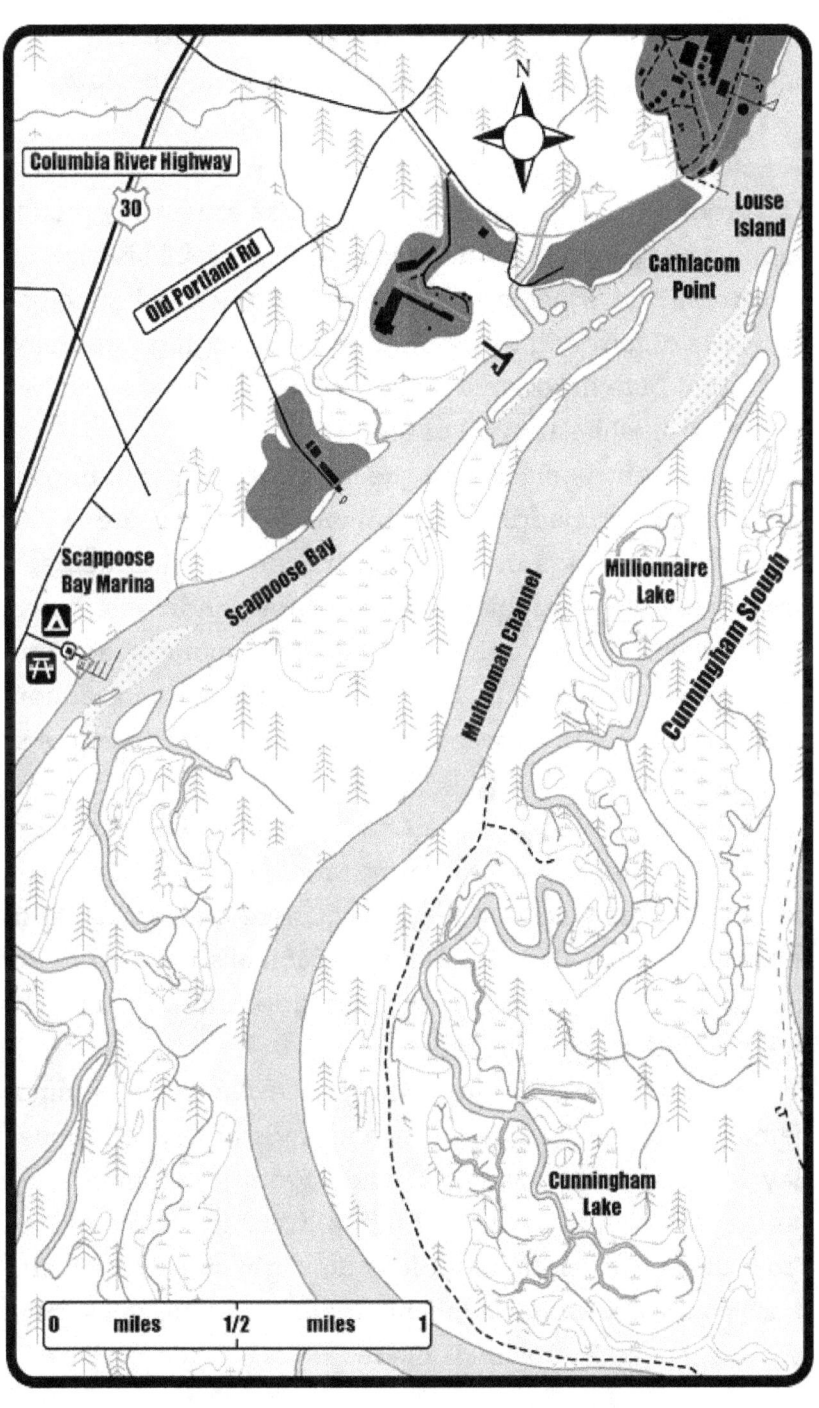

15. Scappoose Bay and Scappoose Creek: Another remote bayou paddle close to Portland

Scappoose Creek is another bayou gem close to Portland. The creek is fairly isolated and the banks are mostly picturesque wetlands lined with Oregon white oaks. This area offers great bird watching as well. On my paddle, I got close up views of four eagles perched in overhanging trees, several great blue herons, white herons, a black oystercatcher, and greater white-fronted geese.

The current is slack and the tide is slight, making for good beginner paddling conditions. But there are a few places where snags in the creek present an intermediate-level challenge, especially in low water conditions. Twice, I was required to kneel and maneuver around snags and branches in the channel, but the obstacles were infrequent and most of the time I was able to stand and paddle free of obstructions.

Unfortunately, Scappoose Creek suffers somewhat from poor water quality. Further up, the creek has a surface sheen and cattle graze close to the water. There are muddy landing spots along this route, but no beaches anywhere in the bay or creek. But do not let this dissuade you from enjoying the remainder of the creek.

Like the paddle through Scappoose Bay and Cunningham Slough, this paddle starts and ends at the Scappoose Bay Marina (not on Sauvie Island). From the launch point (at the marina), you must paddle leftward to reach the bay. From there, turn right and follow the right shore (the mainland) southwestward for one mile, where you will see a small wooden dock. On the left is the mouth of Scappoose Creek.

The paddle along Scappoose Bay is also nice. After leaving the marina, houses on the shore are visible through the wetlands. There are likely to be other paddlers, but the water soon becomes too shallow for motorboats except early in the season (spring and early summer) when the water is high.

About a mile above the mouth, the creek forks. Either or both forks may be impassible due to snags in the channel. When I visited the left fork (when looking upriver) was impassible at the entrance, but I was able to follow the other fork for another 2+ miles further up the creek. Because of the snags, this paddle is better done in higher water conditions, including going both earlier in the paddling season, as well as around high tide. Higher water also extends the navigable distance of the creek, and sometimes it is possible to go a lot farther up the creek.

You can also paddle further up the bay about a mile above the mouth of the creek (southward; see map). The water quality declines here as well, and there are a great deal of aquatic plants that require some navigation to avoid their fin drag hazard.

Difficulty: Easy, but moderate if you want to try navigating the snags up Scappoose Creek.

Distance: 6 miles.

Directions: The Scappoose Bay Marina is accessed from Highway 30, the Columbia River Highway. From Highway 30 about 3 miles south of St Helens and 5 miles north of Scappoose, turn southeast onto Bennett Rd and make an immediate left onto Old Portland Rd. The marina is 0.5 miles ahead on the right. The address is 57420 Old Portland Rd, Warren, OR 97053.

Launch/Return: Scappoose Bay Marina. Parking, toilets, and advice on conditions at the Scappoose Bay Paddle Center, in the marina building. $3 parking fee.

Nearby Rental/Tours: The Scappoose Bay Paddle Center rents SUPs, kayaks, and canoes, as well as offering paddling tours and classes.

Nearby Camping: The Bayport RV Park and Campground is adjacent to the Scappoose Bay Marina. Showers, wifi.

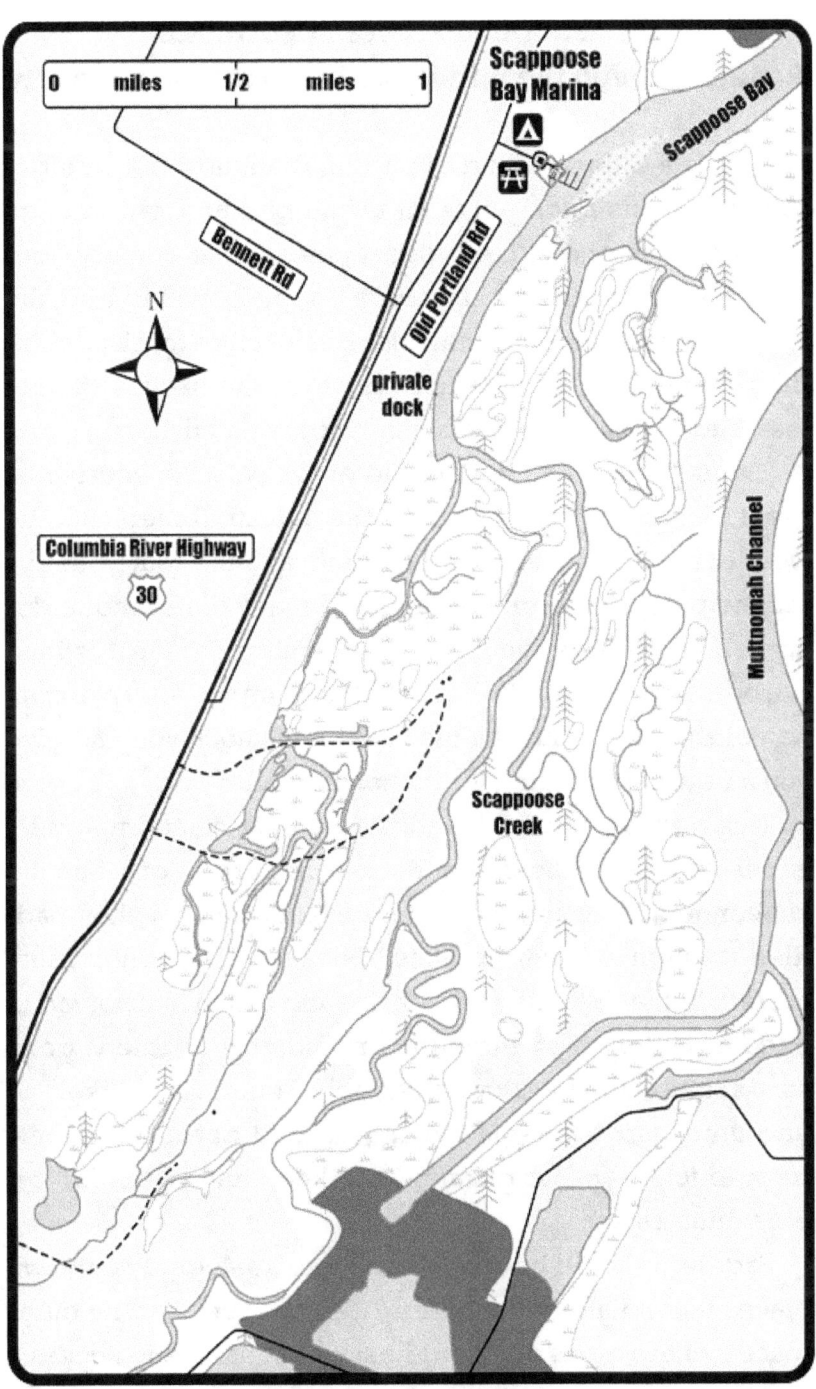

16. Willamette River at Portland:
Paddle through the middle of America's best big city

This is a different kind of paddle than most of those described in this book – it is an urban paddle right through the middle of one of the biggest cities in the country. Your company on the river will include people gawking from the shore, bicyclists and runners, jet boats full of tourists, shipping traffic, recreational motorboaters, the nautical homeless, and occasionally even water skiers and fishers.

There is virtually no nature to enjoy, only the occasional great blue heron hiding among the industrial piers. But the wonders of the human world abound, and the route offers a unique perspective on Portland and many of its landmarks, as well as its large industrial port facilities at the Portland Harbor. Throughout the route, the number of riverfront homeless camps and shanties will both shock you and give you a new appreciation for human ingenuity.

This paddle is difficult and should only be attempted by experienced paddlers. But the rewards are as great as the challenge. Who else among your friends can say they paddled through a Superfund site? Because of the substantial current in the Willamette River, and the distance involved in paddling all the way through Portland, this paddle is done as a shuttle, floating downriver only. You are also likely to encounter large vessels moving up and down the river – be sure to keep your distance and keep an eye out for approaching wakes.

Paddlers should be aware that there are literally only two places to land along the entire 7.5-mile route, and no other places where a paddler could easily get ashore to access a road or trail. Much of the riverfront is either seawall, rip-rap, or private land, and the few land-able places are rocky.

Getting access to the river in the first place is also very difficult. There are only two places to launch in and around downtown Portland, and no good places to launch, with either potential site requiring a considerable walk with the board. But the reason to go through all the trouble is that there are some fantastic sites on the river around downtown.

Start with the USS Blueback (SS-581) submarine, which is docked at the Oregon Museum of Science and Industry (OMSI) just south of the Marquam Bridge. The Blueback is a sleek black missile-shape lurking in the water beneath a conning tower, and you can see it up-close from the river. The Blueback is a decommissioned Barbel-class diesel-electric propelled attack submarine – the last generation before the deployment of nuclear-powered submarines. It was built on the bayous of Mississippi and was in US Navy service in the Pacific from 1960 to 1990, including service in the Vietnam War.

The Blueback is also kinda famous, having appeared in the TV series Hawaii Five-O (the original 70s vintage), as well as Portlandia, and more recently The Librarians. She has also had a career on the big screen, appearing in the blockbuster submarine epic The Hunt for Red October. Really, it's difficult to imagine a higher achievement for a retired submarine than a cameo with Sean Connery, Alec Baldwin, and James Earl Jones. OMSI offers (land-based) guided tours of the submarine for those who are completely free of claustrophobia.

After enjoying the Blueback, you can paddle around the many fine sailing vessels docked at the Riverplace Marina on the western shore (river left). There are also good views of downtown buildings and Tom McCall Waterfront Park, as well as close-up looks at the Hawthorne, Morrison, Burnside, Steel, Broadway, Fremont, Burlington Northern Railroad, and St Johns bridges. There is a great deal of interesting engineering history in these eight Portland bridges. For example, the St Johns Bridge is a replica of the Golden Gate Bridge, scaled down and painted green instead of orange.

You can also paddle past the historic paddle steamer Portland, which is permanently docked on the river between the Burnside and Morrison bridges as part of the Oregon Maritime Museum. According to the Oregon Maritime Museum, the Portland was the last operating sternwheel steam tug in the United States. Like OMSI, entrance to the museum is from land only.

Opposite the Portland lies the Vera Katz Eastbank Esplanade, a floating bike-pedestrian path running adjacent to the eastern shore of the river here. The Esplanade is a very innovative solution to the need for active transportation infrastructure along the Portland downtown riverfront, which is sadly dominated by the I-5 highway on the eastern shore. Paddle over and high-five a runner on your way out of downtown.

As you paddle north, the river transitions to an industrial port, with large silos, storage tanks, docks, ship terminals, cranes, warehouses, shipyards, and other marine industries lining the river. The Portland Harbor officially starts on the north side of the Steel Bridge, where you will see that familiar gigantic grain terminal in front of the Rose Garden. From just below the Broadway Bridge, the river is dredged to a depth of 40 feet to accommodate commercial shipping. Keep an eye out for ships approaching from behind (upriver).

You will feel truly small paddling past the massive cranes and beneath Oregon's longest bridge, the Fremont, which carries eight lanes of interstate highway traffic over 200 feet above your head. Once you are north of the Fremont, you have reached the heart of the Portland Harbor. At the 3.5-mile mark (Rivermile 10), just after the Fremont Bridge and before Swan Island, there is a beach on the eastern shore (river right), popular with dogs and sunbathers, where you can land. Locals refer to it McCarthy Park or the Swan Island Beach. The views of the downtown skyline are good from here on down, just remember to look back from time to time.

After the beach, on the eastern shore are Swan Island and Waud Bluff, from which the University of Portland overlooks the river. On the west side above the harbor is NW Portland, with Washington Park and Forest Park on the ridge above.

Swan Island is an industrial district home to heavyweights such as Daimler Trucks North America. It used to be an actual island, but was filled in and connected to the rest of NE Portland so it could be developed. It also used to be home to Portland's airport – imagine a large plane trying to land on this small strip of land between the river and the bluff. During World War II, Swan Island was used to construct US Navy ships, and it is still home to Oregon's largest shipyard facilities.

This area, from Rivermile 8 to the takeout point at Cathedral Park, is the heart of the Portland Harbor Superfund Site. For nearly a century, businesses dumped poison into this part of the river essentially at will. The term "Superfund" basically refers to a dedication of federal funds to help cleanup the most polluted places in the country. But there isn't enough public money to fix the Portland Harbor, of course. And because "corporations are people," there hasn't been enough private money to do the job, either.

Since 2000, when the Portland Harbor received the Superfund designation, some cleanup has been done, and a lot of lawyers have gotten rich fighting over who polluted what. But a great deal of cleanup and remediation remains undone. Now it seems that, for all the good these industries provided, and for all the profit they made, it will be you and me who ultimately pay for the river to be restored. That is, if we ever get around to dedicating the necessary resources to it.

After passing Swan Island, you will see the Railroad Bridge. Around its base also on the eastern shore, there is another small beach that could be used for landing if you need another break. From here it is less than a mile to the takeout point at Cathedral Park in N Portland, which is right after the St Johns Bridge on the eastern shore (river right).

There are several other options for this paddle. It is possible to see a lot of the sites on the river without doing the entire route. For example, you could put in and take out at the same place in downtown Portland and see the Blueback submarine, the downtown bridges, the Portland steamer, and the Eastbank Esplanade in just a few miles of paddling. You have to be prepared to paddle back upriver, of course, but paddling up just a couple of miles is not too hard, especially on a rising tide.

You could also put in and take out at Cathedral Park, paddling upriver first for as far as you feel comfortable while enjoying the Portland Harbor, Fremont Bridge, downtown skyline, and Forest Park, then paddling back downriver to Cathedral Park.

For a shorter, three-mile float, you could put in at the Swan Island Boat Ramp and take out at Cathedral Park. The Swan Island Boat Ramp is at the southern end of the Swan Island Basin. Be aware that this location is generally very crowded.

For a longer float that would let you avoid the difficulties of accessing the river in SE or SW Portland, you could put in further upriver at Sellwood Riverfront Park or Willamette Park (not shown on the map). These parks are approximately 3 miles from the launch points in SW and SE Portland described above.

Difficulty: Advanced.

Distance: 7.3 miles from SW or SE Portland to Cathedral Park. 10.3 miles from Sellwood Riverfront Park or Willamete Park. Shorter options too (see above).

Directions: See below.

Launch/Return:
In SE Portland under the Hawthorne Bridge: There is no public parking lot for those wishing to access the water or the Eastside Esplanade here, and there is no vehicle access to the single public pier from which a non-motorized watercraft can be launched. To make matters worse, the on-street parking is limited, only allows a two-hour maximum, and requires at least a two-block walk, but more likely a five- or six-block walk, with your board or boat. The best available parking is in a private lot directly under I-5 just north of the

Hawthorn Bridge. It is also possible to park in the Portland Community College lot, which requires a slightly longer walk.

From there, it will be necessary to carry the board across or along the heavily-used bike-pedestrian trail (where the Springwater Corridor Trail and Eastbank Esplanade meet). It is possible to launch from the dirt shore beneath the Hawthorne Bridge on its south side, and this is the closest launch place from most parking, requiring an approximately 50-yard walk with the board.

There are two other possible launch spots at this location. The first is the Portland Boathouse pier right next to the Portland Fire House and similarly close to the private parking lot. The problem with this pier is that it has low rails all along the edge of the pier, requiring a step-over to reach the water, and making the launch more difficult. The second other possible launch spot is the official public pier about 100 yards south of the Hawthorn Bridge. Its only disadvantage is that it requires a significantly longer walk with the board from the parking lots.

On the west side of the river in SW Portland: There is crescent-shaped beach in Waterfront Park between the Hawthorne Bridge and the Riverplace Marina is suitable as a primitive launch/return point. This location also offers very limited parking and requires a significant walk with the board.

In either location, it might be best to get dropped off with the boards, with the driver meeting you at Cathedral Park to complete your shuttle.

If you're not into going through the trouble of launching around downtown Portland, you can add about 3 miles onto the paddle by launching from Sellwood Riverfront Park or Willamette Park.

Sellwood Riverfront Park: Sellwood Riverfront Park is in SE Portland just west of Highway 99E in the Sellwood neighborhood. Bathrooms, parking. No water. No day use fee.

Willamette Park: Willamette Park is in SW Portland off SW Macadam Ave. Toilets, parking. Parking fee of $1/hour for the first five hours, and flat fee of $10 for all-day parking.

Swan Island Boat Launch: Toilets, parking. No day use fee.

Cathedral Park: Toilets, parking. No day use fee.

Nearby Rental: The Portland Kayak Company rents kayaks, canoes, and SUPs and is located adjacent to Willamette Park. Next Adventure, in SE Portland, rents SUPs and kayaks. Oregon River Rentals, in Clackamas, rents inflatable kayaks and SUPs. SUPortland, in the Jantzen Beach neighborhood of Portland, rents SUPs.

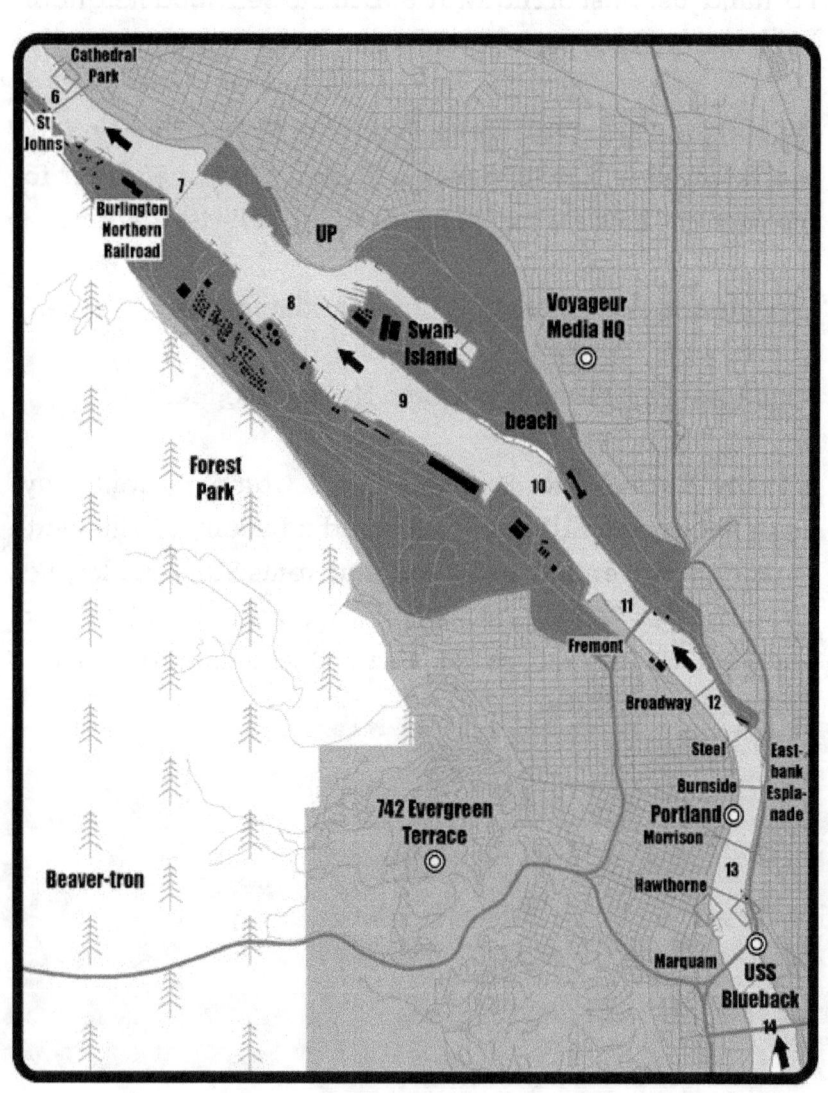

17. Other Good Places to Paddle – The Lower Columbia and Greater Portland

(a)   Lower Columbia River Water Trail Trip Recommendations: The Lower Columbia Estuary Partnership has published detailed descriptions of several paddles on the Columbia River between Astoria and Beacon Rock, upriver of Portland. Some of them overlap with paddles described in this book. Many are excellent paddles, but unfortunately there are no maps. Find the details online at estuarypartnership.org/explore/water-trail-trip-recommendations.

(b)   Columbia River at Hayden Island: There is a lot going on in the area around Hayden Island in Portland, much like the paddle through Portland on the Willamette. The areas is becoming increasingly popular with recreational paddlers, and SUPortland rents boards on the island right below the I-5 bridge. From there, you can explore the extensive houseboats, marinas, and industrial sites of North Portland out of the main channel of the Columbia.

(c)   Kelly Point Park: By launching at this park in North Portland, you can explore the Port of Portland (see the Willamette River at Portland paddle), Multnomah Channel, and the Willamette-Columbia confluence.

(d)   Smith and Bybee Wetlands: Smith and Bybee Lakes are small lakes right in the heart of industrial North Portland. The lakes feature good wildlife viewing, but the water quality is not great and water levels are often too low for paddling. Access is at 5300 N Marine Dr. Check the Metro website for more info on conditions (oregonmetro.gov/parks/smith-and-bybee-wetlands-natural-area).

(e)   Willamette Falls: Willamette Falls is a local site worth seeing, and perhaps the only reason why the Willamette Valley is not the industrial heartland of the Northwest. From the boat launch at Clackamette RV Park just off Highway 99E in Oregon City, you can paddle around the Clackamas-Willamette confluence and Goat Island, where there are some nice beaches. You can also paddle upriver about 1.5 miles to see Oregon City and the falls from below.

(f)   Tualatin River Water Trail: Despite flowing right through one of the most densely populated areas in Oregon, the lower stretches of the Tualatin River offer some good places to paddle. The current is generally slight, but the water quality may not be great. You can find detailed paddle descriptions and maps at the Tualatin River Keepers website (tualatinriverkeepers.org/water-trail/).

III. Willamette Valley

18. Lower Luckiamute & Middle Willamette River: Wildlife and river camping on the Willamette

The informative and well-written Field Guide to Oregon Rivers describes the area around the mouth of the Luckiamute (pronounced "lucky-mute") River as hosting "the richest riparian forest along the Willamette." That's because this area has been permanently protected as part of the Luckiamute Landing State Natural Area, a largely undeveloped state park, where officials and volunteers have undertaken extensive restoration of riparian habitats.

The banks of the Luckiamute between the launch point and its confluence with the Willamette are heavily forested. Paddlers may be lucky enough to encounter river otter, beaver, osprey, and several other species of birds. One species that's no longer found here is the yellow-billed cuckoo, which is a concrete reminder of the consequences of the development of the banks of the Willamette.

There are no roads or trails along this stretch of the river. The river is quite small and the current is slack. At higher water levels, early in the season, the current is stronger, of course. But at lower water levels, which typically start as early as June, snag hazards, including gravel bars, are even more abundant.

From the launch point, it is a nearly three-mile paddle downriver to the confluence with the Willamette. Just before the confluence, you will find a small dead-end bayou on the eastern shore (river right). This used to be a gravel quarry, but it is now, according to the Oregon State Parks and Recreation Department, "some of the best Western Pond Turtle habitat in the Willamette Valley." Paddle in quietly and see if you can see one basking on a log.

When you reach the Willamette, there are more forested shores, as well as some sandy beaches on the far (eastern) shore and on two sand bars around the mouth of the Santiam River. The Santiam can be explored upriver for some distance here, and there are several more sandy beaches along the forested shoreline. At the Santiam's confluence with the Willamette, notice the distinct line between the relatively clear and cold water of the Santiam and the relatively warm and muddy Willamette.

The bulk of the Luckiamute Landing State Natural Area is upriver of the Luckiamute-Willamette confluence between the western shore of the Willamette and the eastern shore of the Luckiamute. (It is divided into two parcels, with the more southerly one not shown on the map.) Just upriver of the Santiam, on the western shore of the Willamette (river left), there is a campground accessible only by boat or trail. If you are up for some board/boat camping, this is a really nice place to spend the night on the river. Once the Willamette completes its big bend around Luckiamute, the shoreline is private land on both sides.

Since this paddle goes downriver first, be sure that you are prepared to paddle back up the Luckiamute after you have paddled around. Or you can do this paddle as a downriver shuttle. You can stop, or take out, at Buena Vista County Park, just 1.5 miles downriver of the Luckiamute-Willamette confluence. This makes for a short 4.2-mile float.

Just below Buena Vista Park and the Buena Vista Ferry (watch out for the ferry boat), is Wells Island, a large island in the Willamette. Wells and the smaller islands surrounding it have several nice beaches, and camping is allowed on the island. The side channel here is a very nice place to paddle, and you can make a loop around Wells Island in about two miles, the island being approximately one mile long.

Another couple of miles or so below Wells Island are American Bottom Landing and Whiteman Bar, two more beautiful sites for riverfront camping. Note that these places are not marked from the river, so they can be difficult to find. Whiteman Bar can be identified by the large sand bar that straddles most of the width of the river on the east side (river left) and the side channel on the same side. As with all paddles, a good GPS is recommended to be sure of your location.

From Whiteman Bar, it's another 7.5 miles to Riverview Park in Independence, which is about a half-mile below the River Road S bridge. This is the best return point for a downriver shuttle.

In between American Bottom Landing and Independence, there are a few places with beaches that make nice places to have lunch, the best being Judson Rocks (an island), Murphy Bar, Independence Bar Landing, and Independence Island. Camping is allowed on Judson Rocks. Sidney Access is ironically named, as there really is not any access to the land and no good place to take out. There is also a formal campground at Riverview Park in Independence ($10/night, not reservable), and the town, though small, has stores and restaurants.

All together, the lower Luckiamute and this 12-mile stretch of the Willamette between the Luckiamute confluence and Independence affords an excellent opportunity for everything from a short day trip to a multi-day, paddle-camping trip right in the middle of the Willamette Valley.

Difficulty: Easy to moderate.

Distance: 4.2 miles downriver from the launch point at Luckiamute Landing State Natural Area to Buena Vista County Park, or about 5.4 miles round-trip to paddle from the launch/return point to the confluence with the Willamette and back. 11 miles downriver from Buena Vista to Independence Riverview Park. 15.3 miles total downriver from the Luckiamute launch point to Independence.

Directions:
Luckiamute Landing State Natural Area Launch/Return Point: From the town of Buena Vista, go south 2.8 miles on Buena Vista Rd and turn right.

Buena Vista County Park: From Willamette Ferry St in the town of Buena Vista, turn south onto Park St one block west of the river/ferry.

Riverview Park (Independence): From Main Street in downtown Indepdnence, turn east onto C St and the park is in one block. Address is 50 South C St, Independence, OR 97351.

Launch/Return:

Luckiamute Landing State Natural Area Launch/Return Point: Toilet, parking. No water. No day use fee.

Buena Vista County Park: Parking, toilets. No water. No camping. No amenities in the town of Buena Vista.

Riverview Park (Independence): Parking, toilets, water, camping. Amenities available in Independence.

Nearby Rental: None.

Nearby Camping: See above.

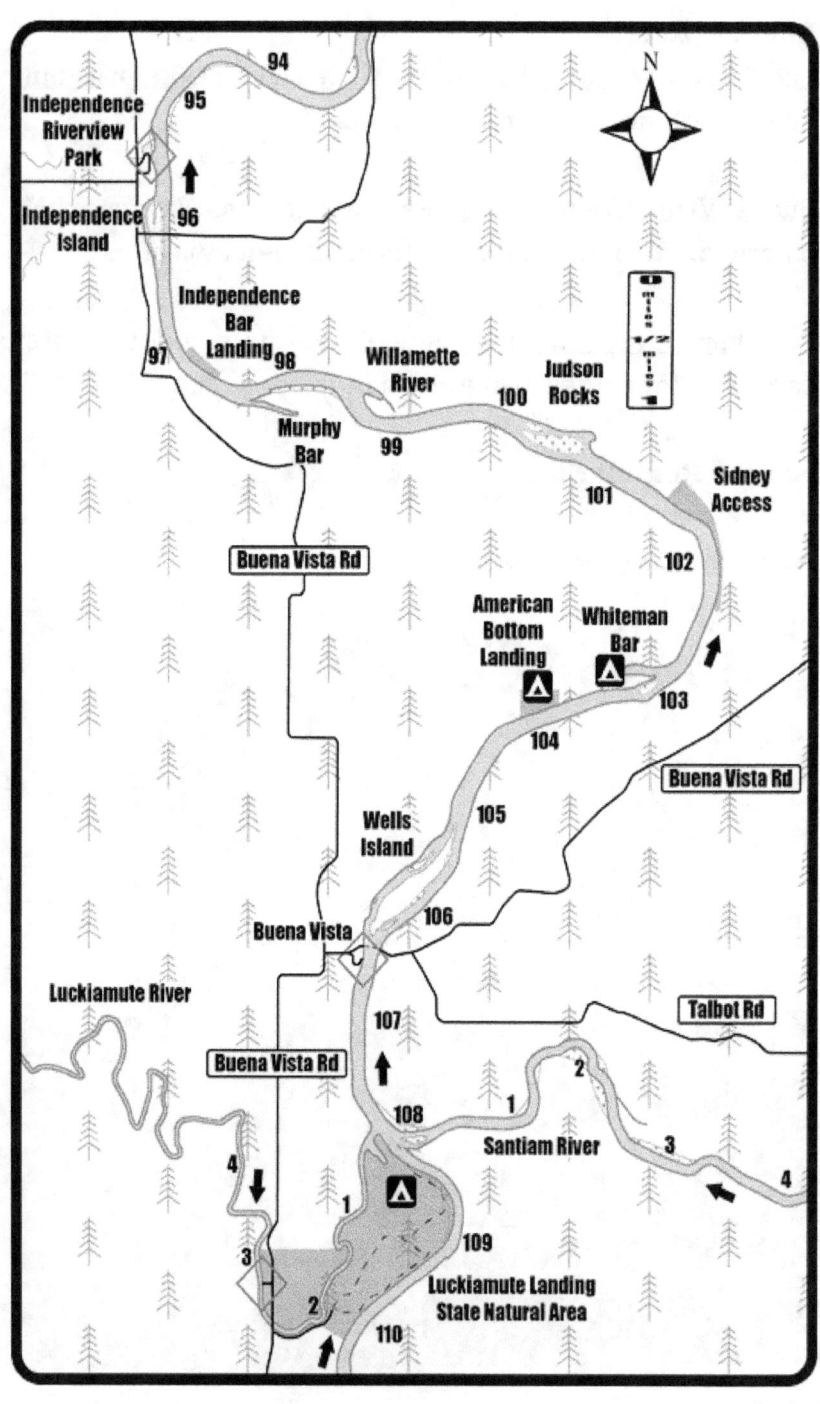

19. Middle Willamette River: Paddle through the heart of the valley

Corvallis is Latin for "heart of the valley." The Willamette Valley, and the Willamette River, are the heart of Oregon, supporting much of the state's population. The Willamette is the thirteenth largest river in the US. Its extensive pollution over the first hundred years of industrialization in the state was the catalyst for a revolution in environmental consciousness in Oregon. Tom McCall's documentation of the pollution, and its effects on people and wildlife, sparked basin-wide remediation efforts and propelled McCall to the Governor's Office in the late 1960s.

Today the Willamette is still stressed, but it retains much of its charm despite being a shadow of its former self in terms of water quality and wildlife habitat. This paddle is a 9-mile, downriver float through the heart of the river, through farmland and small patches of wilderness showcasing the river's wildlife, ending at Corvallis. There is moderately strong current along this stretch of the river, especially in the spring and early summer, and there are many snag hazards along the shorelines, especially during the low-water conditions of late summer and early autumn.

This stretch of river includes a side channel known as the Middle Channel of the Willamette (and, at the lower end, the Bonneville Channel). This channel is quieter and more mellow than the main channel, with less current. However, it is also narrower and has more snag hazards, especially in lower water conditions. The channel extends for 8 miles, so it is essentially another option entirely for doing this paddle.

The main drawback to selecting the side channel for the majority of your paddle is that the main channel along this stretch includes a handful of secluded islands and sand bars that make good places to stop. These places have some nice beaches when the river's flow is not peaking. The best beaches on this paddle are on the two large islands shown on the map (Rivermiles 137 and 134, respectively), as well as the bend on the west side of the river between Rivermiles 134 and 133. This latter area is part of Willamette Park, the same park hosting the takeout point.

The Middle Channel lacks any such places to take a break. It is sufficiently tight that it should only be attempted during higher water conditions. Any time after June may be too low until the winter rains start to swell the river again. It also requires a little more technical skill to navigate due to snags, especially at the entrance, which is often blocked. But there are also sand bars in the main channel that require some navigational skill.

Just after the confluence of the main channel and the Middle Channel/Bonneville Channel, notice the City of Corvallis water treatment plant on the western shore (river left). You can't miss it – it's the big tower in the water right before the island. You are now paddling in the same water that the citizens of Corvallis will soon be drinking and bathing in. It's a concrete reminder that everything in the natural world is connected to our lives.

As you reach the take out point, there is a side channel on the eastern shore (river right) behind the island. It can be explored for a short distance and has an isolated feel due to its forested shores. This is known as the East Channel of the Willamette, though it is no longer an actual river channel. This area is the site of the former town of Orleans, which was completely destroyed in a flood event in 1861. The loss of Orleans was one impetus for decades of efforts to direct and constrict the river's flow, much to the detriment of its ecosystem. The area is now a Corvallis city park, still undeveloped.

Just downriver of the takeout point is the mouth of the Marys River, a small river flowing down from the Coast range. A whole separate paddle could be done here by launching from the return point listed here (Willamette Boat Landing) and paddling up-and-back on the Marys. Once you pass under the bridges at the mouth, it too has an intimate and isolated feel thanks to the forested banks, but it can be difficult to navigate due to the same issues that paddlers encounter in the Middle Channel, including an entrance that may be blocked by debris.

You can also paddle downriver on the Willamette a bit further past the return point. Between the two bridges, you can get a look at downtown Corvallis and its riverfront park on the western shore (river left), and the Orleans Site on the eastern shore. Just be sure you're prepared to paddle back upriver to reach the return point. There is an alternate landing site, Michael's Landing, just north of the second (more northerly) bridges in downtown Corvallis (not shown on the map).

Difficulty: Moderate.

Distance: 9 miles.

Directions:

<u>Peoria County Park</u>: Peoria County Park is on the west side of Peoria Rd at the northern end of the small unincorporated town of Peoria (no services). Look for the "Peoria Park" sign.

<u>Willamette Boat Landing</u>: From Peoria County Park, take Peoria Rd 8.5 miles north to Highway 34. Turn left onto Highway 34. In 0.9 miles, bear left onto the Highway 34 bypass, following the signs for Highway 99W southbound. Merge onto Highway 99W and immediately turn left onto Crystal Lake Dr. In 0.5 miles, turn left onto SE Fischer Ln. The launch point is ahead on the left.

Launch: Peoria County Park. Parking, toilets. No water. No day use fee.

Return: Willamette Boat Landing. Parking, toilets. No water. No day use fee.

Nearby Rental: Peak Sports, in Corvallis, rents SUPs, kayaks, and canoes.

Nearby Camping: The larger river islands (see above) afford primitive camping.

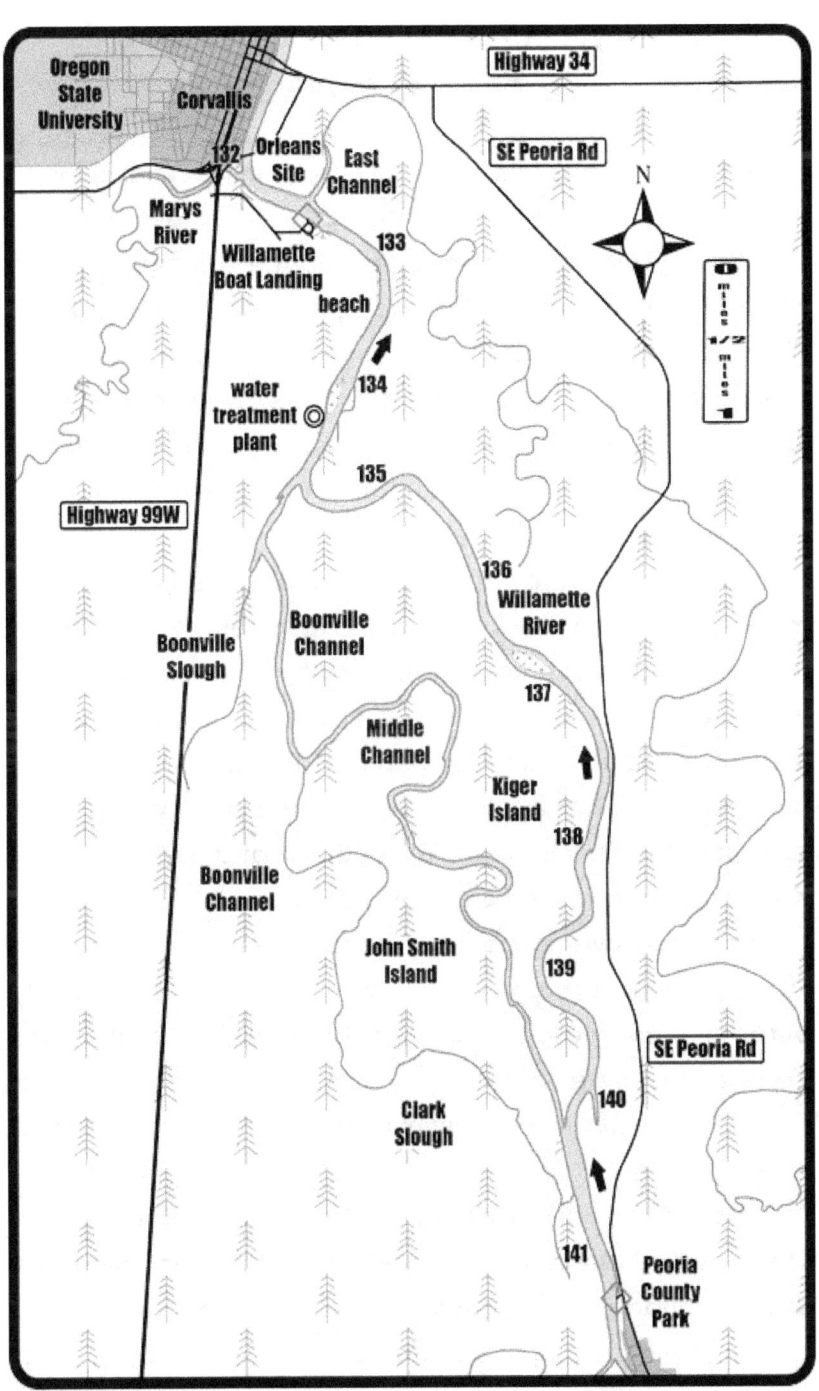

20. Coyote Creek and Fern Ridge Lake: Eugene's bayou

Fern Ridge Lake is a large reservoir just west of Eugene. It was created in 1941 by a dam placed across the Long Tom River. At its highest levels during the summer, it covers about 15 square miles, but it averages only 11 feet in depth. The Atlas of Oregon Lakes puts it perfectly when it says that "Fern Ridge lake is among the most heavily used recreation sites in Oregon and provides for a variety of uses, including swimming, picnicking, and all forms of boating, fishing, and assorted other activities."

Although the lake sees a great deal of use, hosts three marinas, and is surrounded by both suburban and rural residential development, it has many shallow areas that limit access to motorized boats, and much of the shoreline is surrounded by extensive wetlands that provide excellent bird habitat. A vast carpet of mostly reed canary grass, bull rush, and cattails surrounds the lake for long stretches of the western, southern, and eastern shores.

The extensive agricultural and other human activity around the reservoir has had an impact on the water quality, but it is still good enough for swimming. Due to the shallowness, the water gets quite warm in the summer. In fact, Fern Ridge may have the warmest swimming waters in all of Oregon.

Coyote Creek is one of the lake's main inflowing streams. The banks of the creek are mostly forested, and the meandering, muddy water looks the part of a Southern bayou. Launching/returning at Coyote Creek will give your paddle a more secluded feeling at the beginning and end. If you launch here, note that it is necessary to follow the creek until you cross under the highway bridge. After that, you can go left and paddle along the highway until reaching open water. But the best option is to continue straight on and follow the creek through the wetlands all the way out into the lake.

The current in the creek is slack, so returning up the creek is not problematic, but there are some snag hazards at low water. Generally, the reservoir is at its highest between April and June, and high levels are usually maintained through September.

Once you are out onto the lake, you can paddle for a great distance. A trip around the perimeter of the lake would take over 15 miles paddling. In several places, it is possible to paddle up dead-end channels (mostly inlet creeks) in the wetlands.

Difficulty: Moderate to advanced, depending on distance.

Distance: 15+ miles to circle the lake from an access point on the lake, and 21 miles to circle the lake from the launch/return point on Coyote Creek.

Directions: From Eugene, go 8 miles west on Highway 126 to reach Perkins Peninsula Park (or 50 miles east from Florence). To reach the unnamed Coyote Creek launch/return point, turn south off Highway 126 at Perkins Peninsula Park onto Central Rd. Go 0.8 miles and turn left onto Cantrell Rd. Go 1.3 miles and see the pullout on the left.

Launch/Return:

Perkins Peninsula Park: Parking, toilets. No water. No day use fee.

Coyote Creek: This is a pull-out with only a few parking spots along the road and no facilities. Primitive launch requiring a short port.

Nearby Rental: None.

Nearby Camping: None.

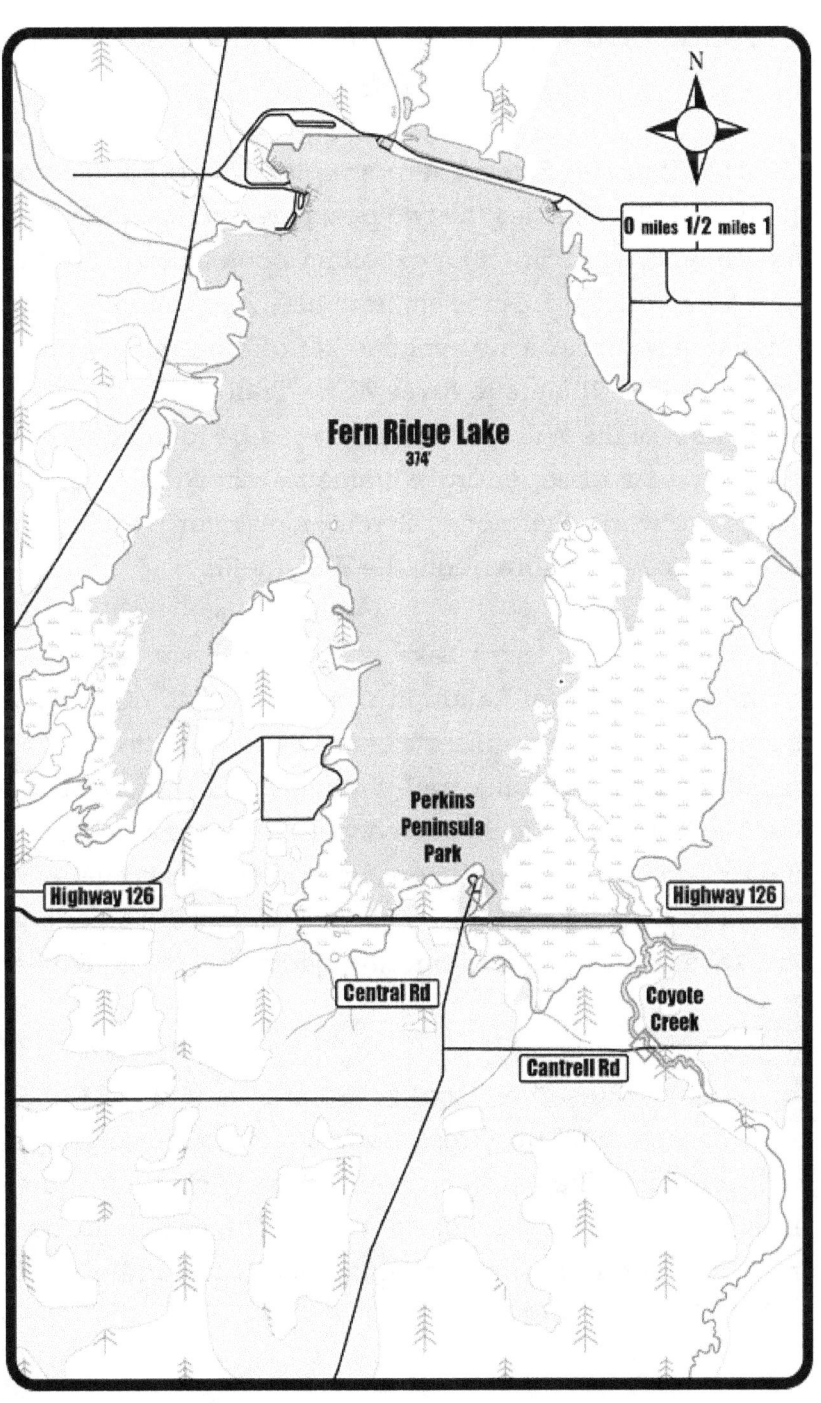

21. Other Good Places to Paddle – The Willamette Valley

(a)   <u>Willamette River</u>: There are other good paddles on the Willamette besides the two described in this book. Travis Williams has written an excellent book called The Willamette River Field Guide that details 12 downriver floats. You can also order a two-volume set of high-quality maps known as the Willamette River Water Trail Guide detailing every inch of the Willamette. Details can be found online at willamette-riverkeeper.org/willamette-water-trail/. These books are worth the money if you enjoy river paddling or just want to know more about the Willamette.

(b)   <u>Hagg Lake</u>: Hagg Lake is a quaint reservoir at the foothills of the Coast Range in rural Washington County. It is a popular place for all sorts of recreation. I try to ride the excellent mountain bike trail circling the lake and pick a few blackberries at least once a year. It's moderately sized and a good place for beginners, but you will likely share the waters with plenty of motorboats. You can rent SUPs, canoes, and kayaks on the lake from Mad Jack's BBQ, Bait, & Boat Rental.

(c)   <u>Dexter Reservoir/Lookout Point Lake and Fall Creek Lake</u>: These are all busy reservoirs not far to the southwest of Springfield. They all feature extensively clearcut shorelines, some rural residential development, and motorboat traffic, but also have some secluded places to paddle, especially Fall Creek Lake.

IV. Cascades – North

22. Lost Lake (Mt Hood): "Heart of the Mountains"

Lost Lake sits quietly in a steep glacial valley on the north side of Mt Hood. It was created by a lava flow from Lava Lake Butte, the forested peak that towers over the lake's eastern shore. The ridge to the southwest is the Cascade Crest, and just on the other side is Bull Run Lake, the main source of Portland's drinking water. This juxtaposition will give Portlanders and others familiar with Bull Run an idea of how clear the water is at Lost Lake.

Lost lake is the deepest lake in the Mt Hood National Forest at 175 feet. The slopes surrounding the lake are covered in a gorgeous mix of Pacific silver fir, mountain hemlock, western red cedar, Douglas fir, and white pine. There are splendid views of Mt Hood from the lake and parts of the shoreline. The Native Americans in the area referred to the lake as "E-e-kwahl-a-mat-yan-ishkt", or "Heart of the Mountains," and the name seems fitting.

Lost Lake is triangular in shape and small in size – a paddle around the shoreline is only a little over three miles. A road runs along the eastern shore of the lake, which hosts a resort with cabins, a restaurant, and a store, as well as a Forest Service campground with a gravel boat launch area and day-use parking. The other two sides of the lake are roadless, but a relatively flat trail circles the lake. There are no beaches, but several of the lakeside campsites offer shore access (and potential launch sites) with charming little rock gardens and wading pools.

The shore is steep and rocky, but there are intermittent takeout sites accessing the trail. Many trees have toppled into the lake along the shore, creating hazards that are easily avoided thanks to the clear water. The lake elevation is just 3,143' but the water is cold and clear, though it does warm up enough in the summer to swim. This is a good lake to spot fish as well. German brown trout, kokanee salmon, brook trout, and rainbow trout are native to the lake. Rainbow and brook trout are stocked.

The lake bottom is rocky except for a marshy area in the northwest corner, where the lake's only inlet creek flows. The lake is also fed by several springs on the eastern and western shores, around which grow vine maple, Devil's club, and deer fern. In the marshy area, we encountered rough-skinned newts laying motionless on the shallow lake floor. River otters and beavers can occasionally be seen in this area as well. The shores sport wildflowers in the summer, and the cut-leaf bugbane is a wildflower native only to this corner of Lost Lake.

The vibe at Lost Lake is quite peaceful. No motors are allowed on the lake, so water traffic is limited to fishers and recreational paddlers. Lost Lake Resort rents rowboats, canoes, kayaks, and SUPs. This makes Lost Lake a near-ideal place to take someone who wants to try learning to SUP or someone who would like to join the paddle but would prefer a different type of watercraft.

Difficulty: Easy; suitable for beginners.

Distance: 3.2 miles around the lake

Directions: From Highway 231, 11.5 miles south of Hood River in the unincorporated town of Dee, turn west onto Lost Lake Rd. Make an immediate left and stay on Lost Lake Rd for 14.3 miles until reaching the lake. Lost Lake Rd makes several turns at intersections. Be sure to watch the street signs to stay on Lost Lake Rd.

Launch/Return: Lost Lake Day Use Area – South. Parking, toilet, water, camping. $8 day use fee. General store and showers ($4) at the Lost Lake Resort.

Nearby Rental: Lost Lake Resort rents SUPs, canoes, kayaks, pedal boats, and even fishing poles (lostlakeresort.org).

Nearby Camping: Camping at Lost Lake Campground and Lost Lake Resort.

Nearby Fun: There are several great hikes in the Mt Hood National Forest, as well as the historic Timberline Lodge, an Oregon must-see. The Columbia River Gorge area offers outstanding hiking, mountain biking, and white water rafting. The picturesque Hood River Valley is regionally famous for its fruit produce and hosts an Oregon Scenic Byway. Hood River has several good restaurants, a brewery or three, and a downtown shopping district. My favorite is employee-owned Hood River Brewing.

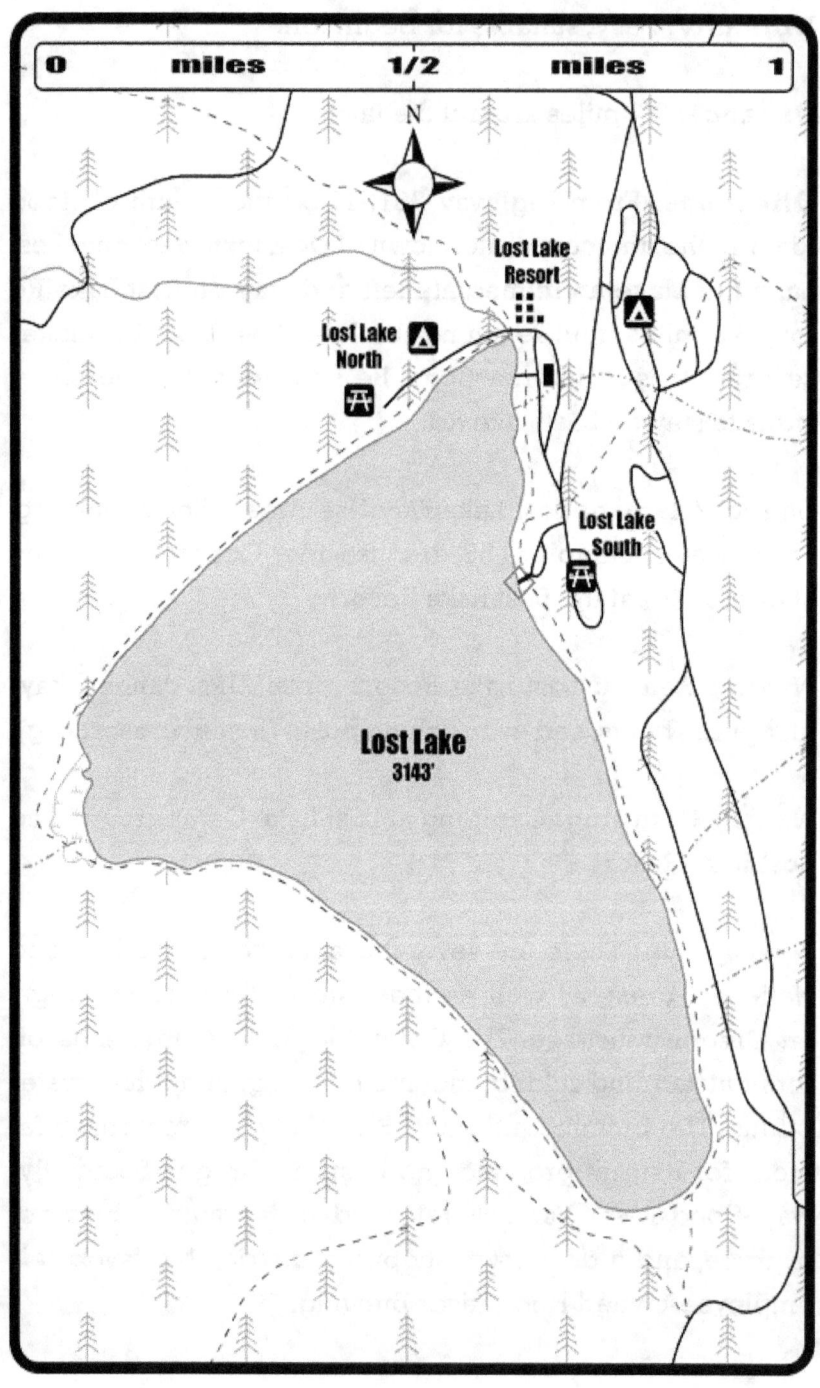

23. Timothy Lake:
By far the best thing about Clackamas County

At one time, Oregonians grazed sheep in a meadow high up on the west side of the Cascades, near the headwaters of the Clackamas River. They spread Timothy grass seed to enhance the summer forage, and the place became known as Timothy Meadows. In 1953, the Federal Power Commission approved Portland General Electric's plan to dam the Oak Grove Fork of the Clackamas River for power generation. PGE subsequently constructed access roads to the site, cleared the timber, and built an earthen dam 110 feet high and 740 feet across the river. The result is Timothy Lake.

Today, the submerged stumps with their long exposed roots look like giant twisted octopuses just beneath the surface. At the north end of the lake, they seem to be hiding in a submarine forest of green aquatic plants. Although Timothy Lake continues to serve as a reservoir, the water level fluctuations are minimal. The water is less clear than some of Oregon's high lakes, but the water quality is good, with 20-30 feet of visibility. And the water is warm enough to be swimmable in summer.

The lake is surrounded by healthy evergreen forests, as well as some older clearcuts. The cone of Mt Hood is visible from certain areas along the southeast shore and in some northern areas, and the tip of Mt Washington is visible from northern parts of the lake.

There are several campsites around the lake that all make excellent launch sites thanks to gently sloping pebble-rock beaches that cover most of the shoreline. Oak Fork, Gone Creek, Hoodview, and Pine Point campgrounds along the southern shore, West Shore Campground on the western shore, and North Arm Campground on the northern lobe, all feature waterfront campsites and near-waterfront campsites that can be used as informal launch sites. The south shore campgrounds also have formal boat ramps, not that you would need one.

The Meditation Point Campground is aptly named. It is a rare hike-in or boat-in primitive campground consisting of four campsites and a restroom. It is located on the peninsula on the northern side of the main southern circle of the lake. Each site has a picnic table and offers some seclusion at an otherwise popular place.

Motorized craft are common on the lake, mostly fishers. There is a 10 mph speed limit. The lake is stocked with rainbow trout and cutthroat trout, and there are naturally-sustained populations of kokanee and brook trout. The best fishing is later in the summer, and fly fishing near the mouths of the tributaries at the northern end of the lake has been described as "excellent."

Because the lake is a reservoir, there are many near-shore stumps. Most are submerged, but many breach the surface or are close enough to be a snag hazard. All are visible, at least to some degree, because the water is fairly clear. At lower water levels, these may be more of a problem. There are also some fallen trees in the water near the shore at various places around the lake. The lake tends to get sustained winds and concordantly large waves in the afternoon.

The larger, southern circle of the lake is far busier than the neck and the northern lobe. The northern lobe is too shallow for most motorized craft and is nearly roadless, making it very secluded. It is also the most scenic part of the lake, featuring clear views of the lake bottom, wetlands, and lots of aquatic life, including the intrepid rough-skinned newt.

The northern lobe is fed by two main inlet creeks. The creek to the north, Cooper Creek, is navigable for a short distance. The most remarkable feature of the lake, however, is the unnamed creek flowing in from the east, from Little Crater Lake and its surrounding springs. The springs are artesian, welling up frigid 34°F water from deep within the Cascade Mountains. The water is still nearly that cold as it enters Timothy Lake, so cold that I was unable to wade in the creek for longer than about 30 seconds! Unfortunately, this creek too is navigable for only a short distance.

But do yourself a favor and visit Little Crater Lake by land. It can be accessed via a short path off of Forest Service Road 58, which runs on the northeast side of the lake (not shown on the map). The Atlas of Oregon Lakes refers to Little Crater Lake as "a geologic curiosity formed by the force of an artesian spring washing away the overlying siltstone." Put simply, it is a 45-feet deep blue pool full of crystal-clear water that is better seen than described, one of Oregon's smallest and least-known geological wonders.

For shorter trips (2-3 miles) in the northern lobe, the best launch point would be at North Arm Campground, though there is no formal launch area there. From the campsites on the south shore, a paddle along the shore to the top of the northern lobe and back is about 7.5 miles. A trip around the whole shoreline would be slightly longer, just over 10 miles.

And if you really want to paddle Timothy Lake in style, consider staying at the Clackamas Lake Historic Ranger Cabin. It was built in 1933 by the Civilian Conservation Corps. It is a lovely home, even if temporary, and it is truly a piece of American history. It is two stories, 1,380 square feet with a fireplace in the living room, a large dining table, a fully equipped kitchen, sun porch, three large bedrooms (one with a bunk bed), and a single bathroom. The kitchen appliances and hot water heater run on propane, but there is no power for other plug-in appliances or electronics.

The cabin costs $140-160 a night and has to be reserved six months in advance. It usually becomes booked as soon as it is available. It can be rented from Memorial Day weekend through the third week in October. Minimum stay is two nights and maximum is seven. Maximum capacity is eight people, and no pets are allowed.

Difficulty: Easy to moderate; suitable for beginners.

Distance: 2 to 10.2 miles. 7.5 miles to circle the southern lobe of the lake, and 10.2 miles to circle the southern lobe and the northern arm.

Directions: On Highway 26, 4.2 miles south of the junction with Highway 35, and 41.2 miles north of Warm Springs, turn west onto Forest Service Road 42/Skyline Rd. Look for the "Timothy Lake" sign. The road changes to Forest Service Road 57, and there are some turns at intersections. Follow the signs for Timothy Lake and reach the campgrounds on the south shore in approximately 10 miles.

Launch/Return: Any of the campsites can be your launch/return point (except Meditation Point). See above.

Nearby Rental: None

Nearby Camping: There are several campgrounds around the lake. See above.

Nearby Fun: See above for details on Little Crater Lake and the Clackamas Lake Historic Ranger Cabin.

There are several great hikes in the Mt Hood National Forest, as well as the historic Timberline Lodge, an Oregon must-see. The Columbia River Gorge area offers outstanding hiking, mountain biking, and white water rafting. The picturesque Hood River Valley is regionally famous for its fruit produce and hosts an Oregon Scenic Byway. Hood River has several good restaurants, a brewery or three, and a downtown shopping district. My favorite is employee-owned Hood River Brewing.

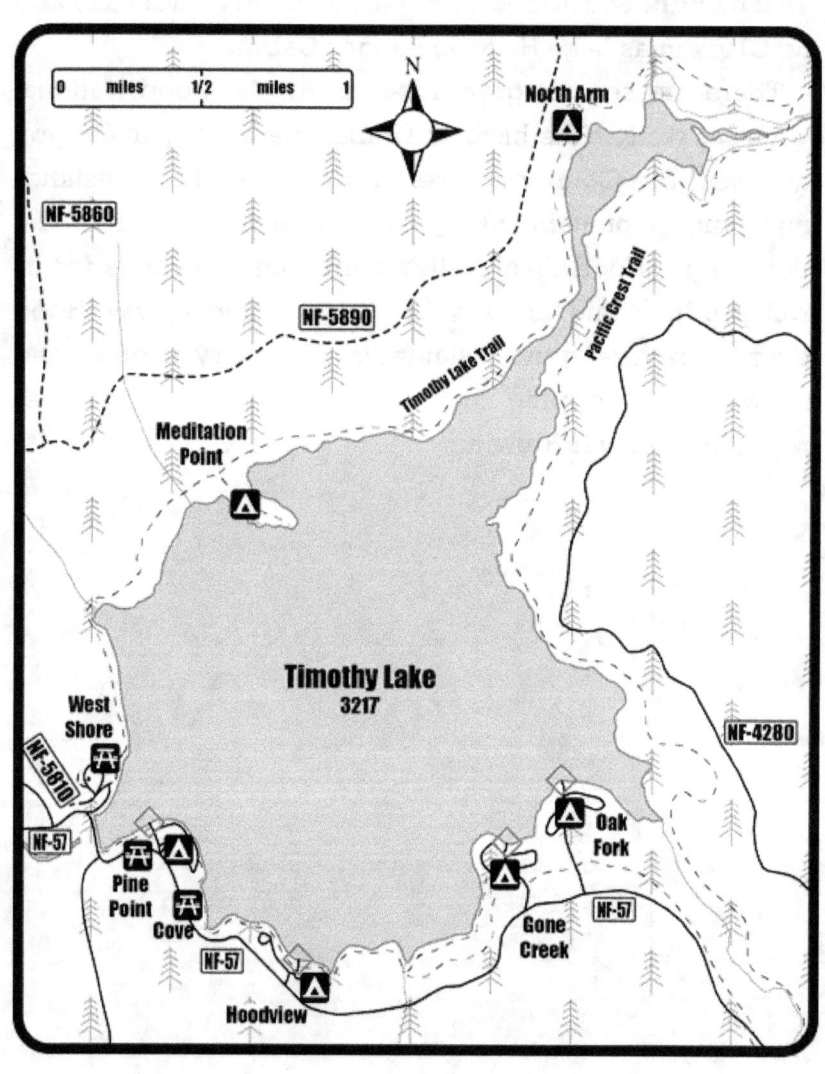

24. Olallie Lakes:
A group of small but fantastically secluded mountain lakes

The term "Olallie Lakes" is my catch-all for a group of four small lakes, and a fifth nearby lake, in the Bull of the Woods Wilderness near the crest of the Cascades just north of Mt Jefferson. These lakes are very isolated, with no cell phone coverage and no motorboats, making for some fantastically secluded, though tragically short, paddles.

Olallie, Monon, Horseshoe, and Breitenbush Lakes line up from north to south along a rough road that becomes rougher as you go southward. Beyond Monon Lake, the road becomes impassable to all but high-clearance four-wheel drive vehicles. Elk Lake is separated from this lake cluster by about 15-20 miles, as the crow flies, and is also isolated due to the rough access road. (Elk Lake is not shown on the map.)

On the bright side for paddlers, it is virtually impossible to bring a big boat trailer on one of these roads. So the reward for a slow, bumpy ride near the end of the trip is miles of secluded, motor-free paddling in clear mountain waters.

<u>Olallie Lake:</u>
As with Elk Lake, Olallie Lake has a popular name. Many geographical features in the Cascades use the name Olallie, which means berries in the Chinook jargon. Sometimes the term refers to a particular type of berry, like salmonberries or huckleberries. Not surprisingly, the shores of Olallie Lake are covered with huckleberries that ripen in late summer.

Olallie Lake is the largest of a group of over 200 small lakes near the base of Olallie Butte, all the product of the retreat of Pleistocene Epoch glaciers. If you want to see them all at once, consider hiking the trail to the top of Olallie Butte. It offers outstanding 360-degree views of the high Cascades.

The water at Olallie Lake is so clear that paddlers can almost read the labels on the several beer cans left on the bottom of the lake through 30 or 40 feet of water. Even the deepest point in the lake, 43 feet below the surface, is clearly visible from a board. The rest of the bottom is mud, rocks, and snags, as well as a few fish and rough-skinned newts. There is also some grass in the shallows at the southern end of the lake.

Olallie Butte dominates the shoreline to the east, and Mt Jefferson dominates to the south. The surrounding forest has suffered greatly from the mountain pine beetle, which has thinned areas along the eastern shore and totally deforested the southern shore, leaving unsightly gray snags standing instead.

The shore is rocky but the slope is slight. There are shallows in the many small bays along the shore, and there are occasional rock-pebble beaches. There are a lot of places to land, but swimming was banned at Olallie Lake (though it was once allowed) because lake water is used for drinking water at the resort.

I guess five or six cases-worth of disintegrating beer cans and a few old tires don't impact the drinking water quality as much as a human would taking a ten-minute dip in the cold water. And it's a shame too, because almost one-third of the lake is less than 10 feet deep, which allows the water to warm nicely for swimming in the summer.

No motorboats are allowed on Olallie Lake, but the resort rents rowboats and paddleboats. This would be a great place to learn to paddleboard, but falling would arguably violate the "no swimming" rule, so it cannot be recommended for beginners.

Despite the availability of human-powered boats, most people at the lake fish from the shore. The paddling is quiet and serene. And even though Olallie is the largest lake locally, it is only an approximately 3.8-mile paddle around the perimeter. There are boat launches at the resort and at Peninsula Campground. There are two other campgrounds, Camp Ten and Paul Dennis, as well as dispersed camping on the eastern shore.

Monon Lake:

Monon Lake is right next to Olallie and very similar in character, but it has no formal campground and no swimming ban. Monon is just as clear as Olallie, but much shallower. It also harbors several pretty pebble-rock beaches, and its beautiful waters are swimmable in summer.

Perhaps best of all, it attracts even fewer people than Olallie. When we visited, there were no other paddlers and only two campers. We paddled in utter silence with osprey for escorts. These features make Monon a good place to learn to paddle. There are several beautiful shallow rocky bays on the northern shores of the lake that are challenging to navigate.

Access is accomplished via pullouts on the road running along the western shore, which allow for both primitive camping and launching. A paddle around the lake will take 2.5 miles. Unfortunately, its surrounding pines also suffer from beetle-kill, with almost half of its shoreline deforested. There is good fishing for stocked rainbow trout and brook trout.

Horseshoe Lake:
Unless you have a high-clearance vehicle, you cannot go past Monon. The road up to Horseshoe Lake is a four-wheel drive track. Are Horseshoe and Breitenbush worth the trouble? Perhaps only for the true-die hard paddler.

Horseshoe Lake is tiny, far too small by itself to justify an entry in this book. It is so small that it doesn't even have an entry in the Atlas of Oregon Lakes. Any paddling you do here will be brief, but it is stunningly beautiful, featuring crystal clear waters hemmed in by steep forested slopes.

Underwater boulders are dotted about the shallow water. The far shore has some small pebble-rock beaches. The back side of the lake (unseen from the launch/return point) features a sheer rock cliff and a boulder-laden scree field at the edge of the water. There are some nice lakefront campsites in the hardly-used Horseshoe Lake Campground. The water is great for swimming. The lake's shallowness and protection from the wind makes it a great place for beginners to learn.

Sadly, even little Horseshoe Lake suffers from the beer can scourge. But if you have a high-clearance vehicle and want to see one of the most beautiful places in Oregon, it is definitely worth the trip. The little channel at the back of the U looks inviting but is not navigable. A paddle around Horseshoe is just 1.1 miles.

Breitenbush Lake:

The road between Horseshoe and Breitenbush is much worse, and much longer, than from Monon to Horseshoe. Even in my indestructible Toyota Tacoma, it is a jarring 2mph crawl. If you do decide to go all the way to Breitenbush, it's a toss up as to whether to go back the way you came or continue on Skyline Road back to Forest Service Road 46, completing the four-lake loop. Both ways feature similar lengths of truck-crawling.

Like the other nearby lakes, Breitenbush makes for a beautiful, serene paddle. Unlike the other nearby lakes, and every other lake mentioned in this book, it is in the Warm Springs Indian Reservation. The Warm Springs folks have seen fit to prohibit swimming in the lake and to close entry to the shoreline (except at the campground), without any explanation.

But, as with the rest of the lakes described here, Breitenbush is beautiful. And it offers its own charms. The outlet creek channel on the eastern shore is navigable for a short distance through wetlands. There is a more extensive wetland around the outlet area at the southern end of the lake featuring a network of defined channels passing through aquatic grasses. We watched schools of small fish flitting up and back in the channels. There are also views of Mt Jefferson to enjoy.

Though the pebble beaches are inviting, the prohibition on landing is not a problem since a trip around the lake can be completed in just 2 miles.

Elk Lake:

Elk Lake is much closer to Detroit than the other lakes described here, but it is well-hidden at the end of a gravel track. The last four miles of the access road are not maintained and are quite rough. Though the road is too rough for a boat trailer, it can be traversed by a passenger car, slowly. The lake's lack of popularity comes solely from the difficult access. The water is sufficiently clear that the deepest point can be seen clearly at 30 feet below the surface.

Unlike the other lakes, Elk Lake has a grass and shrub shoreline that offers very few places to land. Once again, the short distance of just 2.1 miles around the lake mitigates this issue. The lake is clear and deep, with steep forested shores. There is a beautiful rock wall at the inlet on the western end, as well as a lovely wetland area hosting many fish and rough-skinned newts. The sediment in the shallows near the outlet at the eastern end of the lake sparkles a beautiful golden color in the sun. A few of the campsites at the lakeside campground have direct shore access, though there is also a primitive launch with just two day-use parking spaces.

Only electric motors are allowed on the lake. It is stocked with rainbow trout, and there are native kokanee. It is another great spot for beginners.

Difficulty: Easy, all lakes are suitable for beginners except Olallie and Breitenbush.

Distance: Olallie is 3.8 around, Monon is 2.5, Horseshoe is 1.1, Breitenbush is 2.0, and Elk Lake is 2.1.

Directions:
Olallie, Monon, Horseshoe, & Breitenbush: From Highway 22 in Detroit, turn west onto Forest Service Road 46/Breitenbush Rd. Signs for the road say "Breitenbush Resort." Go 24

miles on NF-46 and turn right onto NF-4690. Stay on NF-4690 for 8.1 miles and turn right onto NF-4220. Go 5.1 miles on NF-4220 before reaching the northern end of Olallie Lake.

Elk Lake: Note that there is a far larger and better-known Elk Lake in Deschutes County. This is not that Elk Lake. From Highway 22 in Detroit, turn west onto Forest Service Road 46/Breitenbush Rd. Signs for the road say "Breitenbush Resort." Go 4.4 miles before turning left onto NF-4696. In 0.1 miles, turn left onto NF-4697. The road dead-ends at Elk Lake in 7.5 miles.

Launch/Return: See above for details on each lake. All day use parking is $5 or use the Northwest Forest Pass.

Nearby Rental: At Olallie Lake, the private resort rents rowboats and paddleboats (olallielakeresort.com).

Nearby Camping: See above for details.

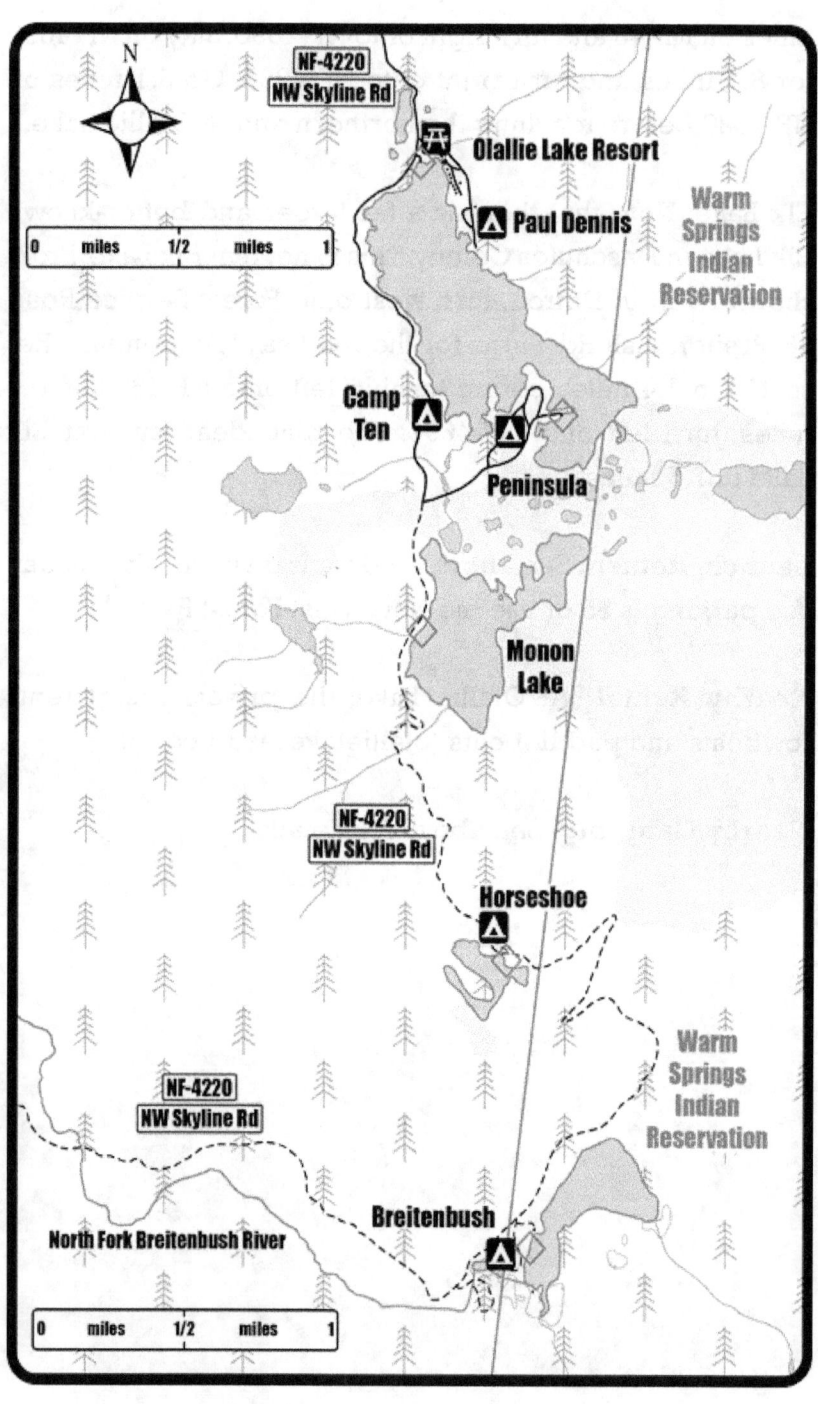

25. Other Good Places to Paddle – The Cascades – North

(a) <u>Clear Lake (Mt Hood NF)</u>: Clear Lake is a small reservoir just off Highway 26 south of Mt Hood. The water is not particularly clear, but there is lakeside camping and beaches at lower water levels. Watch for submerged stumps. I must question, in the strongest terms, the decision to locate portable toilets on the shoreline within view from the lake. Note that this is not the other Clear Lake (McKenzie River) described as paddle 28.

(b) <u>Detroit Lake</u>: Detroit Lake is one of the best-known lakes in Oregon. It is a huge lake and sits in an immense mountain canyon on the western slopes of the Cascades. It is definitely worth a visit (perhaps on your way to the Olallie Lakes), but is usually very busy with motorboaters and fishers.

V. Cascades – Central

26. Leaburg Lake / McKenzie River:

See one of Oregon's few remaining historic covered bridges and enjoy the McKenzie without the rapids

There are a lot of beautiful rivers in Oregon, but the McKenzie is far and away my favorite for its impressive waterfalls, gurgling crystal-clear water, and lush green shores shaded by old-growth forest. The Tamolitch Pool is one of the most beautiful things I have ever seen.

For those few who have not visited it (and there seem to be very few, indeed), the McKenzie disappears underground for about three miles before re-emerging into a brilliant blue pool over 30 feet deep. The color of the water can be described with words like iridescent topaz or electric blue, but it has to be seen to truly be appreciated.

The hiking and mountain biking along the McKenzie is excellent, as is the whitewater paddling. And thanks to the Leaburg Dam, you can add flatwater paddling to the list of things to do when visiting the McKenzie. The paddle here is short, hemmed into the 1.5 miles between the dam and the riffles upriver. But that short stretch is quite scenic, with homes dotting the shore along the forested slopes of the McKenzie canyon. The current is slack, and you will have the opportunity to get a unique perspective one of Oregon's last remaining covered bridges.

The Goodpasture Bridge is at the upriver end of the paddle. It is 165 feet long, making it the second longest covered bridge in Oregon and one of 17 in Lane County. The bridge was built in 1938 and is named after a local pioneer. It has ten Gothic style louvered windows on each side, and is still open to traffic.

Above the bridge are riffles that can be hazardous.

Difficulty: Easy.

Distance: 3.2 miles round-trip between the Leaburg Dam and the Goodpasture Covered Bridge.

Directions: The EWEB Goodpasture Boat Landing is about 19 miles east of Springfield (Spring-field! Spring-field!) on the McKenzie River Highway, Highway 126, or 29.3 miles west of the Highway 126-Highway 242 junction. The sign is small and can be difficult to find.

Launch/Return: EWEB Goodpasture Boat Landing. Toilets, no water. No day use fee.

Nearby Rental: None.

Nearby Camping: None, but there are several campgrounds another 30 or so miles eastward on the McKenzie River Highway.

Nearby Fun: This is the only paddle in the book with a pizza place on the route. There is no bigger fan of The Simpsons than me, and Ike's Lakeside Pizza features a set of life-sized (and super-creepy) Simpsons family characters in the restaurant, as well as a sasquatch. Stop in, have a slice, and get your picture taken with Homer.

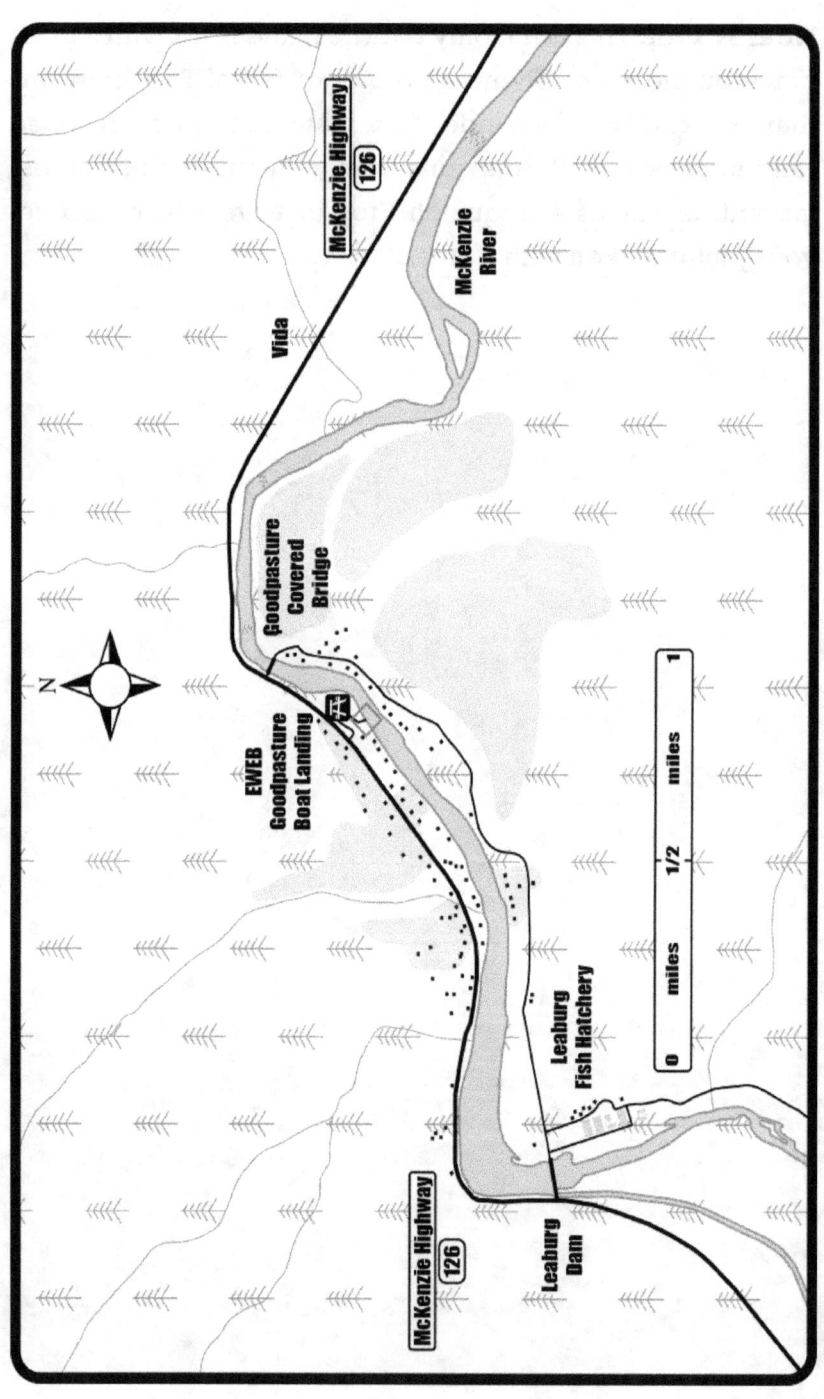

27. Blue River Lake:
Paddle through an isolated conifer canyon

Blue River Lake is a huge reservoir on the western slopes of the Cascades created in 1968 on a tributary of the McKenzie. The shores are very steep and heavily forested with Douglas fir and western hemlock. The shores are so steep that development, and even shoreline access, is very limited. The lake has 17 miles of shoreline, but only a single campground.

Launching from the boat ramp at the campground is difficult by late summer due to the annual drawdown of the lake, which leaves the sandy, stump-studded lake bottom exposed and the entire 88 square miles of the lake nearly free of motors and virtually everyone else. If you want to enjoy nearly limitless paddling in near-total isolation in the warmest and sunniest months of the year, then hike along the rugged shoreline or wade through the shallow, rocky inflowing creek to reach the water. You're welcome.

The water is clear and suitable for swimming. In low water conditions, there are some sandy beach areas. There are two other boat ramps on the lake, and even when the boat ramp at the campground is usable, most of the other users are in small fishing boats, although there are occasionally water skiers. Fortunately, the lake is so large that it is easily possible to find isolated spots.

Perhaps the only downside is the unsightly stumps and bare shoreline in low water conditions. Still, that is a small price to pay for summer solitude on the water.

Difficulty: Easy to advanced, depending on distance and water level.

Distance: 17 miles to paddle around the entire lake.

Directions: To reach the informal ramp at the Blue River Dam (on the western end of the lake), from the McKenzie River Highway, Highway 126, 32.8 miles east of Springfield, and 13.8 miles west of the Highway 126-Highway 242 junction, turn north onto Cascade St in the unincorporated town of Blue River. Go five blocks, and turn right immediately after crossing the river onto Blue River Rd (aka Lucky Boy Rd). The ramp is on the right in 1.5 miles.
To reach the Lookout Campground and Boat Launch, from the McKenzie River Highway, Highway 126, 35.5 miles east of Springfield, and 11.1 miles west of the Highway 126-Highway 242 junction, turn north onto Blue River Reservoir Rd (aka Old Scout Rd and NF-15). The boat launch is on the left in 3.6 miles.

Launch/Return:

Lookout Campground and Boat Launch: Toilets, parking. No water. $5 day use fee or Northwest Forest Pass.

Blue River Dam and Saddle Dam: Informal launch areas with no facilities. $5 day use fee or Northwest Forest Pass.

Nearby Rental: None.

Nearby Camping: Lookout and Mona Campgrounds are both on the northeastern lake shore. Delta Campground is near the lake just off the McKenzie River Highway, and there are several more campgrounds further east on the highway.

Nearby Fun: For a glimpse of the ancient, pre-colonization forest that once covered most of western Oregon, check out the Delta Old Growth Grove Nature Trail. It's a half-mile walk through a stand of massive old growth Douglas fir. These trees are over 650 years old and tower over native understory vegetation along a lovely stream. The grove is right next to Delta Campground just off Highway 126 near Blue River Lake.

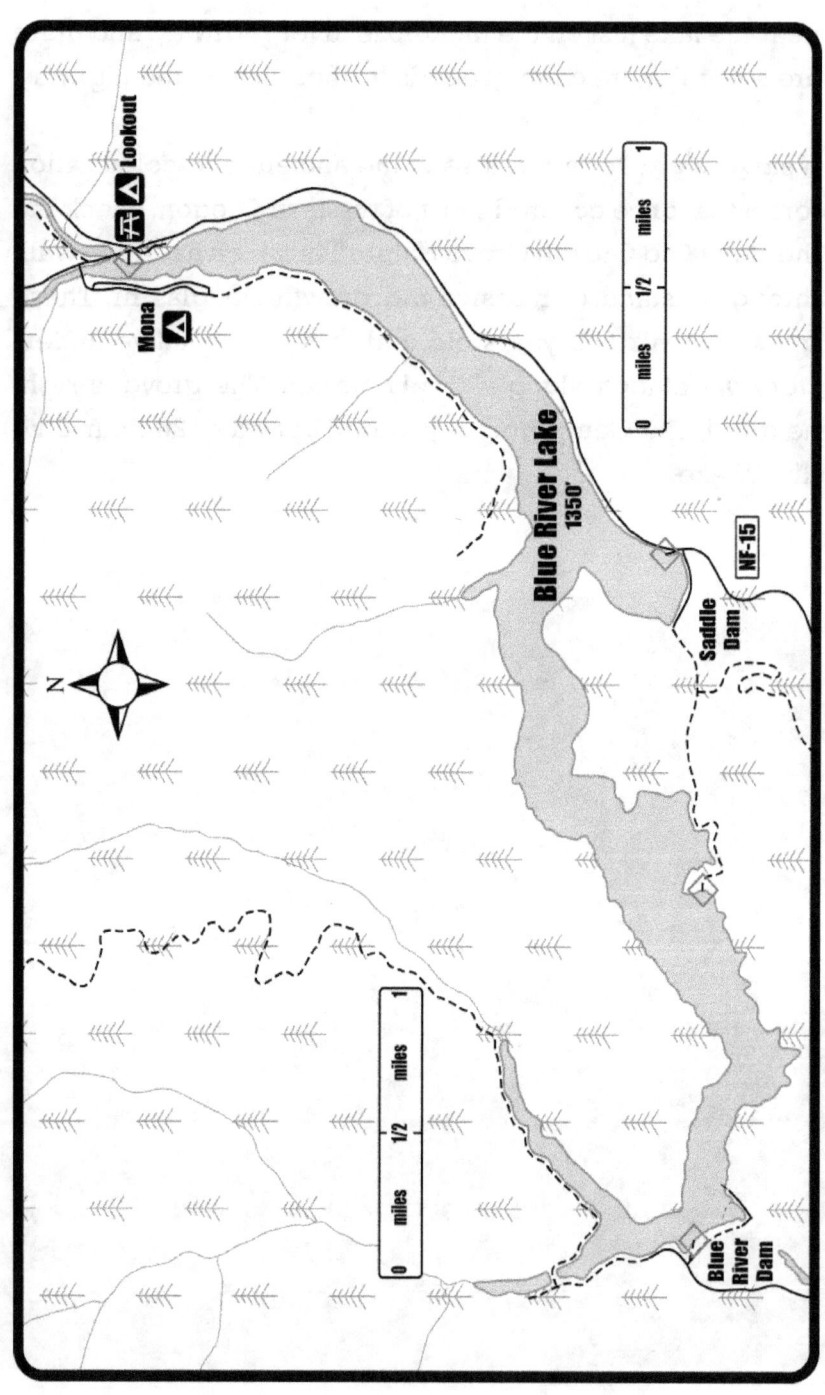

28. Clear Lake (McKenzie River): The best small lake paddle in Oregon

The term "clear" does not do justice to Clear Lake. Let me explain it to you this way: You will spend nearly your entire time at Clear lake gawking at the bottom of the lake. There you will see, with absolute clarity, through many feet of water, huge Doug fir snags, intricate lava rock structures, and schools of fish, all set in brilliant hues of blue and green. Clear Lake is epically beautiful.

Clear Lake is the headwaters of the McKenzie River. It was formed about 3,000 years ago when a lava flow dammed the McKenzie and inundated a forest of Douglas fir. Paddlers can still see many of the trees in this underwater forest. They are not petrified, but are well-preserved thanks to the low level of biological activity in the lake. Paddlers can also still see the relatively young lava flows, both along the banks of the lake and below it's surface. The round hole that looks like a drain in the lake bottom at the southern end is actually where the cooling lava flow enveloped a tree trunk, the tree now gone.

Clear Lake is fed by several springs, including most notably Big Spring, which is sufficiently big to form a short inlet creek to the lake. The inlet from Big Spring is in the northwest corner of the lake. Be sure to feel the temperature of the water coming out as you paddle past. The term "ice cold" does not do that temperature justice either. This lake could just as creatively have been named "Cold Lake." The lake is deep too, averaging 80 feet and maxing out at 175 feet. Because of these factors, I do not recommend this as a place to learn to paddleboard.

Despite the cold, there is a native population of cutthroat trout, as well as stocked rainbow and eastern brook trout. That fish population helps keep osprey hanging around the lake. And despite the piles of lava rock comprising much of the shoreline, there are still several good places to land. A trip around the lake will take you 3.5 miles.

There is a small resort on the western shore, with a dock at the narrows of the lake. The resort rents rowboats only. No motors are allowed on the lake.

Difficulty: Easy.

Distance: 3.5 miles around the lake.

Directions: The turnoff for the Coldwater Cove Campground from Highway 126, the McKenzie River Highway, is 4.5 miles south of the Highway 126-Highway 20 Junction, or 65 miles east of Springfield. Note that there are 11 "Clear Lakes" in Oregon and there is one other described in this book.

Launch/Return: Coldwater Cove Campground. Parking, camping, water, toilets. $5 day use fee or Northwest Forest Pass.

Nearby Rental: The lodge at the lake rents rowboats only.

Nearby Camping: Coldwater Cove and Clear Lake campgrounds are right on the lakeshore. The Clear Lake Resort rents rustic cabins on the lakeshore as well. Ice Cap Campground is just a few miles south on Highway 126, and Fish

Lake Campground is just a few miles above. There are several other campgrounds along the McKenzie River Highway as well.

Nearby Fun: The McKenzie is an Oregon destination for hiking and mountain biking, and a must-see when doing this paddle. Perhaps the best section of the trail, the one featuring Koosah and Sahalie Falls, as well Tamolitch Falls a little further along, is right next to the lake.

The Tamolitch Pool is another must-see, certainly one of the most beautiful things in the Northwest. See the Leaburg Lake/McKenzie River paddle for more info.

When the McKenzie Pass (Highway 242) is open (check the ODOT website), I highly recommend a visit to the Dee Wright Observatory to enjoy its 360-degree views of the central Cascades.

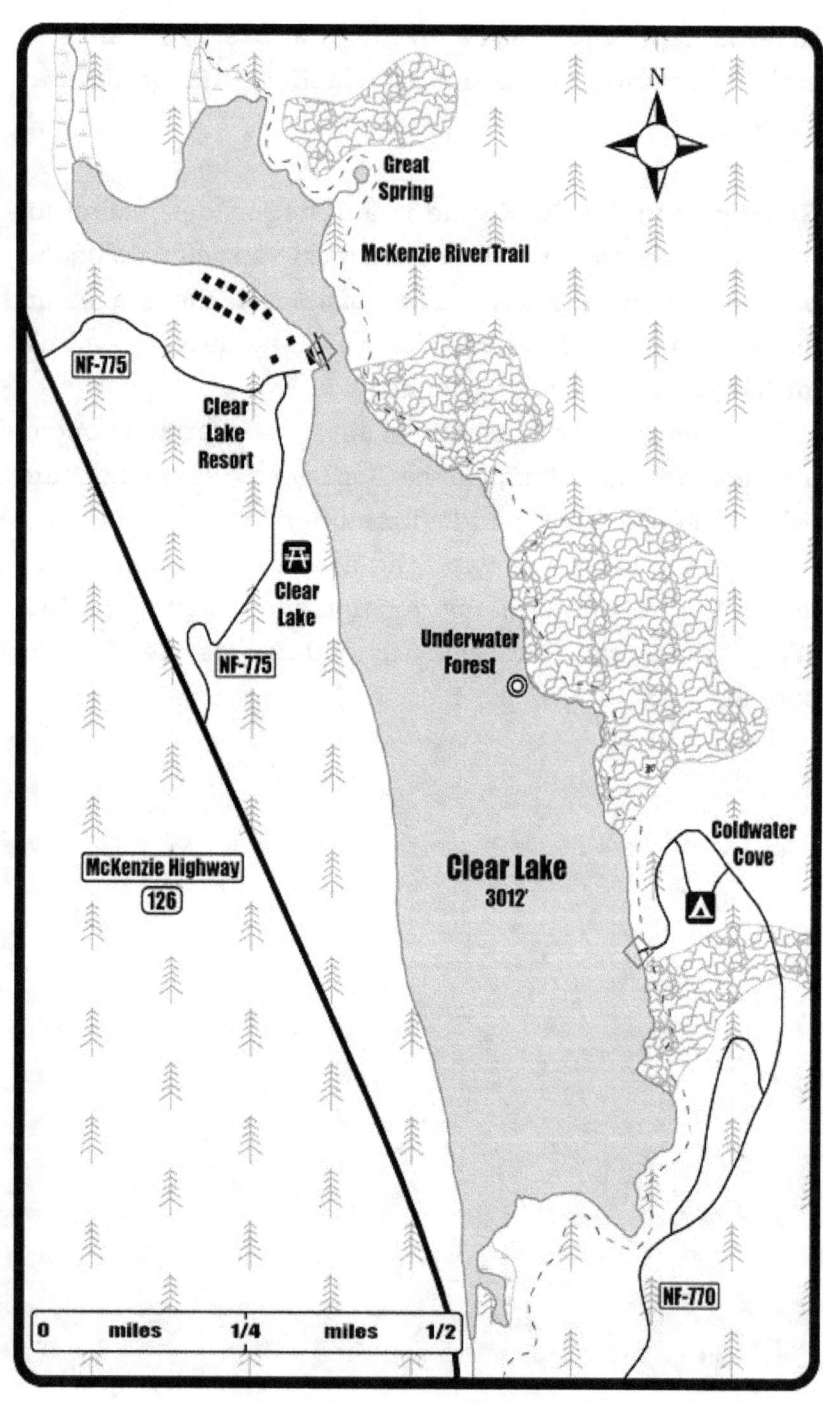

29. Big Lake:
Great swimming, great views, and nice beaches, not particularly big

The Atlas of Oregon Lakes is an excellent reference book. It dares to ask, and answer, the probing question, "How big is Big Lake?" The answer is, "Not particularly." Big Lake is actually one of the smaller lakes described in this book by both area and volume. But it is a great place to paddle, even if the name is suspect. A trip around the lake is just 3.1 miles.

The water at Big Lake is very clear, and near the shore it is shallow and warm in the summer, making it eminently swimmable and a good place to learn to paddle. There are several nice sandy beaches along the northern and western shores, some associated with the many lakeside campsites. There are also a few nice beaches along the isolated south shore. Unfortunately, about 40 percent of the shoreline forest has been deforested by fire, but the open landscape also brings summer wildflowers.

Big Lake features close-up views of Mt Washington to the south, as well as the Hoodoo Butte ski mountain and the distinctive Hayrick Butte to the north. Hayrick Butte looks different than all the other mountain peaks in Oregon. It is a rare type of flat-topped, steep-sided volcano known as a tuya. Tuyas form when lava erupts through a glacier, which must have been quite a sight to see from Big Lake long ago. Hayrick Butte is a textbook example of a tuya, with a flat, half-mile wide top and near-vertical walls rising 700 feet above the lakeshore.

Although motors are allowed on the lake, we encountered none when we visited. Because Big Lake is at the crest of the Cascades, it can get quite windy, even early in the day. Fishers can catch kokanee, brook trout, and cutthroat trout. A Seventh-Day Adventist youth camp, known as the Big Lake Youth Camp, is on the eastern shore.

Difficulty: Easy; suitable for beginners.

Distance: 3.1 miles to circle the lake.

Directions: The turnoff for Big Lake is on Highway 20, 5.1 miles east of the Santiam Junction, the junction of Highways 22 and 20/126, and 20.5 miles west of Sisters. Look for the signs for Hoodoo Ski Bowl. Turn south onto NF-2690 and follow it for 3.3 miles before reaching the lake.

Launch/Return: Big Lake Campground & Day Use Area. In addition to the formal boat ramp, many lakeside campgrounds have informal areas to launch. Toilets, parking, water. $5 day use fee or Northwest Forest Pass.

Nearby Rental: None.

Nearby Camping: Big Lake Campground is on the northwestern shore of the lake. Other campgrounds are at Suttle Lake, which is 7 miles east on Highway 20, and along the McKenzie Highway, Highway 126, about 10 miles west on Highway 20.

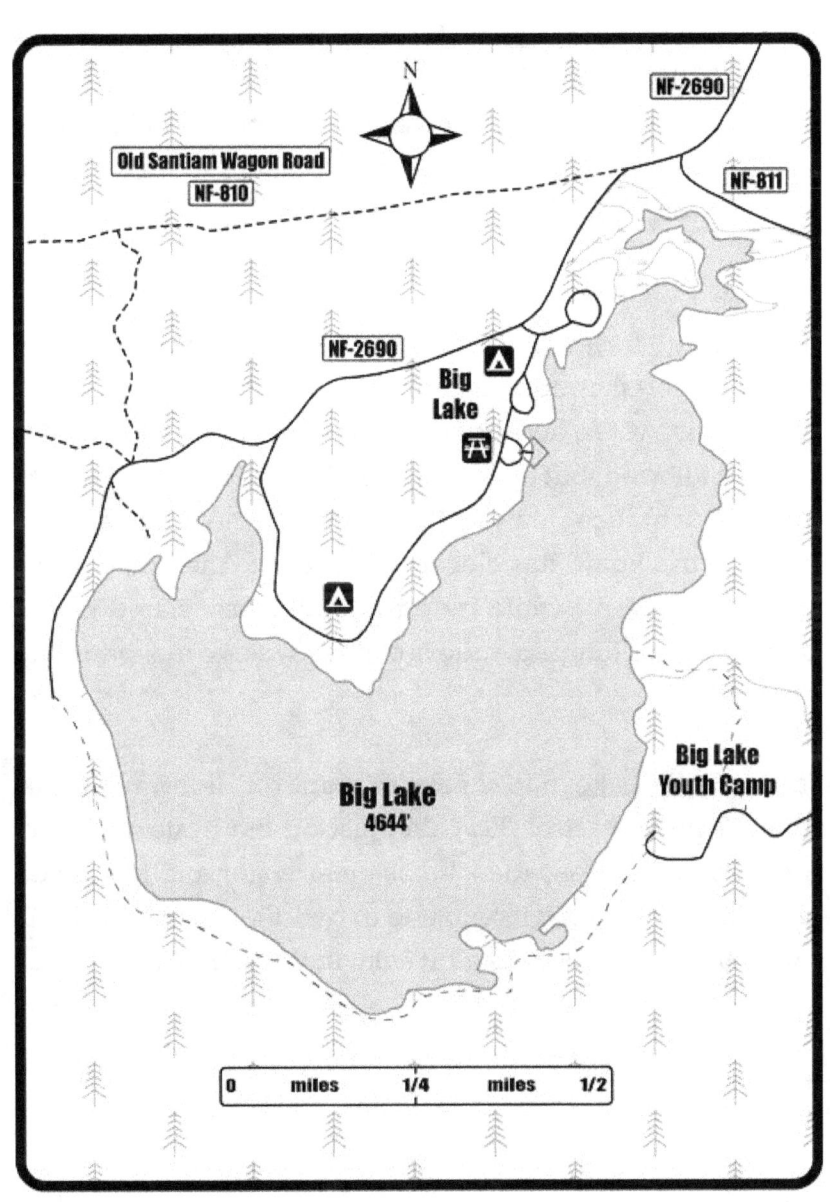

30. Other Good Places to Paddle – The Cascades – Central

(a)   <u>Green Peter Lake</u>: Green Peter Lake is a huge reservoir in the foothills of the Cascades about 17 miles west of Sweet Home. There are many miles of coves and inlets to explore, and some isolated places along the shore thanks to its large size. It also has some good beaches at lower water levels.

(b)   <u>Smith Reservoir</u>: This place is somewhat of a tragedy. It is a finger-shaped reservoir with steep, forested shorelines, clear water, and boat-in camping opportunities. Motors are allowed, but the access road is narrow and steep, so motorboat traffic is limited. Unfortunately, the Eugene Water and Electric Board has closed all access to the lake for five years (from 2017) while it upgrades the associated power plant. Perhaps future paddlers can enjoy this great paddling spot.

(c)   <u>Suttle Lake</u>: Suttle Lake is right on Highway 20/126 about 7 miles east of Big Lake, just on the eastern side of the crest of the Cascades. It has clear water and a forested shoreline. It is a very nice place to paddle, but is a bit small for a full-day and suffers a bit from highway noise.

VI. High Cascade Lakes

31. Sparks Lake:
Lava fjords!

"Lava fjord" is a term I coined after paddling Sparks Lake for the first time. It refers to a canyon-like water channel through a crack in a lava flow or between lava flows. And Sparks has two excellent lava fjords that can be paddled, in addition to others around the lakeshore that can be waded or explored on foot. These lava fjords are largely unique to Sparks Lake and truly a highlight of paddling in Oregon.

Sparks is also a great place to try some backcountry camping from your board or boat, as the southern end of the lake abounds with primitive campsites both on the shores and hidden within the lava hills surrounding the lake. Oh, and Sparks has some of the best mountain views of any of water body in Oregon. South Sister towers 5,000 feet above the lake just about 5 miles to the north, making quite clear where all that lava originated. Broken Top lies next to South Sister, its jagged spires showing the explosive power of the Cascade volcanoes. About the same distance to the south is the symmetrical butte-cone shape of Mt Bachelor, where the ski runs are clearly visible.

Sparks is one of the few lakes in Oregon that has a volume, 960 acre-feet, that is very close to its area, 779 acres. That is a complicated way of saying that Sparks is very shallow. The average depth is less than two feet, and the maximum depth is just seven feet, and that is even with a low dam at the outlet constructed to maintain lake levels. If you listen closely in the lava fjords, you can hear the lake draining through the many cracks in the lava. The Forest Service and Oregon Department of Fish and Wildlife actually tried to plug some of these holes in the lava, but you know what they say about the little boy who put his finger in the dyke.

Sparks is so shallow that it is best to paddle early in the season, as soon as the Cascade Lakes Highway opens in late June. Usually by mid-August, the first 200 yards from the launch/return point is barely navigable. The best approach in such conditions is to stay to the left on the way out and skirt the base of the lava rock wall, as this is the deepest area in this part of the lake. You will also encounter shallows in what looks to be open water adjacent to the marshes along the northern shore.

Unfortunately, the entire northern lobe of the lake becomes unreachable by mid-summer due to the shallow water. That's partly because, on October 7, 1966 a glacial moraine at the foot of Crook Glacier on Broken Top broke, sending an estimated 10,000 to 20,000 tons of sediment down Soda Creek, across the Cascade Lakes Highway, and into the northern lobe of the lake.

Although the lava fjords and miles of good paddling are in the main, southern portion of the lake, the northern lobe is outstanding in it's own right. It is surrounded by pristine alpine wetlands that are buzzing with life early in the summer. Last time I paddled here, I had a frog (unknown species) actually jump onto my board as I paddled past the wetlands in the channel connecting to the northern lobe. The channel comes with a decent current early in the summer. Also, early in the season this water is recently melted snow and is very cold.

In low water conditions, following the river channel through the southern portion of the lake is the best strategy to avoid running aground. The southern shores of the lake are roadless, and largely trailless, with nice sandy beaches in the southeast corner ideal for camping or picnicking. There are also many landing sites in the lava rock that can be explored.

Motors are allowed at Sparks, but most of it is too shallow for all but the smallest boats. Instead, it is very popular with paddlers of all types, and hopefully the reasons why are clear by now. So be prepared to share the water with lots of paddlers and campers if you visit on a weekend or a holiday. The lake is stocked with eastern brook trout and rainbow trout for fishers.

Difficulty: Easy; suitable for beginners.

Distance: 4.8 miles round-trip from the launch/return point to the southern end of the lake. Another 5 miles round-trip to the northern lobe of the lake.

Directions: The turnoff to Sparks Lake is 23 miles west of Bend on the Cascade Lakes Highway, Highway 372, and 44 miles north of the junction of Highway 372 and Crescent Cutoff Rd. After the turnoff, bear left and go another 1.6 miles on the dirt road to reach the day use area.

Launch/Return: Sparks Lake Day Use Area. Toilets, parking. No water.

Nearby Rental: Bend Kayak School in Bend rents SUPs and kayaks. Wanderlust Tours in Bend offers canoe and kayak tours on some of the High Cascade Lakes.

Nearby Camping: The Soda Creek Campground is at the northeast corner of the lake. There are several other campgrounds along the Cascade Lakes Highway.

Nearby Fun: The Green Lakes Trailhead is on the northern shore of the lake. Green Lakes is widely regarded as one of the most beautiful hikes in the state, as it climbs up to alpine lakes between the Broken Top and South Sister peaks.

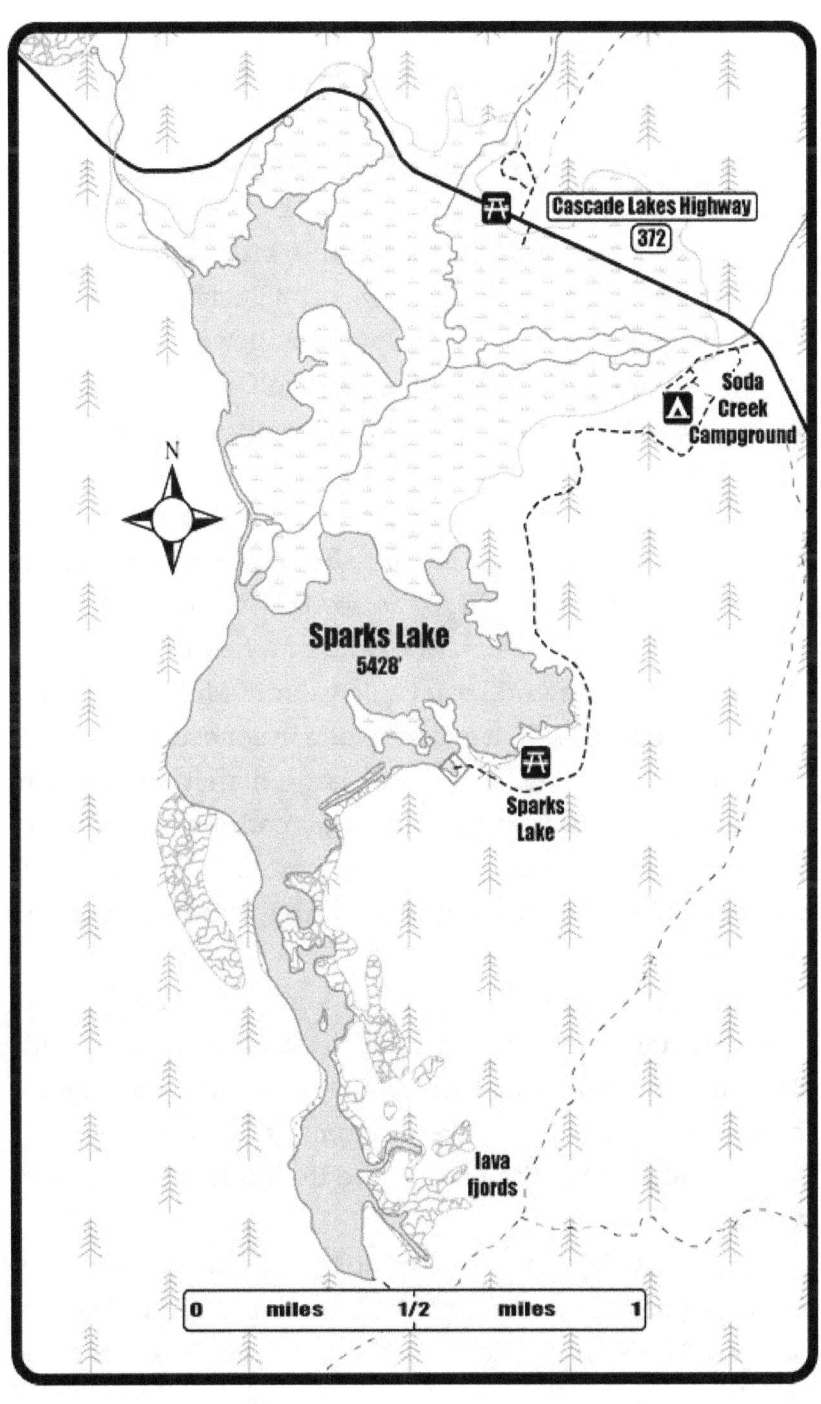

32. Hosmer Lake:
The best wetland paddle in Oregon

Of all the places to paddle in the Northwest, Hosmer Lake has to be at the top of every list. Thanks to the shallow water and extensive marshes, the wildlife viewing is truly outstanding. There are close-up views of Mt Bachelor and South Sister everywhere. And no motors are allowed on the lake. Even the unique structure of the lake itself creates a sense of discovery and adventure. Paddling Hosmer is like paddling through a living labyrinth.

But Hosmer is a quick 30-minute drive from Bend, making it a very popular destination for fishermen and recreational paddlers. So expect to share the serenity with a lot of other folks if you visit on a warm weekend or a holiday.

Hosmer was created by lava flows from Mt Bachelor that impounded the creek. It is now a lake in senescence, meaning that it is slowly turning into a large marsh surrounding a small creek bed. To the present-day paddler, the lake appears as two open-water areas at either end of the lakebed, connected by a channel that winds through the encroaching marsh.

From the launch/return point at the South Campground, on the southern lobe of the lake, paddle next to the reeds along the southern shore before turning north. This area is the deepest part of the lake, bottoming out at just 12 feet. It is the only part of the lake where the bottom is not easily visible.

As you paddle north, the lily pads, reeds, and other aquatic plants (known as macrophytes) close in and the channel narrows. The average depth of the lake is only about three feet and visibility is good, so aquatic plants are nearly everywhere in the lake. The marshes are far more extensive than most maps show, especially in the middle part of the lake.

As you paddle through the channel, red-winged blackbirds flit through the reeds. You may also be able to get close-up looks at great blue herons, nesting ducks, egrets, gulls, and terns. The plants along the connecting channel are so tall and close in places that at times it feels like paddling through a tunnel. The plants beneath the surface create many nooks and crannies where paddlers can see fish hiding from the anglers. The lake is stocked with Atlantic salmon and brook trout.

After a short distance heading north in the channel, it forks. To the right is a channel that dead-ends in one of the lake's outlets. Near the end of the channel, the water percolates through a wall of lava and down through a large lava fissure. Exploring the area around the outlet will reveal a few good places to take out and some secluded picnic or campsites.

The main channel winds around before making a sharp right turn and opening into the northern lobe of the lake. The northern lobe is the bigger of the two open-water areas and is dotted with marshy islands. People are not permitted on many of these islands – they are designated as wildlife habitat.

Paddle counter-clockwise around the northern lobe to examine the many islands and the steep northeast shore. There are some more good take out places and campsites near the northern end, where landing is permitted.

Quinn Creek, the lake's only inflow, is at the northern tip of the lake. The lake becomes increasingly shallow near the mouth of Quinn Creek and when we visited in drought-ridden 2015 this area was so shallow that we ran aground before we could approach the mouth of the creek. Paddling earlier in the summer, soon after the Cascade Lakes Highway opens in June, is your best chance of reaching the secluded northern end of the lake.

Difficulty: Easy; suitable for beginners.

Distance: 5.5 miles to paddle around the lake.

Directions: The turnoff to Hosmer Lake, NF-4525, is 32.6 miles west of Bend on the Cascade Lakes Highway, Highway 372, and 34.8 miles north of the junction of Highway 372 and Crescent Cutoff Rd.

Launch/Return: South Campground. Toilets, parking. No water. $5 day use fee or Northwest Forest Pass.

Nearby Rental/Tours: Bend Kayak School in Bend rents SUPs and kayaks. Wanderlust Tours in Bend offers canoe and kayak tours on some of the High Cascade Lakes.

Nearby Camping: South and Mallard Marsh campgrounds are both on the lake shore. There are several other campgrounds along the Cascade Lakes Highway.

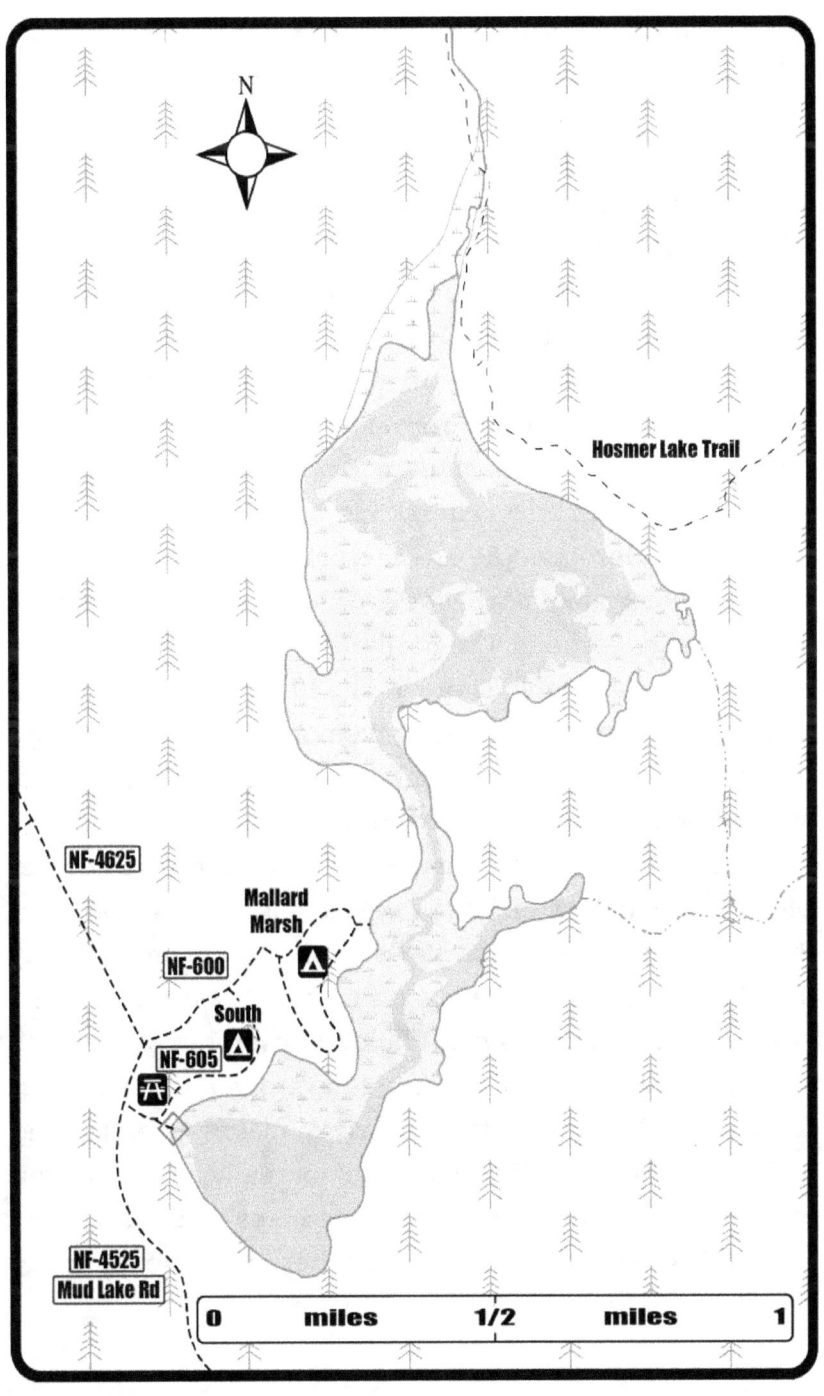

33. Lava Lake, Little Lava Lake, and the Blue Pools: Paradise at the headwaters of the Deschutes River

Both Lava Lake and Little Lava Lake are pretty small lakes suitable for beginning paddlers. A trip around Lava Lakes takes around 2.5 miles, and around Little Lava Lake is only about a mile. The resort at Lava Lake rents SUPs, as well as canoes, kayaks, and boats.

Both lakes have great views of Mt Bachelor, and relatively warm and clear water. Motorboats are allowed on Lava Lake, but the lakes' size keeps motors to a minimum. The 10 mph speed limit eliminates waterskiing and the most annoying motorboats. Here, people are interested chiefly in fishing.

The southern and northwestern shores of Lava Lake have some patches of reeds. The northern and eastern shores are mostly steep lava rock. There are no beaches. The highlight of Lava Lake is the marsh along the northwestern shore (opposite the launch/return point), which sports pink flowers and flitting red-winged blackbirds.

The highlight of Little Lava Lake is the gorgeous powder blue color of the water. Little Lava Lake is the headwaters of the Deschutes River, which starts flowing south immediately out of Little Lava Lake before doing a 180-degree turn and heading north upon leaving Wickiup Reservoir.

The Blue Pools are the name I have given to a series of three cascading pools that the river makes after leaving Little Lava Lake. The Blue Pools are not really a thing, meaning that they do not appear on most maps and hardly anyone even knows they're there. And there isn't even much to paddle. But what there is to paddle is gorgeous.

To reach the first pool, you have to wade with your board through an approximately 30-yard stretch of the frigid Deschutes headwaters as the river leaves Little Lava Lake as little more than an alpine creek. This part is definitely not for beginners. After dodging snags and boulders in the shallow creek, the channel deepens and becomes navigable as it enters into a wide wetland meadow. The water is crystal-clear and a vibrant blue, with the aquatic plants and other features of the river bottom clearly visible. The pool itself is only around a half-mile long, but I have spent hours here by myself watching raptors hunting for fish and deer grazing at the edge of the meadow.

As tantalizing as it is to continue on, the second pool cannot be reached on foot from the first pool, and certainly not with a board. The second pool can be accessed separately by road. It is equally beautiful, but with mostly forested shores. At the northern end there is a large wetland meadow, as well as a deep section of water where the bottom is positively mesmerizing. There are some truly fantastic back-country (and free) riverfront campsites along the shore of the second pool as well.

The third pool is even smaller, and inaccessible by car, board, or even foot (as far as I know). Just appreciate that it exists, and keep that pristine state as the ideal for visiting these other two tiny treasures. The Lava Lakes and Blue Pools might not afford a great distance of paddling, but the paddling they do offer is of the highest in quality. I hope doing this paddle gives you a new appreciation for the beauty of the High Cascade Lakes and the upper Deschutes, or just a nice lake or two to learn on.

Difficulty: Easy. Lava Lake and Little Lava Lake are suitable for beginners.

Distance: 2.5 miles to paddle Lava Lake, 1.1 miles to paddle Little Lava Lake, and less than a mile in the two blue pools.

Directions: The turnoff to the Lava Lakes, NF-500, is 38.4 miles west of Bend on the Cascade Lakes Highway, Highway 372, and 32 miles north of the junction of Highway 372 and Crescent Cutoff Rd. The lakes are a mile off the highway. The dirt road to the second blue pool is unmarked. It is 1.5 miles south of the turnoff to the Lava Lakes.

Launch/Return:
Lava Lake: Lava Lake Resort or the Lava Lake Campground. The Lava Lake Resort has toilets, parking, general store, gas station, showers, and laundry. $5 day use fee or Northwest Forest Pass.

Little Lava Lake: Little Lava Lake Campground. See above for amenities.

Second Blue Pool: Some primitive launch sites down the unmarked dirt road associated with good backcountry campsites. No day use fee.

Nearby Rental/Tour: Bend Kayak School in Bend rents SUPs and kayaks. Wanderlust Tours in Bend offers canoe and kayak tours on some of the High Cascade Lakes. Lava Lake Resort has boat rentals.

Nearby Camping: Lava Lake and Little Lake campgrounds are on the lake shores. There are several other campgrounds along the Cascade Lakes Highway.

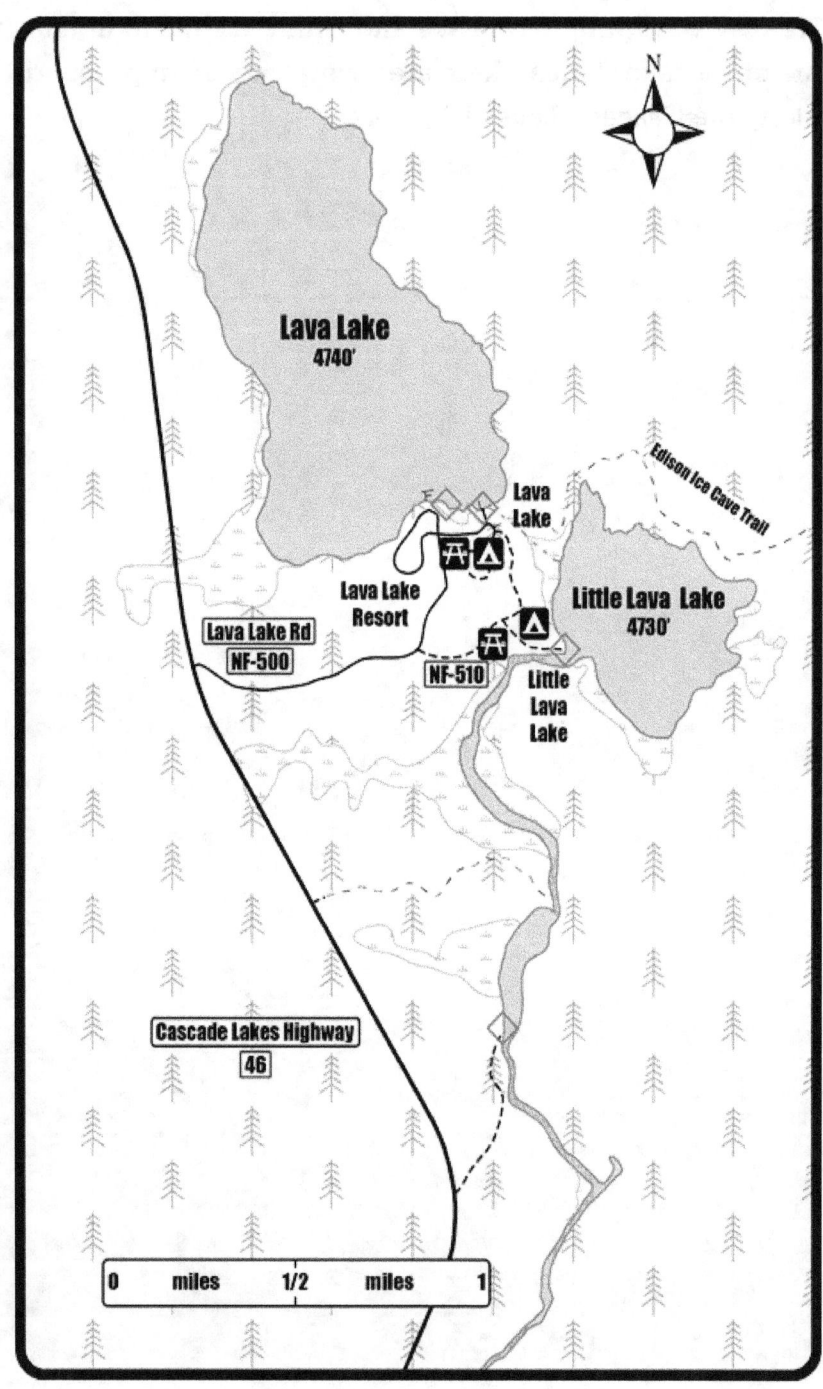

34. Little Cultus Lake:
A quiet lake, good for learning

Cultus Lake is a big, clear lake high in the Cascades surrounded by dense forest. It's just a little too busy for chill paddling, with so many other great paddles so close. Cultus is popular with water skiiers, jet skiiers, sailors, and fishers. It hosts a resort with a restaurant, as well as three Forest Service campsites.

Right next to Cultus is Little Cultus Lake. Little Cultus is less than one-quarter the size of Cultus, with a single campground and an otherwise undeveloped shoreline. There is a 10 mph speed limit for motorboats, so it attracts only a few fishers. There are also fly fishers vying for the stocked populations of rainbow trout and brook trout. Most of the lake is shallow, making the water warm enough for swimming in the summer. The inlet creek on the northwestern end hosts a small but pleasant wetlands area.

The light traffic, clear, warm water, and nice views of Cultus Mountain make this a great place for beginners to paddle. You can paddle around the lake in about 2.2 miles.

Difficulty: Easy; suitable for beginners.

Distance: 2.2 miles to circle the lake.

Directions: The turnoff to Cultus and Little Cultus Lakes, NF4536, is 38.1 miles west of Bend on the Cascade Lakes Highway, Highway 372, and 25.7 miles north of the junction of Highway 372 and Crescent Cutoff Rd. Little Cultus Lake is 3.9 miles from the highway.

Launch/Return: Primitive launch area at or near Little Cultus Lake Campground. Toilets, parking. Amenities available at nearby Cultus Lake. $5 day use fee or Northwest Forest Pass.

Nearby Rental/Tour: Bend Kayak School in Bend rents SUPs and kayaks. Wanderlust Tours in Bend offers canoe and kayak tours on some of the High Cascade Lakes.

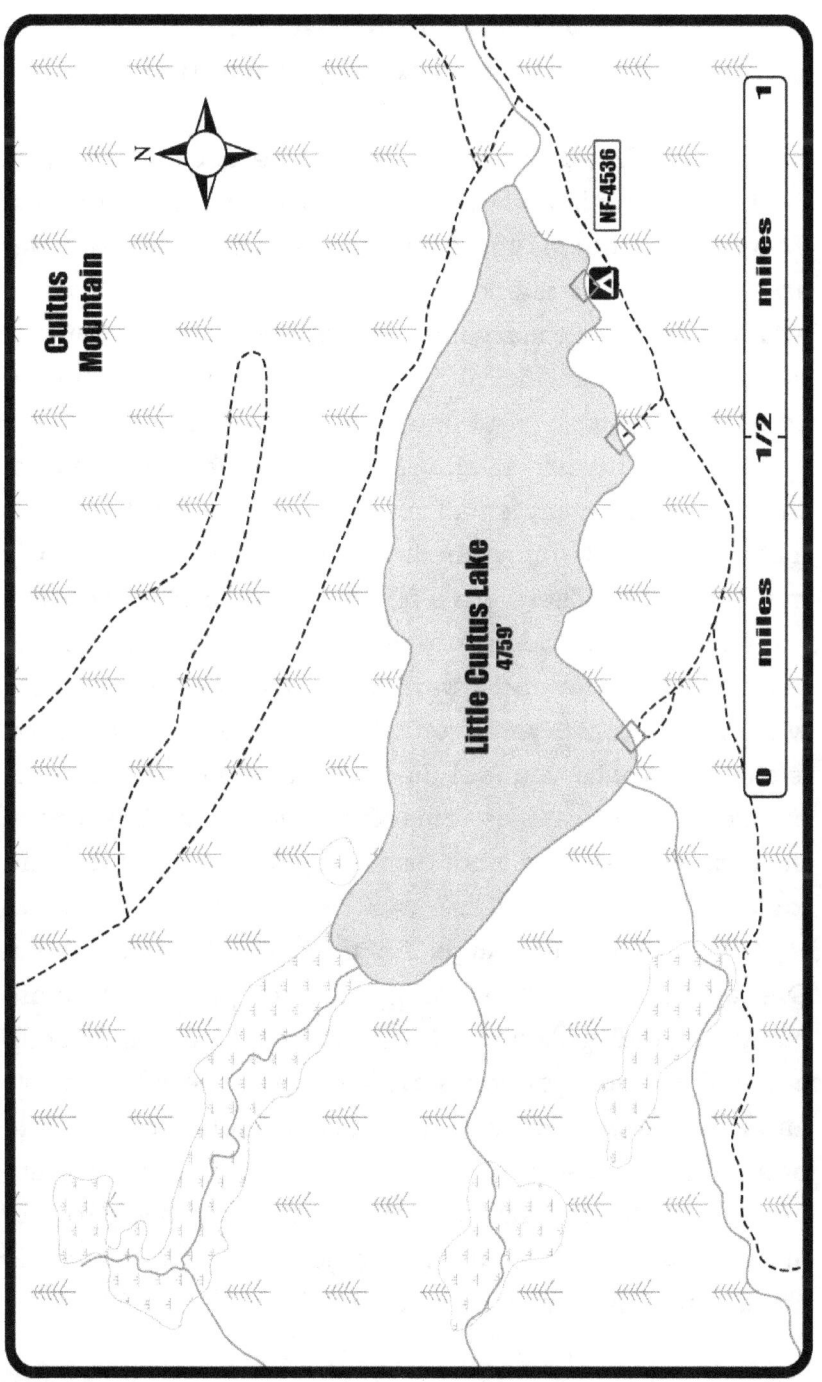

35. Waldo Lake – North:
The crown jewel of Oregon paddling

They say Crater Lake is the crown jewel of Oregon's lakes. But because it's in a national park, it isn't open to paddling. Waldo Lake, then, is the crown jewel of Oregon's paddleable lakes. Waldo is one of the clearest lakes in the world and will leave you marveling at how far down you can see through the water. Visibility extends over 50 feet, and the color of the water is a sublime, deep cobalt blue.

Waldo really has it all. The easily-accessible eastern shore features many small rocky islands and other areas that are perfect for sunbathing, picnicking, and playing in the shallows. There are a few small white sand beaches dotted around the lakeshore that, when combined with the crystal clear water and a warm day, may fool you for a little while into thinking you're on a tropical island. That illusion is shattered once you feel the temperature of the water, of course, but the water is remarkably warm (for Oregon) in the shallow areas. On a hot day, it's the perfect temperature for a cool-off.

Waldo Lake is also huge. It is the second largest lake in Oregon, and over 400 feet deep in some places. There are many isolated spots around the lake to take out and set up camp. Once you get some distance from the parking lots and campgrounds on the eastern shore, solitude is easy to find. Perhaps best of all, internal combustion engines are banned on Waldo Lake to protect the incredible purity of the water, so there are no wakes or jetskiis to dodge, and no noise to interrupt the solitude.

From the launch/return point at the North Waldo Campground, it is difficult to get a good view of the lake. An unnamed island sits in the way, but after going around the island, you will see a bevy of nearby small, rocky islands, the deforested northern shore, the crest of the Cascades, Diamond Peak, and the remainder of the massive lake stretching into the distance.

In 1996, the Charlton fire left most of the northern shore deforested. This may make it less attractive to some paddlers, but this area includes a few sunny, small, and very secluded beaches situated in coves with shallow water suitable for swimming. The fire has not harmed the water quality here, either. But it does allow you to watch mountain bikers zoom along the lake trail as you paddle along the northern shore.

At Waldo, the further you paddle, the more isolated you become. For the first time, you may realize how peaceful and serene it is when there are no motors on over 6,000 acres of water. The entire western shore is designated wilderness, and there are no roads anywhere along the shoreline except adjacent to the three launch/campground areas. Waldo is the perfect place for backcountry board camping, for spending a quiet afternoon on a gorgeous beach, or for paddling for hours in near silence.

The only downside to paddling at Waldo is the wind. Because it is right at the crest of the Cascades, it can get very windy in the afternoon. Because it is so big, it also can get large, wind-driven waves. Don't try to cross the lake once the wind comes up unless you are an expert paddler. Mosquitos can also get quite bad at Waldo, but you can avoid them (mostly) by paddling here later in the summer or early fall.

Difficulty: Easy to advanced, depending on distance.

Distance: 5 miles round-trip from the launch/return point to the northwestern corner of the lake.

Directions: NF-5897, the turnoff for Waldo Lake, is 23.5 miles west of Oakridge on Highway 58, the Willamette Highway, and 13.9 miles east of the Highway 58-Crescent Cutoff Rd junction. Go 12.2 miles on NF-5897, then turn left onto FS-5898, following the signs for the North Waldo Campground. In 0.4 miles the road Ts. Go Right onfo NF-514, again following the signs for North Waldo. The campground and boat launch is 0.4 miles ahead.

Launch/Return: North Waldo Campground and Boat Launch. Toilets, parking. No water. $5 day use fee or Northwest Forest Pass.

Nearby Rental: None.

Nearby Camping: North Waldo, Islet, and Shadow Bay campgrounds are all on the eastern shore of the lake. Primitive camping is allowed elsewhere around the lake.

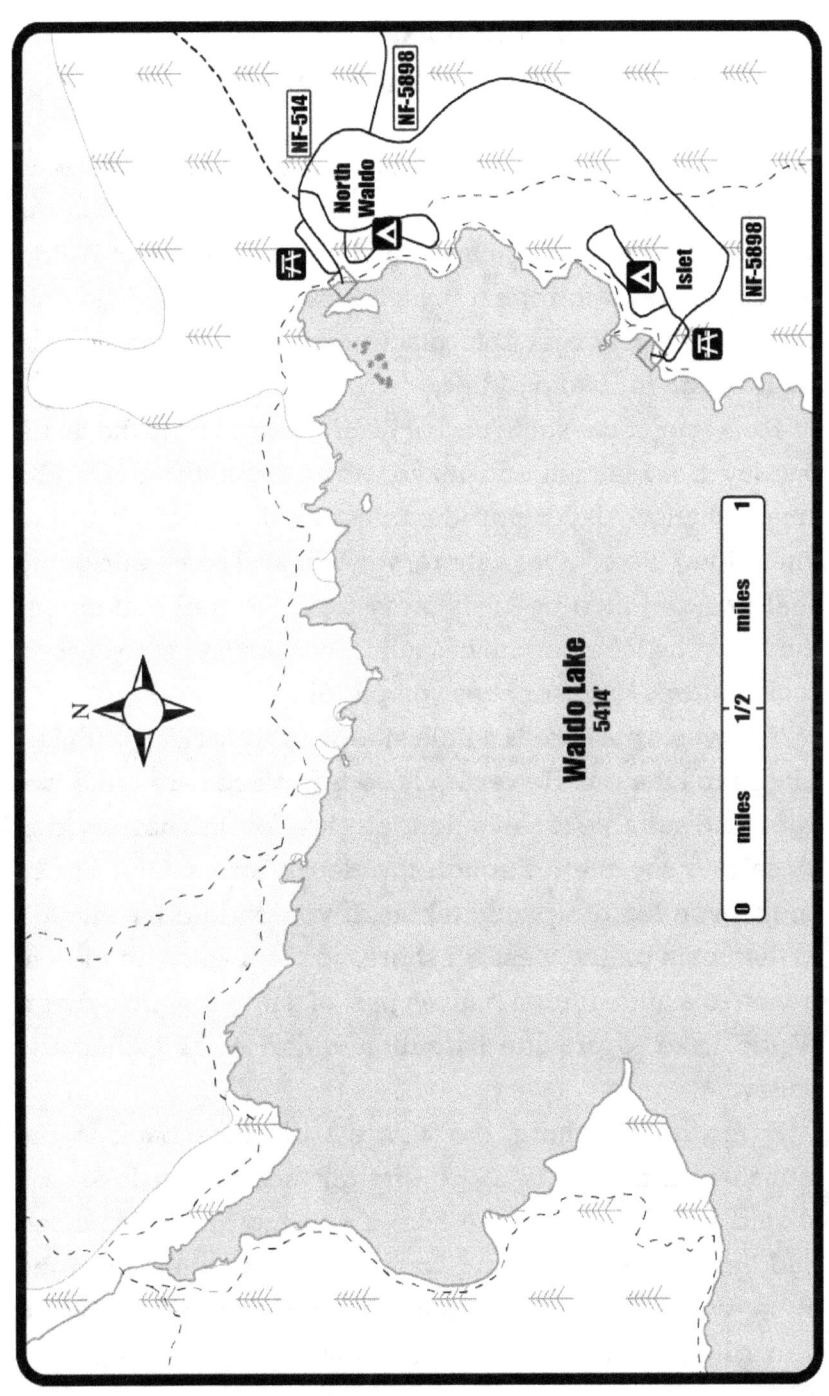

36. Waldo Lake – South:
The crown jewel of Oregon paddling, Part II

In conjunction with reviewing this paddle, please read the Waldo Lake – North entry to hear a little bit about the lake itself. I can gush on and on about the beauty of Waldo, but I don't want to repeat myself here. Suffice it to say that Waldo is an unforgettable place to paddle and more than big enough for two paddles.

For a tour of the south end of Waldo, launch from the Shadow Bay boat launch and make a quick circuit around the small, shallow bay before heading south along the shoreline. Along the southern shore, you will find some intriguing shallows and nice beaches away from the trail that circles the lake. The lake bottom has numerous logs and interesting rock features to observe as you paddle.

The western shore is a little steeper and rockier, with few places to take out. However, those few places are quite isolated and suitable for an extended stay. You will have to look closely to see them through the dense forest. One or two spots even feature picnic tables. If you paddle far enough to the north on the western shore, you will also see the entrance to a huge tunnel built as part of a failed plan to divert Waldo Lake to provide irrigation water to the Willamette Valley.

From the far shore, the shortest distance back to the launch/return spot is to go straight across the lake. You should only go across the lake if you are an experienced paddler, as the winds and waves can get quite big in the open water. We once found ourselves crossing Waldo through whitecaps, and gazing down into the deep blue abyss made me acutely aware that crossing open water at Waldo Lake is serious work.

The eastern shore north of Shadow Bay is a delight, lined with shallows, small beaches, and rocky islands perfect for wading, sunbathing, or getting comfortable on your board. This is also the area around the campground. If you are looking for shorter paddle, head north along the shore from the launch/return point to enjoy this area.

Difficulty: Easy to advanced, depending on distance. Suitable for beginners.

Distance: 5 miles round-trip to paddle around the southern lobe of the lake.

Directions: NF-5897, the turnoff for Waldo Lake, is 23.5 miles west of Oakridge on Highway 58, the Willamette Highway, and 13.9 miles east of the Highway 58-Crescent Cutoff Rd junction. Go 6.7 miles on NF-5897, then turn left onto FS-5896, following the signs for the Shadow Bay. The boat ramp is ahead in two miles.

Launch/Return: Shadow Bay Campground and Boat Launch. Toilets, parking. No water. $5 day use fee or Northwest Forest Pass.

Nearby Rental: None.

Nearby Camping: North Waldo, Islet, and Shadow Bay campgrounds are all on the eastern shore of the lake. Primitive camping is allowed elsewhere around the lake.

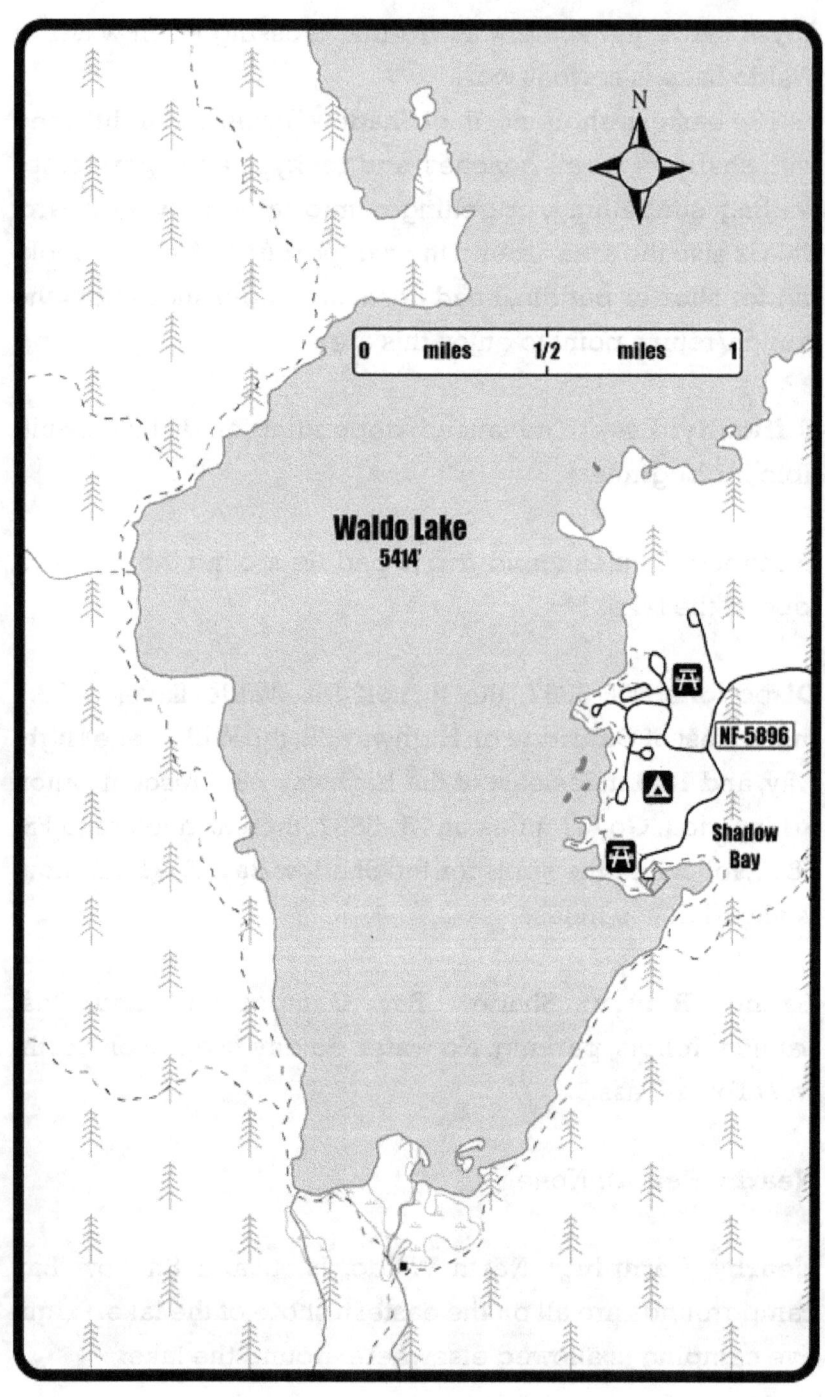

37. Gold Lake:
Yes, it really is golden!

Yes, Gold Lake really is golden in color, making it the most aptly named lake in Oregon. The color is the result of a unique combination of factors. Before reaching the lake, the inlet stream, Salt Creek, passes through a subalpine sphagnum bog. The clear water mixes with organic matter from the bog, and reflects off the sandy lake bottom, creating uniquely colorful shades. In many places, the water has a brownish hue, though it is clear. When the sun catches it, the water and the lake bottom appear to be a brilliant warm golden color.

The banks are heavily forested with Engleman spruce and subalpine fir. The shallows of the lake support large, red-and green-leafed lily pads. The area around the bog, along the northern shore, is home to Cascade frogs and western spotted frogs. You might also see beavers, which are so populous here that their dams effectively support water levels in the lake and the bog. The lake is stocked with brook trout and rainbow trout. It is popular with fishers, but no motors are allowed.

The bog itself is full of rare plants and is protected as the Gold Lake Bog Research Natural Area. Five species of rare plants in the bog are carnivorous, catching and digesting insects with stalks that are covered with sticky, viscous liquid. A permit is required to enter the bog, and inquiries can be made at the district ranger station in Oakridge.

The only downside to this gorgeous lake is that it is small, only about a half-mile in length and 1,200 feet wide. So, not much of a paddle. I have included it here for its outstanding color and biological diversity, so if you're paddling any of the other great lakes in the area, I recommend stopping in to see it for yourself.

Difficulty: Easy.

Distance: Less than a mile around the lake.

Directions: NF-500, the turnoff for Gold Lake, is 26 miles west of Oakridge on Highway 58, the Willamette Highway, and 11.5 miles east of the Highway 58-Crescent Cutoff Rd junction. The boat ramp is ahead in two miles.

Launch/Return: Gold Lake Campground. Toilets, parking. No water. $5 day use fee or Northwest Forest Pass.

Nearby Rental: None.

Nearby Camping: Gold Lake Campground is the only campground on the lakeshore. There are several campgrounds on the shores of Crescent and Odell lakes, which are a few miles west on Highway 58.

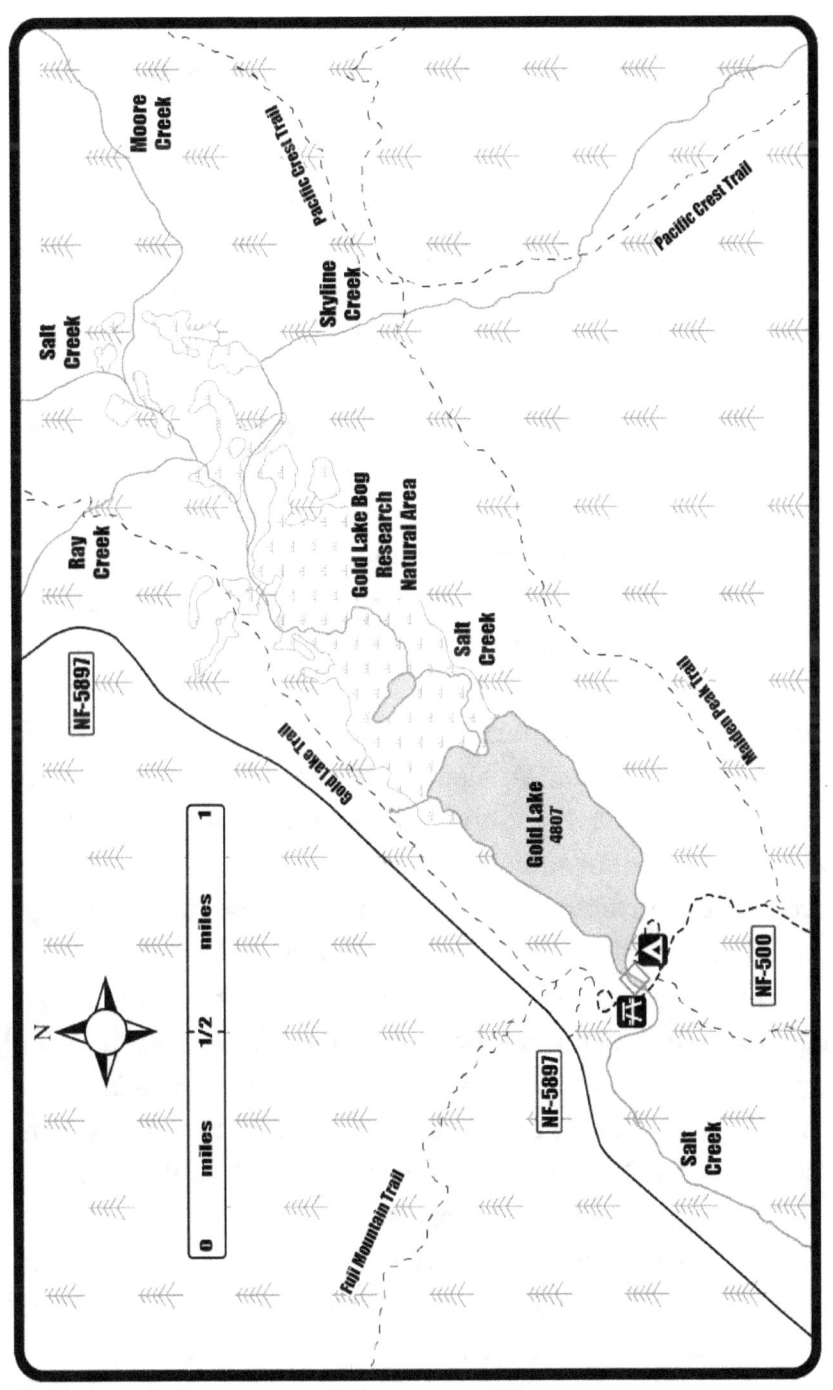

38. Davis Lake:
Solitude, wildlife, lava fjords, and electric green water

Davis Lake is a great place to paddle for birding or for fishing – or just fish watching, which is a thing now that SUPs exist. And it's a good bet that Davis will offer you a serene environment to do your fish- and bird-watching. Although motors are allowed, the lake often has no motorized boats on it because the lake level gets too low later in the summer. The lake also benefits from being at the far southern end of the Cascade Lakes Highway, straddling the Klamath County line, placing it farther away from Bend than most of the other High Cascade Lakes. As a result, it also has outstanding views of the Cascade volcanoes to the north.

We paddled Davis Lake on a Saturday and found only a few kayakers and fishermen at the southern end of the lake – and no one else! We also found very shallow but pretty clear water. The lake bottom is a patchwork of aquatic plants and bare sand. In some areas the water takes on a brilliant golden-green color that B accurately described as "just south of Gatorade." You have to see it to believe it.

Throughout the trip, we watched fish dart away from our boards. Some of the rainbow trout and largemouth bass we spotted schooling in Odell Creek and in the reeds at the north end of the lake were shockingly big and fat, demonstrating why Davis Lake is regarded as one of the best "fly fishing only" lakes in the Northwest.

And the birding is as good as the fishing. We saw ducks, Caspian terns, Canada geese, redwing blackbirds, osprey, American white pelicans, a red-tailed hawk, and some eagles. In fact, part of the lake's eastern shore was closed on our visit to protect nesting eagles (look for signs at the campgrounds).

The most impressive were the large groups of American white pelicans. These birds have wingspans as wide as nine feet, making them the second-largest in north America, after the California condor. They migrate from Baja, wisely spending their summer in the High Cascade Lakes. They can usually be seen standing in large groups in the shallows, but their fishing is impressive too. They coordinate by swimming in circles around schools of fish, surrounding them and then going to town with their huge, foot-long beaks.

The Forest Service says several other species of birds are prevalent at Davis Lake as well, including other types of terns (Forester's and black), four types of grebes (pied-billed, horned, eared, and western), black-backed woodpeckers, and great gray owls. There are also many bird types that are rare in Oregon, including the scissor-tailed flycatcher, northern parula, and semipalmated sandpiper. Many birds seem to hang around the marshy western shore, where human presence is minimal.

The most interesting natural feature of Davis Lake is the large, extremely young lava flow that formed the lake by damming Odell Creek. This lava flow is estimated to be only about 6,000 years old, and it shows. It now forms the lake's northeastern shore.

The piles of lava that form the shore are steep and almost completely treeless, with jutting rock spires, including "the old man of Davis Lake." See if you can spot the craggy face as you paddle past. The flow includes two really neat lava fjords where the golden-green water contrasts sharply with the dark gray rock walls.

The main downside we encountered at Davis Lake was a general lack of good places to stop along the shore. The prominent point of land on the eastern shore south of Lava Flow Campground appeared to offer a solid shoreline and some shade, but was closed for the eagles. The lava flow is so young that there are no sandy or flatter spots to land a board. The few inviting, slightly less vertical places we did find along the lava flow were muddy and had lots of flotsam near the shore. The remainder of the lakeshore is either blocked by large tracts of reeds or is very muddy, with knee-deep sink levels in many places. So be prepared to stay out on the water once you get going.

Access to the lake can also be challenging due to low water levels. The ideal place to launch for exploring the lava flow would be Lava Flow Campground, but when we visited, the lake was sufficiently low that launching from there was pretty difficult. It required carrying the board while rock-hopping along the base of the lava flow for 20-30 yards before reaching a narrow clearing in the reeds that appears to offer floatable passage to open water if you care to wade into some pretty thick mud.

We decided to pass on that option and headed instead to East Davis Lake Campground, one of two campgrounds at the south end of the lake. The nice part about launching at East Davis is paddling on Odell Creek, which is clear and full of fish. However, the mouth of the creek was very shallow and we had nearly 50 yards of hike-a-board to reach navigable water in the lake. In my opinion, this is a small price to pay for being motor-free.

West Davis Lake Campground sits right at the mouth of the creek and so largely avoids this problem, but it requires a bit farther of a drive to reach. Nevertheless, West Davis is your best bet for a clean launch on Davis Lake in low water conditions. The difficulties at Davis are well worth the trouble. Our only real complaint is that the pelicans wouldn't allow us to get close enough to get better pictures of them.

Difficulty: Moderate.

Distance: 7.3 miles to circle the lake. This figure is for low water conditions, when the lake has the wetland boundaries shown on the map. In higher water conditions, it would take significantly longer to circle the lake.

Directions: The turnoff to East Davis Lake Campground is 61 miles southwest of Bend on the Cascade Lakes Highway, Highway 372, and 6.4 miles north of the junction of Highway 372 and Crescent Cutoff Rd. Turn west off Highway 372 and go 0.6 miles before turning right. The campground is ahead in 0.4 miles. The turnoff to the West Davis Lake Campground is 64 miles southwest of Bend on the Highway 372, and 3.3 miles north of the junction of Highway 372 and Crescent Cutoff Rd. Turn west off Highway 372 and go 3.7 miles before turning right. Turn right again in 0.4 miles, and the campground is ahead in 1.6 miles.

Launch/Return: East Davis Lake Campground or West Davis Lake Campground. Parking, toilets. No water. $5 day use fee or Northwest Forest Pass.

Nearby Rental: None.

Nearby Camping: There are three campgrounds on the lakeshore, East Davis Lake, West Davis Lake, and Lava.

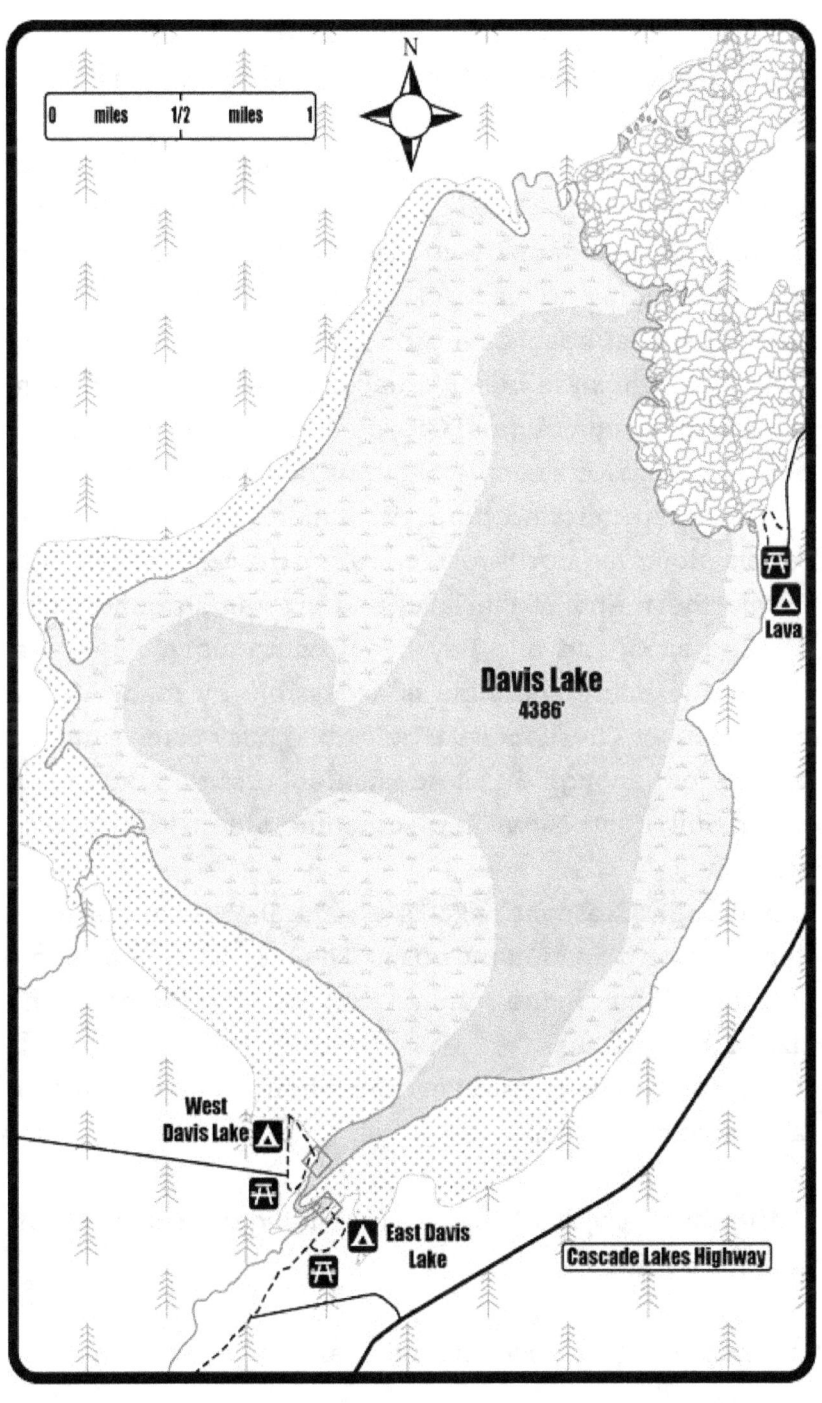

39. Crescent Lake:
Beautiful sandy beaches waiting for you!

Crescent Lake is just another gorgeous, large, clear lake high in the forests of the Cascade Mountains, perfect for paddling. It also happens to have the best beaches of any lake in Oregon. And the sand is a wonderfully warm orange color. The best beaches are on the southern shore, where many campsites are beach-adjacent. The water gets warm enough for swimming, and Crescent Lake makes the perfect place to camp for a couple of nights in the late summer.

Motors are allowed here. Also, there are 70 recreation cabins along the northwest shore, a privately-run resort at the northern end of the lake, and six campgrounds, four day-use sites, and one Boy Scout camp along the shore. Nearly the entire shoreline is accessible by road. As you might expect, Crescent Lake gets quite busy in the summer, but it is big enough that it doesn't feel crowded out on the water. Still, it is best visited sometime other than summer weekends.

Although Crescent Lake is a natural lake, it has been dammed for irrigation purposes. The lake level goes down several feet late in the summer, but that only increases the size of the beaches.

There are many miles of paddling here – a trip around the lake takes is 10 miles.

Difficulty: Easy to advanced, depending on distance. Suitable for beginners.

Distance: 10.2 miles to circle the lake.

Directions: The turnoff to Crescent Lake is 33.4 miles east of Oakridge on Highway 58, the Willamette Highway, and 3.6 miles northwest of the junction of Highway 58 and Crescent Cutoff Rd. Turn west and go 2.3 miles to reach the Crescent Lake Resort. Continue another 0.5 miles to reach the lake.

Launch/Return: There are numerous campgrounds and day use areas around the lake to launch, as well as the Crescent Lake Resort (see map). Crescent Lake Resort has a bar and restaurant, and there is a general store on the Willamette Highway near the turnoff (in the unincorporated town of Crescent). There is $5 day use fee or Northwest Forest Pass for the campsites and day use areas.

Nearby Rental: Crescent Lake Resort rents SUPs, kayaks, and aqua cycles.

Nearby Camping: See the map for a list of the many campgrounds on the lakeshore. Crescent Lake Resort rents cabins on the lake.

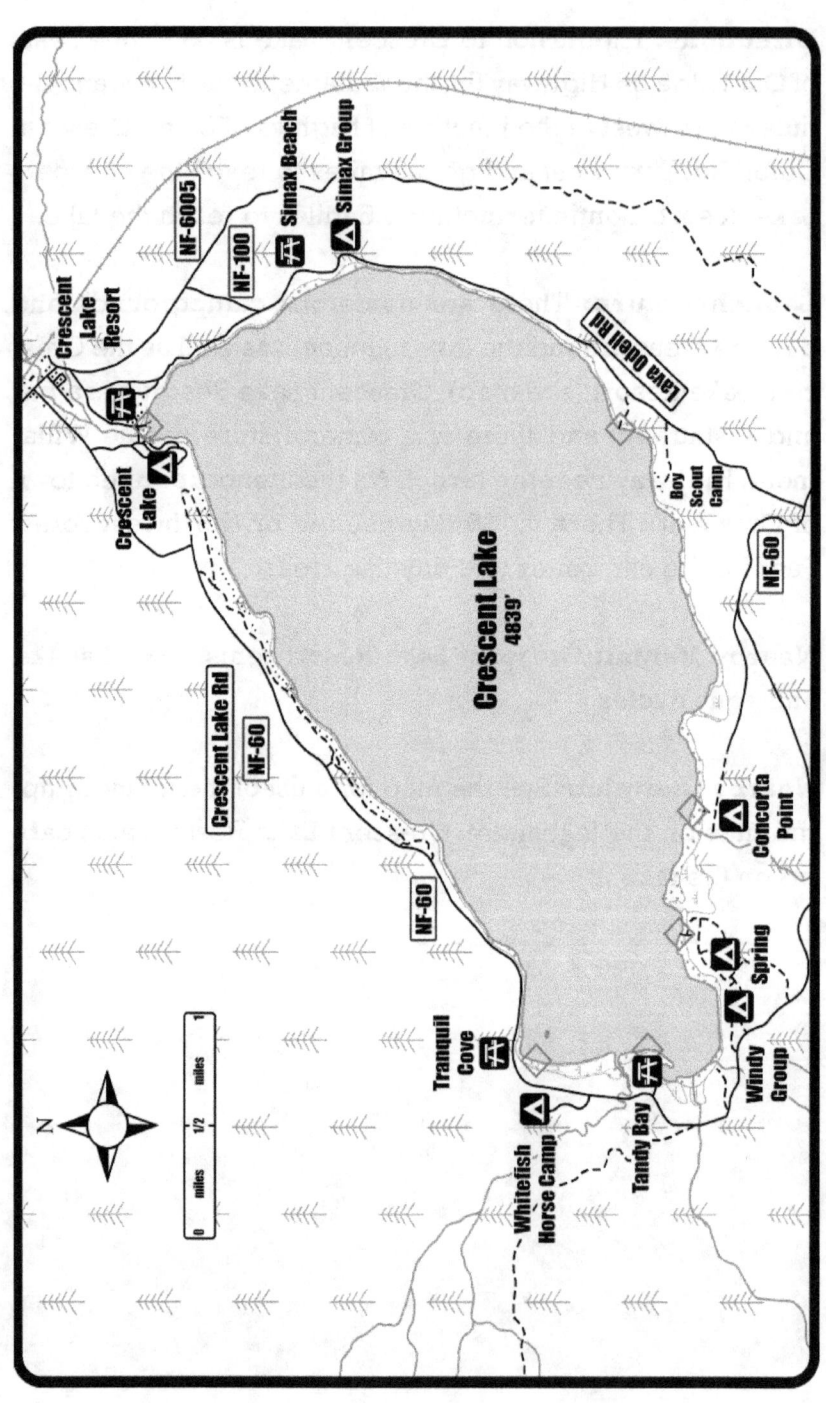

40. Summit Lake:
The best paddle in the whole state!

After paddling at nearly 70 places in Oregon, I declare that Summit Lake is the best, or at least my favorite, paddle in the entire state. That's because it is as beautiful as Waldo, but even more secluded. The road to and around Summit is rough, and there are no developed campsites and no developed access to the water. The entire shoreline is ringed by dense coniferous forest, and the road comes close to the lake only briefly in one location. Because of its situation at the crest of the Cascades, it is only accessible by road for three or four months each year (roughly July, August, and September).

Summit is known as an "ultra-oligotrophic" lake, meaning that its water is so pure that there is hardly enough biological activity to support fish and other aquatic animals. For this reason, the lake does not attract a lot of fishers, nor a great deal of birds. The water has a gorgeous turquoise color.

The northern shore is an epically beautiful place to paddle. It is heavily forested and features two isthmuses, several peninsulas, an archipelago, several rocky islands, and a blue lagoon! The water is shallow with many aquatic plants, and there are many rocky coves to explore. The blue lagoon is well-hidden but a delight to stumble upon.

Most of the shoreline is rocky but not steep, though there are several coves and a handful of small but very pretty beaches tucked away along the shoreline. The crystal-clear water is warm enough for swimming at times.

This is the most isolated moderate-length paddle in the state. You will paddle about 6.7 miles to circumnavigate the lake. The only negatives to paddling here are strong afternoon winds (it is at the summit of the Cascades, after all) and a healthy mosquito population.

Difficulty: Easy to moderate, depending on distance.

Distance: 6.7 miles to circle the lake.

Directions: Take the turnoff to Crescent Lake, which is 33.4 miles east of Oakridge on Highway 58, the Willamette Highway, and 3.6 miles northwest of the junction of Highway 58 and Crescent Cutoff Rd. Turn west and go 7.2 miles along the shoreline of Crescent Lake. Turn left onto NF-6010 and go another 6.2 miles to reach the Summit Lake Campground.

Launch/Return: Summit Lake Campground. Toilets, parking. No water. There are also numerous primitive campsites along the northeast and western shores (look for pullouts) where you can camp and launch.

Nearby Rental: None.

Nearby Camping: See above.

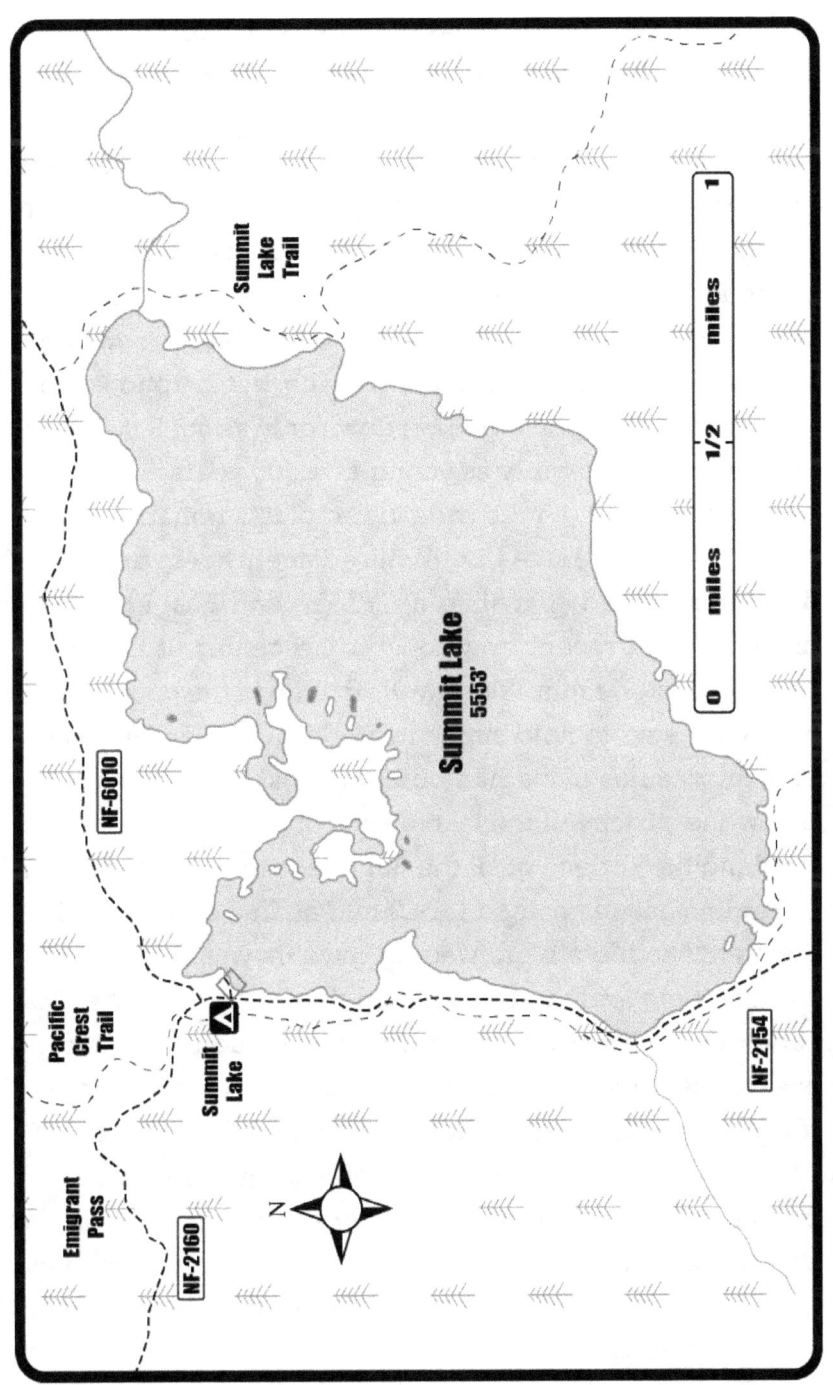

41. Paulina Lake and East Lake:
Paddle in the crater of a volcano, soak in hot springs

Newberry Volcano is a massive, 20-mile wide shield volcano east of the main line of Cascade volcanoes in central Oregon. The vast volcanic field spreading north from Newberry to the edges of Bend includes more than 150 cinder cones, or buttes, as the 150- to 500-feet-high cones are known. Newberry is a dormant volcano, but eruptions there are very recent, with large lava flows only about 2,000 years old and others possibly as young as 1,000 years.

In the nearly five-mile wide crater of this remarkable volcano are two large lakes, both with adjacent hot springs. Paulina (pronounced "paw-line-uh") Lake and East Lake were once one, but recent eruptions in the center of the crater have separated them. Water wells drilled in the center of the crater are said to hold super-heated water over 600°F. Several cubic miles of magma boil away just about three miles below the surface of the lakes. As cool as all this is, it is just touching the surface of all the fun things to do at Newberry.

Paulina Lake is named for Chief Paulina, a Northern Paiute man who led a band waging guerilla war against European settlers and the US Army on the east side of the Cascades in the 1860s. Its hot springs are unique and a soak is essential to any paddle at Paulina. On the north shore of the lake is an extensive black pebble beach. Hot water, 96-113°F, bubbles up through the pebbles. Some areas are dug out and marked with driftwood. By digging around in the pebbles and mixing the warmer water from below with the colder lake water, you can create the perfect water temperature for a soak!

Paulina Lake is deep, with steep shores forested primarily with lodgepole and ponderosa pine. Nevertheless, there are many places to takeout. Because of the depth and the elevation, Paulina can get windy and wavy. Motors are allowed, and there are some recreational boaters, but most boaters are fishing. The lake is stocked with German brown trout, rainbow trout, and eastern brook trout, and is a very popular fishing destination. A paddle around the lake is a moderate distance of about 4.8 miles.

East Lake is essentially the same as Paulina in all respects, though it is smaller at about 3.8 miles to paddle around. It has a few small beaches. It is also more popular with fishers since it was once home to a record-setting German brown trout (22 pounds, 8 ounces) caught way back in 1982. Perhaps most significantly, the hot springs at East Lake are more traditional looking and can be viewed after a short hike on the lakeshore, but cannot be soaked in.

Both lakes have small resorts where you can rent a board, kayak, or canoe, enjoy a lakeside beer and meal, and buy some supplies.

Difficulty: Easy to moderate, depending on distance. Suitable for beginners.

Distance: 4.8 miles to circle Paulina, and 3.8 miles to circle East.

Directions: The turn off to Newberry, Paulina Lake Rd/FS-21, is 22.3 miles south of Bend, and 6.1 miles north of La Pine, on Highway 97. Turn east onto Paulina Lake Rd and Paulina Lake is 12.6 miles ahead.

Launch/Return:
Paulina: Paulina Lake Lodge is perhaps the easiest place to launch. Parking, toilets, restaurant, general store. No day use fee. Little Crater Campground also has a day use area, and two other campgrounds also have primitive launch areas. $5 day use fee or Northwest Forest Pass.

East: East Lake Resort. Parking, toilets, restaurant, general store. No day use fee. There are also several campground launch sites, including East Lake, Hot Springs, and Cinder Hill (two places) campgrounds. $5 day use fee or Northwest Forest Pass.

Nearby Rental:
Paulina: Paulina Lake Lodge rents motor boats for fishing only, row boats, SUPs, kayaks, and canoes. Bend Kayak School in Bend rents SUPs and kayaks.

East: East Lake Resort rents boats, SUPs, kayaks, and canoes.

Nearby Camping:
Paulina: Paulina Lake, Newberry Group, and Little Crater campgrounds are all on the lakeshore. Paulina Lake Lodge rents cabins.

East: East Lake, Hot Springs, and Cinder Hill campgrounds are all on the lakeshore. East Lake Resort rents cabins and has a restaurant and a general store.

Nearby Fun: Drive the steep dirt road up to the top of Paulina Peak for fantastic views of both lakes, the whole volcanic crater, and the large lava flow and cinder cones to the north.

Visit the Big Obsidian Flow (also visible from Paulina Peak), where you can walk around through gleaming, razor-sharp boulders made of black glass. The rim trail is an epic mountain bike ride, and the falls are also worth a visit.

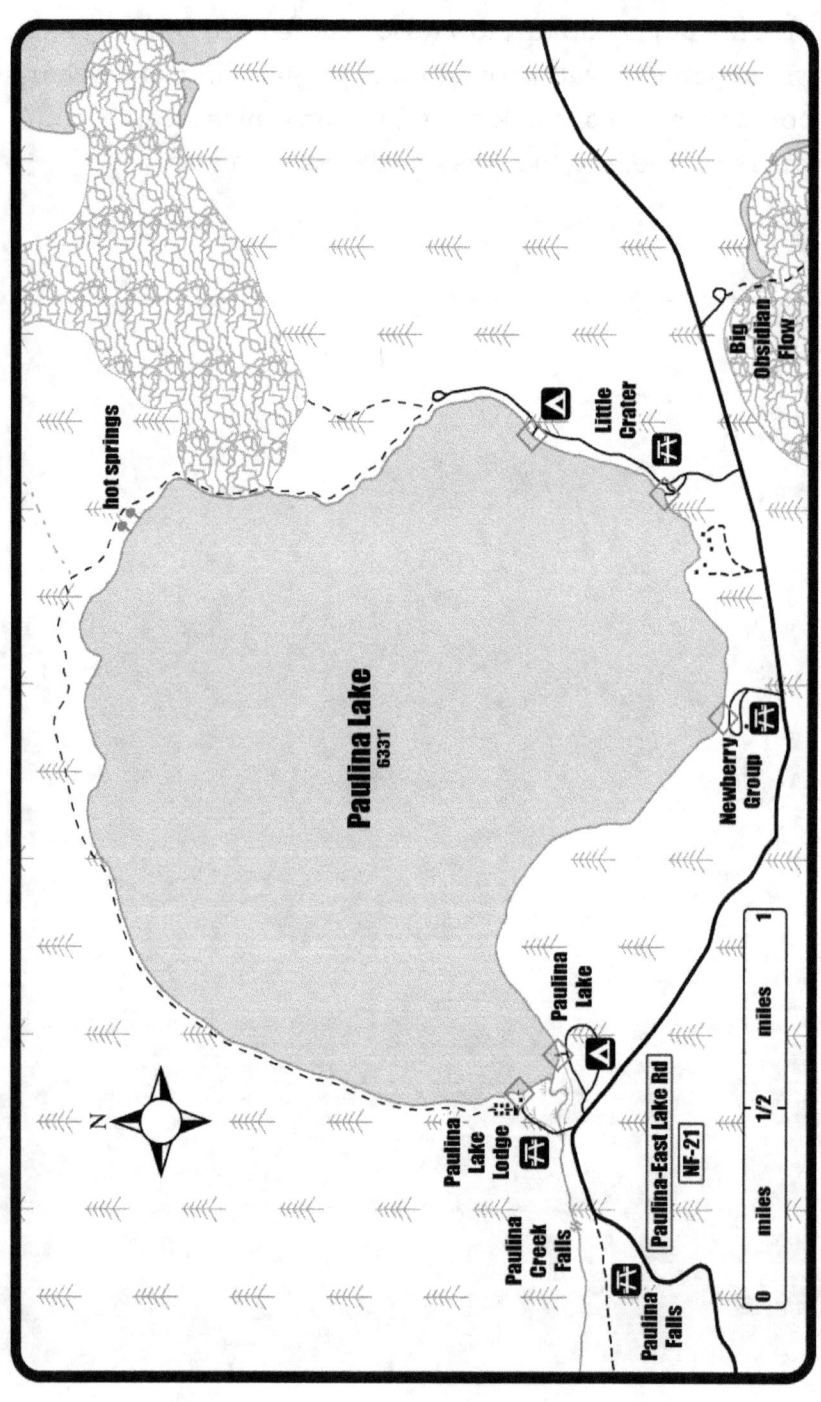

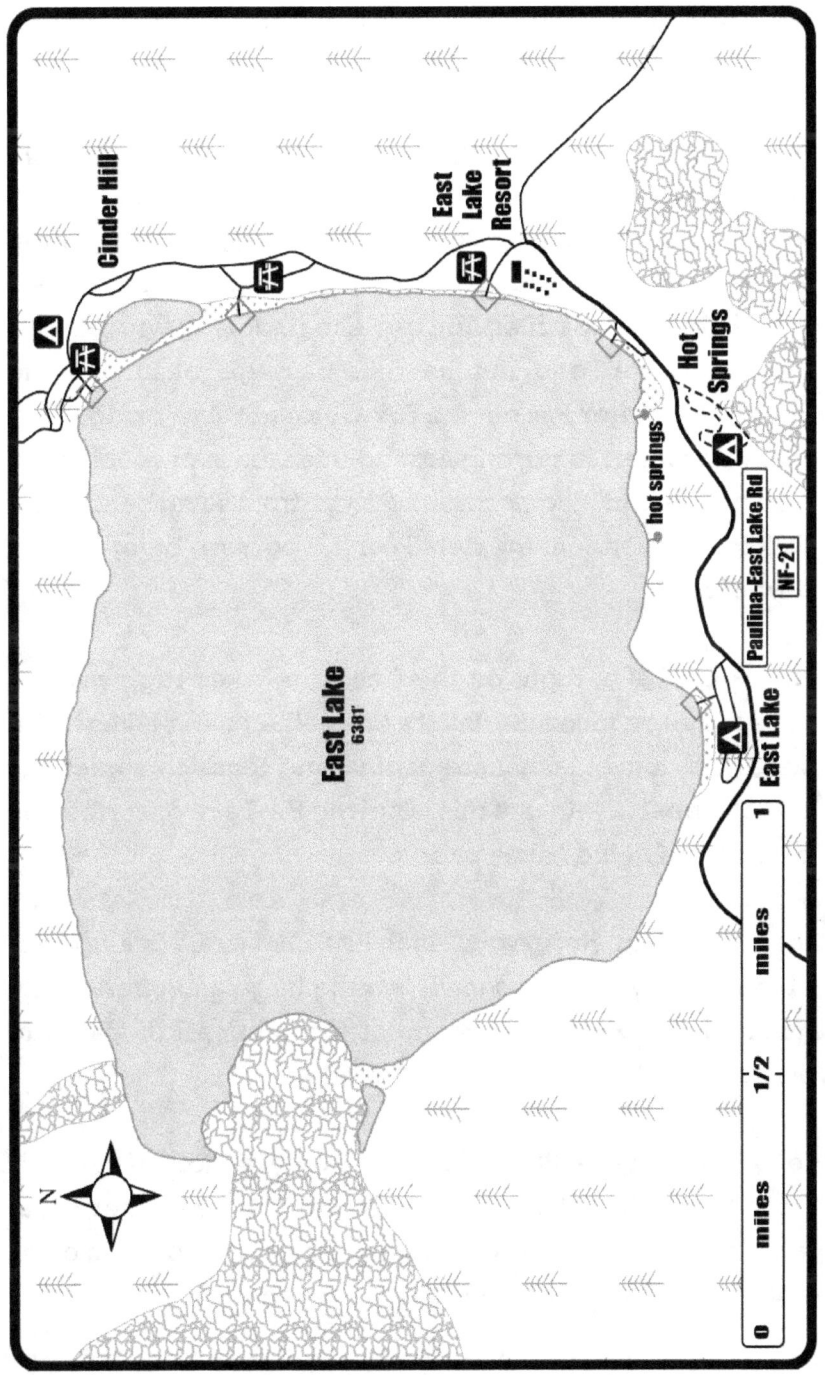

42. Other Good Places to Paddle – The High Cascade Lakes:

(a)   <u>Deschutes River at Bend</u>: This one isn't in the high lakes, but it is close. Tumalo Creek Kayak and Canoe in Bend rents SUPs, kayaks, and canoes. From there, you can paddle a few miles upriver through Bend before the river becomes impassible due to riffles. You can also paddle downriver and through Mirror Pond, but the "safe passage" channel at the Bend Whitewater Park at the SW Colorado Ave bridge isn't really flatwater, so porting around this area is probably necessary. You can also access the river from Riverbend Park. Talk to a local about the details of the portage before going downriver.

(b)   <u>Elk Lake</u>: Right on the Cascade Lakes Highway, Elk Lake is quite a nice lake. But it's one of the busier lakes in the state, with lots of lakeshore cabins, and tends to attract lots of motorboats. Note that this is not the Elk Lake described as part of the Olallie Lakes paddle.

(c)   <u>Wickiup Reservoir</u>: Much like Elk Lake, Wickiup Reservoir is busy but pleasant. It is quite large and offers many miles of paddling near many of the other High Cascade Lakes.

(d)   <u>Odell Lake</u>: Places like Odell only get left off the "featured" paddles list because there are so many other great lakes nearby. The lake is right on Highway 58 but has clear water and a forested shoreline.

(e) <u>Lake Billy Chinook:</u> Lake Billy Chinook is also not in the high lakes, but it is near them, and it is stunningly beautiful, ringed by sheer rock walls rising hundreds of feet above the lake. Although it feels like the paddles in eastern Oregon, it is right in the heart of the central Oregon population and is quite popular with motorboaters and waterskiiers. It's big enough to get some space from the crowds, but plan your visit for some time other than a warm weekend or summer holiday.

VII. Southern Oregon

43. Squaw Lakes:
A tiny, hidden beauty with sweet rope swings

The Squaw Lakes are hidden away at the top of the beautiful Applegate Valley, at the end of a long road just on the right side of the California border. The lakes are surrounded by steep slopes forested in dry oak, Manzanita, and fir. There is some nearby private land on the far eastern shore of Little Squaw, but otherwise the shorelines are public, undeveloped, and accessible. The water is warm, moderately clear, and still. The shallows are filled with aquatic plants and flowers. There is good fishing for rainbow and cutthroat trout, crappie, bluegill, largemouth bass, black bass, yellow perch, and catfish.

There is no vehicular access to either lakeshore, and motors are prohibited on both lakes. Fishers and hike-in campers visit, and the campsites often fill up during the height of the summer, but the feeling is calm and quiet. The only drawback to paddling the Squaw Lakes is their tiny size. You can paddle around Squaw in just 1.3 miles and Little Squaw in just 0.6 miles.

The road to Squaw Lake is gated roughly 200 yards from the shore, requiring paddlers to carry their watercraft and gear down (and up) a moderately steep slope. Access to Little Squaw Lake is similar, except it is via shorter but steeper trails, and the launch/return points are more primitive. As you can imagine, this portage requirement probably lowers the number of paddlers coming to the Squaw Lakes.

My favorite part about this paddle is the many rope swings on Squaw Lake. The lake has the perfect combination of steep, wooded shores and deep, warm, near-shore water. In fact, Squaw has the warmest water I encountered of all of the paddles described in this book. It is perhaps the best natural place to swim in the whole state.

My least favorite part about this paddle is the lakes' name. The term squaw is pejorative and many Native Americans find it offensive. At the request of the Confederated Tribes of Warm Springs, in 2001 the Oregon Legislature passed a law removing the term from over 170 geographical features across the state.

Since 2001, the Oregon Geographic Names Board has removed the term from many place names. For example, in 2015 it renamed a Squaw Lake in Harney County "Puhi-Pane Na-De Lake," which means "pretty blue lake."

But 15 years after this law passed, the Squaw Lakes are still the Squaw Lakes. Why? The name-change process occurs via proposals from the public. Anyone can propose a new name. If you do enjoy this paddle, consider submitting a proposed new name based on your experience. You can do so at the Oregon Geographic Names Board's website.

Difficulty: Easy; suitable for beginners who don't mind carrying their board or boat a little ways.

Distance: 1.3 to circle Squaw Lake and 0.6 miles to circle Little Squaw Lake.

Directions: From I-5 in Medford, take Highway 238 west for 14.5 miles. In the unincorporated town of Ruch, turn left onto Upper Applegate Rd. Follow Upper Applegate Rd for 15 miles to Applegate Lake. Turn left onto French Gulch Rd (across the dam) and go 1.4 miles, bear right onto NF-1075 (aka Squaw Creek Rd), and the lakes are ahead in 6.7 miles.

Launch/Return: There are informal launch areas on both lakes. No amenities. The closest amenities are at the Har-Tish General Store at the Har-Tish Campground on the western shore of Applegate Lake (0.6 miles past the turnoff onto French Gulch Rd). Note that there are two other options for carrying gear to the lakeshore. For $10, the camp host (if available) will haul gear for you in an ATV. For $5, you can rent a cart and carry it yourself.

Nearby Rental: None.

Nearby Camping: There are 19 hike-in campsites (4 designated for groups) around the lakes. 16 of the sites are on Squaw Lake, with two on Little Squaw Lake, and one on the connecting creek. Reservations must be made at least three days in advance at reserveamerica.com or 877-444-6777. $15/night. You must also check in at the Har-Tish General Store (see above) and take your reservation confirmation with you to the campsite.

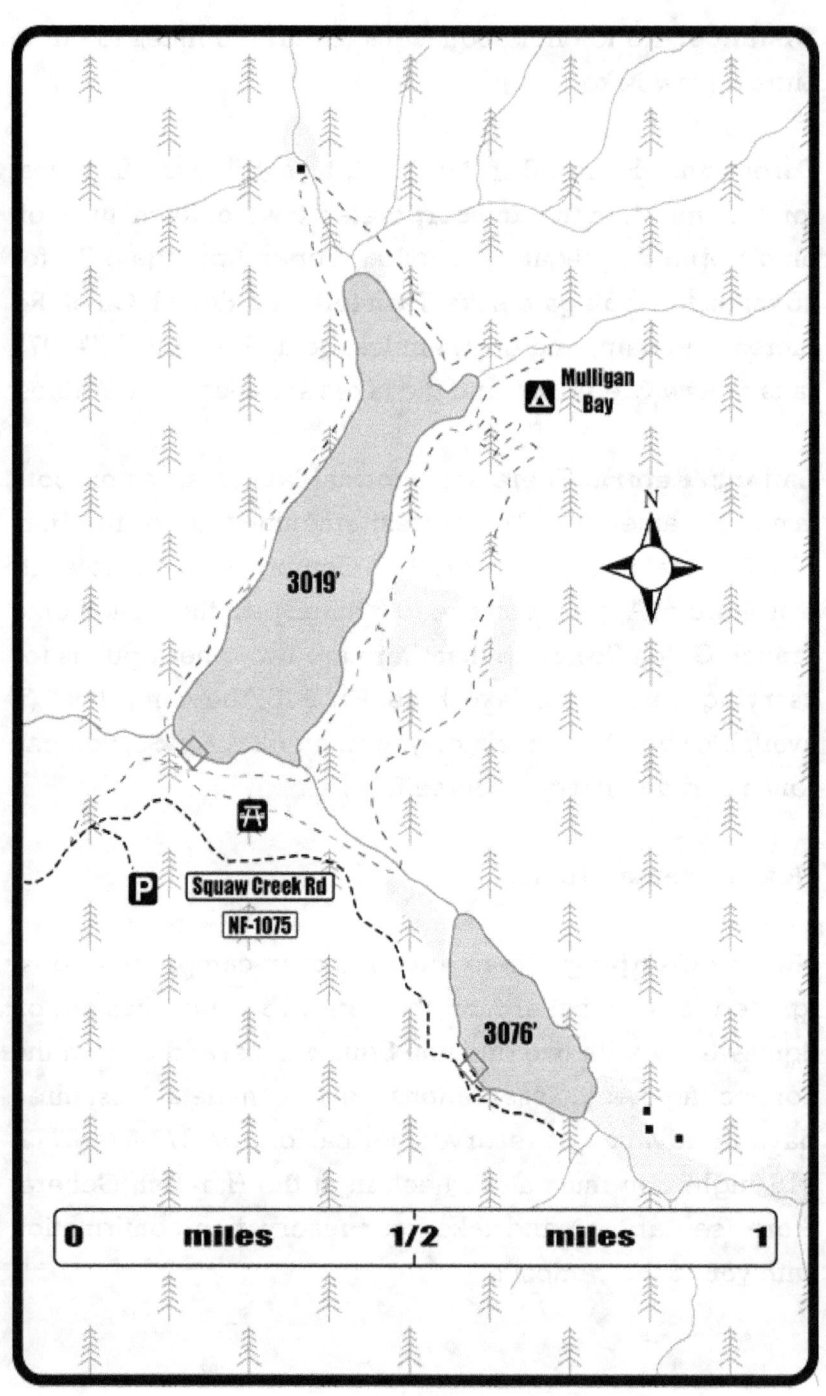

44. Wood River:
A challenging paddle on a crystal-clear, spring-fed creek

Wood River is a difficult paddle due to the combination of strong current, frequent snags in the river, frigid water, and a narrow, shallow, and twisting channel. Do this paddle only when you are very comfortable on the board, and only in warm weather. Consider kneeling on the sharper bends, which require fast and strong paddle strokes to change direction quickly. Also, this paddle should be done only as a downriver shuttle because paddling upriver for long distances in the current is extremely difficult.

Fortunately, the Wood River offers a relatively short but satisfying 3.9-mile mile shuttle paddle from Jackson F Kimball State Recreation Site at the headwaters to the Forest Service's Wood River Day Use Area. This paddle is definitely stretching the definition of "flatwater," but this place is too beautiful to leave out of a "best of Oregon" paddle book. Frankly, it's probably best suited to a kayak.

The Wood River comes, somehow, from Crater Lake. It flows underground for about 20 miles before emerging in a large spring, which is a beautiful blue pool surrounded by quaking aspen where this paddle starts. The water is crystal clear and so cold it is hard to believe it can maintain its liquid form. The launch point is a little below the headwaters spring, so paddle up and back on the river at this point to enjoy the entire headwaters spring area.

Downriver of the spring, the shoreline is mostly open meadow, with stands of ponderosa and lodgepole pine along the eastern shore. The banks were once wetlands but have since been converted into cow grazing pastures. The shoreline is mostly undeveloped, though there are some ranches along the way and occasionally structures near the shore. The meadows along the banks have blooming wildflowers in the early summer.

The Wood River is known as an excellent fly-fishing river (catch and release and barbless hooks only). It has populations of brook, brown, coastal rainbow, and Great Basin redband trout. You may also see beaver, river otter, and muskrats in the water, as well as martens, red and gray fox, bobcats, and black bear along the banks. Of course, there are also a great deal of waterfowl, including wood ducks, mallards, cinnamon teal, great egrets, meadowlarks, and yellow warblers. There are raptors too; bald eagles, osprey, and northern harriers.

The Wood River's name probably comes from all the wood in the river, and there is a lot. You will need to pick your line carefully at many spots. You will also need to read the channel to avoid shallow gravel bars in the lee of the many turns along the way. If you paddle early in the summer, you can enjoy higher water and avoid the worst of the snag hazards, but you will also face a greater current. So, choose your poison. The challenge comes with ample reward.

There is one spot about halfway along the route where you will need to crouch very low or port around a weir with metal bars across the river. Fortunately, you can see it coming well ahead and the port is only a few feet long.

You can watch a video of people kayaking the Wood River by searching on Youtube.

Difficulty: Advanced.

Distance: 3.9 miles downriver.

Directions: From the town of Ft Klamath on Highway 62, go north 2.4 miles and turn right onto Dixon Rd. You will soon cross part of the Wood River that is on this paddle route. In 1.6 miles, the road Ts. Go left and the entrance to Jackson F Kimball State Recreation Site is immediately on the left.

Launch/Return: Jackson F Kimball State Park. Parking, toilets. No water.

Nearby Rental: None.

Nearby Camping: The Jackson F Kimball State Recreation Site is on the paddle route and hosts 10 campsites.

Nearby Fun: You are just about 20 miles from Crater Lake National Park. Take the boat ride around Crater Lake, hike to the top of Mt Scott, or just enjoy views of the lake from the lodge.

You can also visit the Ft Klamath Museum, which is at the site of a historic US Army fort that operated from 1863 to 1889.

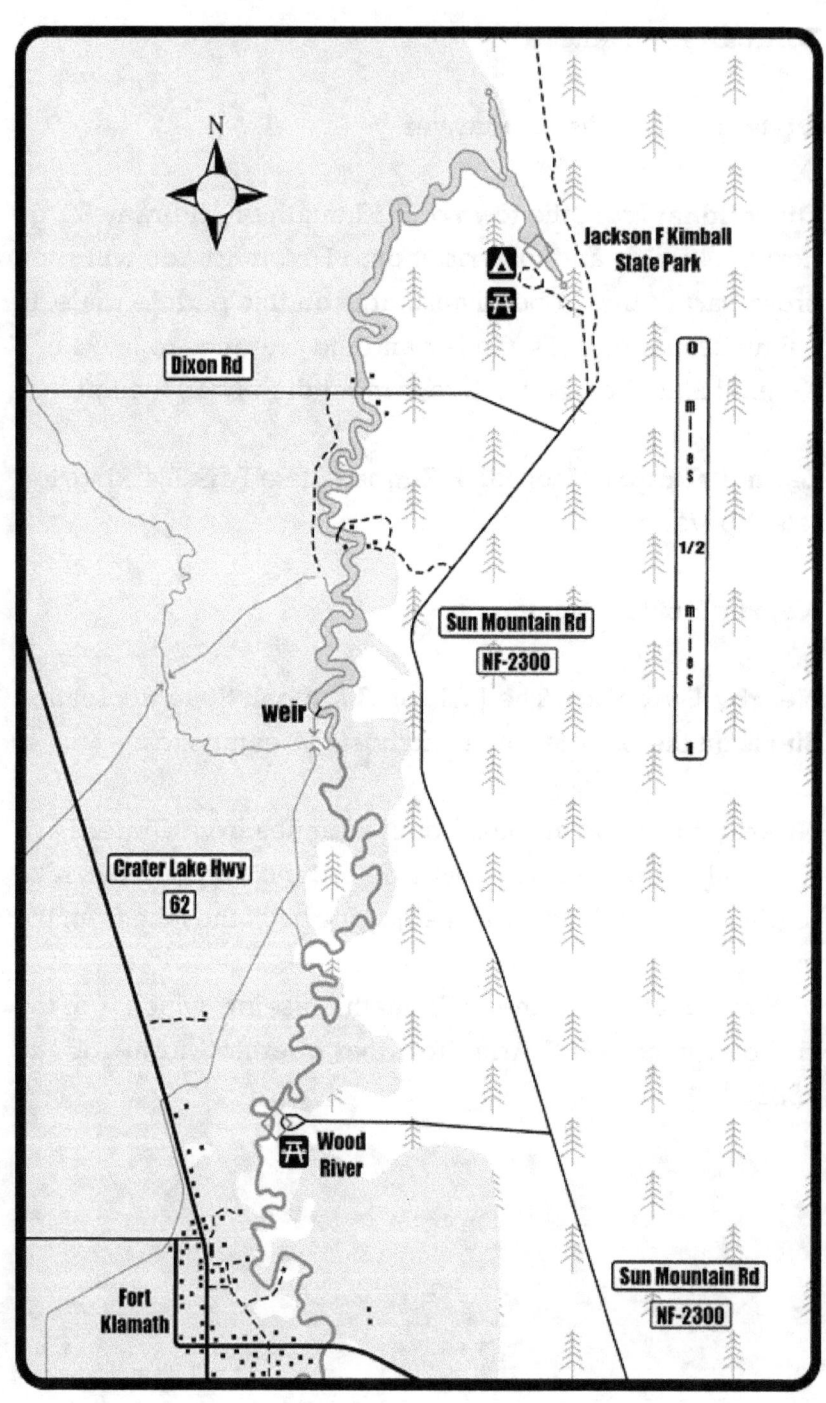

45. Upper Klamath Canoe Trail:
Endless wetlands filled with wildlife

When I was a kid growing up in the South, the bayou seemed to stretch forever. The wetlands in the Upper Klamath Lake are the only other place I have felt the infinity of wetland wilderness. There is no other paddle in this book, or anywhere in Oregon, like this one. The entire route goes through isolated wetlands filled with wildlife. Water traffic is limited – only the smallest boats can ply the bayous that comprise the canoe trail. While the wetlands seemingly extend forever to the east, there are good views of Mt McLoughlin as well.

The Upper Klamath marsh is massive; 15,000 acres of wetlands adjacent to Agency Lake and Upper Klamath Lake. Most of it is protected as part of the Upper Klamath National Wildlife Refuge, and the canoe trail extends into the Refuge. Be sure to stay on the trail when paddling. Areas within the refuge are closed to entry, except on the designated trail, to protect nesting birds.

The diversity of bird species found here is quite impressive. I counted nearly 30 species that are commonly reported, from huge American white pelicans to the tiny hermit warbler. The most common species are probably the wood duck, the red-winged blackbird, or the red-necked grebe, but there are also some big names, such as great egrets, osprey, and bald eagles. My favorite is the belted kingfisher, which can often be seen perched like a silent sentinel on posts and tall reeds before diving head-first into the water for fish and other aquatic prey.

The trail offers perhaps one of the best chances in Oregon to see beavers and river otters in the wild. If you visit in the spring, amongst the bullrushes and cattails you will see the huge yellow flowers of the wocus lily, also known as the Rocky Mountain pond lily. These beautiful flowers are common in Oregon wetlands and their seeds, ground into flour, were once a staple food for the Klamath people.

The trail is made up primarily of two southerly flowing creeks, though the current is negligible. Crystal Creek originates at Crystal County Park and diverges, with Recreation Creek to the west of the continuing Crystal Creek. Below the divergence, a gap in the wetlands known as Wocus Cut connects the two creeks, as does Pelican Bay, where both creeks end. There is 12.8 miles of paddling total in the area. Here is the mileage of each section, from north to south:

- Crystal Creek between Crystal Creek County Park and Malone Springs is 4.4 miles.
- Crystal Creek between Malone Springs and the divergence with Recreation Creek (north of Wocus Cut) is 2 miles.
- Crystal Creek from the divergence with Recreation Creek to the junction with Wocus Cut is 1.3 miles.
- Recreation Creek from the divergence with Crystal Creek to the junction with Wocus Cut is 1 mile.
- Recreation Creek from the junction with Wocus Cut to Rocky Point is 1 mile.
- Crystal Creek from the junction with Wocus Cut to Pelican Bay is 2 miles.
- Pelican Bay between Crystal Creek and Recreation Creek is 1.1 miles.

Water levels drop later in the summer and fall, which can cause navigability issues and exacerbate snag hazards. Wocus Cut often becomes impassible late in the year. The best time to paddle is late spring and early summer, but the mosquitos are brutal then. They are not as bad on the water, but at the launch sites you will need a double-coat of bug spray. The mosquitos are much less of a problem late in the season, but you may be in for a shorter paddle.

On the trail, look for small, brown signs sticking a few feet out of the water. They have a picture of a canoe and the words "CANOE TRAIL." Note that the stretch of Crystal Creek between Crystal Springs and Malone Springs is not part of the official canoe trail and so is not signed.

You can find videos of people paddling the Upper Klamath Canoe Trail on Youtube.

Difficulty: Easy to advanced, depending on distance.

Distance: 12.8 miles total, with lots of different length options. Can even be done as a one-directional float (north to south).

Directions: Westside Road is off Highway 140 25 miles west of Klamath Falls, and 43.5 miles east of White City (measuring from either end of Highway 140). Turn north onto Westside Road and go 3.3 miles to reach Rocky Point, 6.4 miles to reach Malone Springs, and 10.3 miles to reach Crystal Creek.

Launch/Return:
Crystal Creek County Park: Toilets, parking. No water.

Malone Springs Day Use Area: Toilets, parking. No water.

Rocky Point Day Use Area: Toilets, parking. No water. The adjacent Rocky Point Resort has a restaurant and general store.

Nearby Rental/Tours: Rocky Point Resort (adjacent to the Rocky Point Day Use Area) rents canoes, kayaks, and paddle boats.

Nearby Camping: Rocky Point Resort (adjacent to the Rocky Point Day Use Area) rents campsites and cabins.

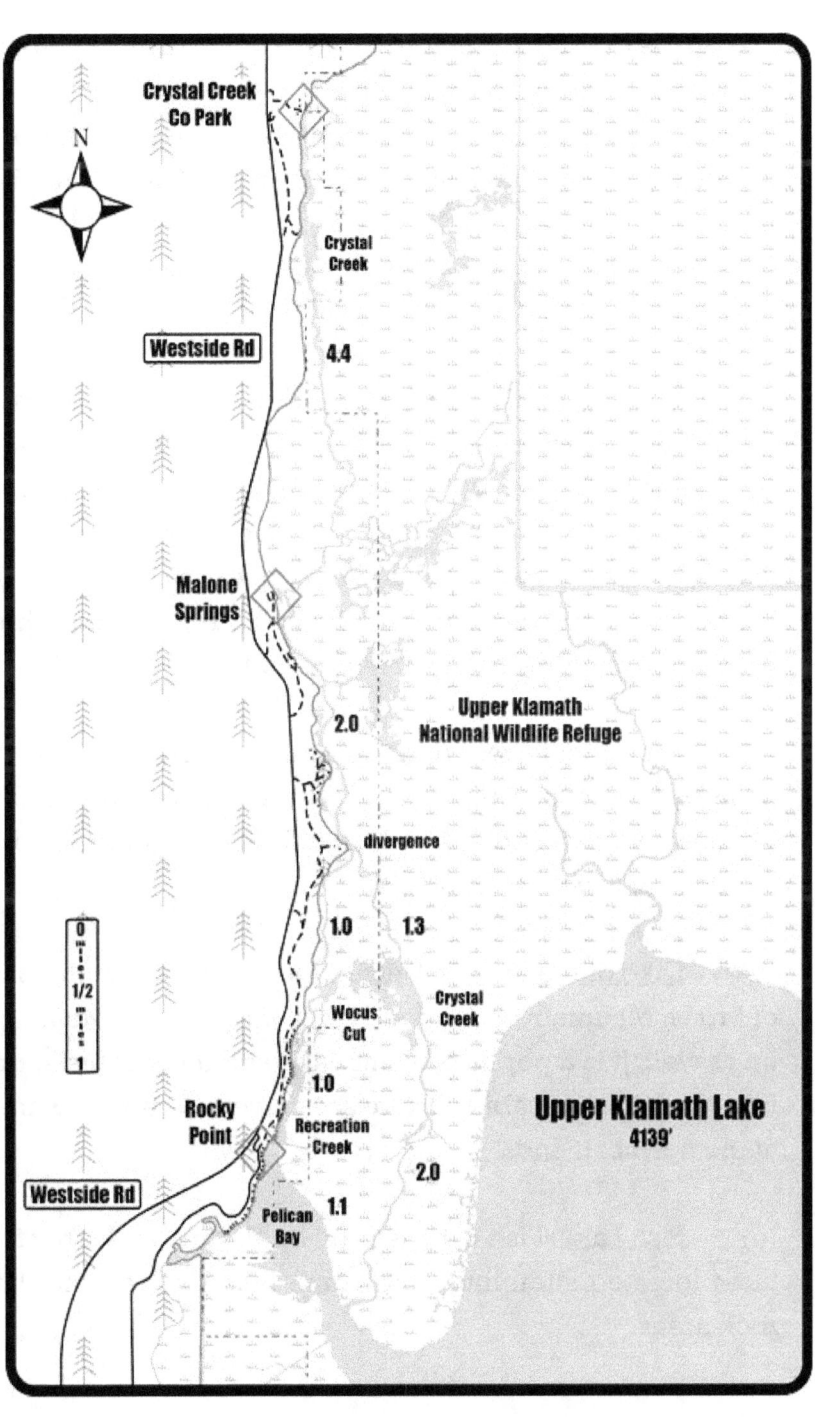

46. Other Good Places to Paddle – Southern Oregon

(a)   Applegate Lake: Applegate Lake is an isolated reservoir near the California border west of Medford/Ashland and on the way to the Squaw Lakes paddle. It tends to get busy only on summer weekends and has on-site kayak rentals.

(b)   Emigrant Lake: Emigrant Lake is a large reservoir just a few miles southeast of Ashland. It sees a good deal of recreational use, but has a lot of secluded coves, nice views, and some good wetland areas at both southern arms of the lake. The best access point for paddlers is probably the Songer Wayside, off Highway 66, the Green Springs Highway, on the southeastern corner of the lake.

(c)   Fourmile Lake: Fourmile Lake is a reservoir at the base of Mt McLoughlin. It sees less motorized traffic than the nearby Lake of the Woods and Fish Lake and has some beaches at lower water levels.

(d)   Lake of the Woods: Lake of the Woods sits at the base of Brown Mountain with good views of nearby Mt McLoughlin as well. It is a popular fishing lake and most of the shoreline hosts fishing cabins. There are some nice wetland areas at the northern end.

(e)   Fish Lake: Fish Lake is right on Highway 140, but features forested shorelines and some nice wetland and lava rock areas.

(f) <u>Upper Klamath Lake</u>: Upper Klamath Lake is gigantic. There are many miles of paddling between the Upper Klamath Canoe Trail at the northern end and the town of Klamath Falls at the southern end, with lots of coves to explore and even a couple of islands. But it is "open water," windy and wavy in the afternoons, with plenty of motorized traffic during the summer.

VIII. Eastern Oregon

47. Wallowa Lake:
A majestic lake in The Alps of Oregon

The majesty of Wallowa Lake is difficult to capture in words. It sits snugly surrounded by the Wallowa Mountains, frequently referred to as "The Alps of Oregon," and the views of these snow-capped peaks from the northern end of the lake are fantastic. The lake is a textbook-quality example of what's known as a ribbon lake, a finger-shaped lake formed by a glacier. The huge moraine left by the glacier towers 900 feet over the lake's eastern shore.

The water is so clear, it looks like the glacier melted only yesterday. Look for the huge boulders submerged near the northwestern shore of the lake. They were carried here near the end of the last Ice Age by the glaciers coming down the steep mountain valleys. You may also see some of the fat resident kokanee salmon hanging out in the shallows.

Wallowa is large enough for a full day of paddling – a trip around the lake is about 8 miles. There are small beaches at either end of the lake, and floating island docks around the middle of the lake on the eastern side (most of which are private – look for signs prohibiting landing/use). There are not a lot of other places to land, due to a shoreline that is either rocky, private, or both. If you want to get a more intimate feel for the water, look for the rope swing near the island docks on the eastern shore.

Wallowa is the only lake in Oregon where you will see paragliders dropping seemingly out of nowhere, flying right over your head, going for a landing spot on the south shore. Perhaps the only downside is that motors are allowed, and the lake is pretty popular with fishers and motorboaters. On the bright side, the lake is big enough to get some space, and there are a lot of other fun things to do near the lake. For the best views, paddle clockwise around the lake. The lake is a popular vacation destination regionally and there are hotels, restaurants, and stores at the south end of the lake.

Although Wallowa Lake is natural, its outlet, at the northern end of the lake, was dammed in 1916. The water is used for irrigation, supporting most of the economic activity in Wallowa County. Unfortunately, the dam killed the entire native salmon run. That is now being remedied with the introduction of fish passage. The lake hosts a native resident population of kokanee, as well as stocked rainbow trout.

Difficulty: Easy to moderate, depending on distance. Suitable for beginners.

Distance: 7.9 miles to circle the lake.

Directions: From I-5 in La Grande, take Highway 82 north and east, over the Wallowas, until the end of the road. Highway 82 goes through the small towns of Wallowa, Lostine, Enterprise, and Joseph before turning into Highway 351 and reaching the lake in 71 miles.

Launch/Return:
Wallowa County Park: Toilets, parking. No water. No day use fee. Amenities are available in Joseph, just a mile north.

Wallowa Lake State Park: Toilets, parking. No water. No day use fee. Amenities are available nearby at the south end of the lake.

Nearby Rental: The Wallowa Lake Marina, adjacent to Wallowa Lake State Park at the south end of the lake, rents SUPs, kayaks, canoes, and row boats.

Nearby Camping: Wallowa Lake State Park is at the south end of the lake. There are also several hotels at the southern end of the lake.

Nearby Fun: Imagine if you could drive to the bottom of the Grand Canyon. Well, Hells Canyon is even deeper than the Grand Canyon, and you can drive to the bottom of it, at least if you have a high-clearance four-wheel drive vehicle. From Joseph, take the Imnaha Highway west, then turn north onto Little Sheep Creek Highway to the village of Imnaha. From there, Lower Imnaha Rd gets progressively rougher, skirting cliff edges, until reaching the bottom of the canyon, the Snake River at Dug Bar Landing. This last 25 miles takes nearly three hours to traverse. Call or stop by the Hells Canyon Ranger Station in Joseph for information on road conditions before going.

If you are brave enough to drive this road, you will be rewarded with amazing views of the deepest river gorge in North America, as well as likely sightings of big horn sheep and rattlesnakes. You may also see rafters and jet boats on the river. There is a campground here, trails along the river and up to an overlooking cliff, and an abandoned mine site. This place is also known as Nez Perce Crossing, as it was a traditional crossing place for the native Nez Perce and the place where the legendary Chief Joseph lead the remaining Nez Perce people out of the Wallowa Valley for the final time under threat of murder at the hands of the US Army.

At the south end of the lake, take the Wallowa Lake Tramway up to over 8,000 feet of elevation at the top of Mt Howard for fantastic views of Hells Canyon and Washington and Idaho beyond. There are some nice short trails at the top, allowing you to get a taste of the alpine environment of the Wallowas.

For a more close up look at the high country in the Wallowas, there are some excellent hiking trails leaving from the south end of the lake into the Eagle Cap Wilderness. You can even hire a guide and visit the Eagle Cap on horseback.

Perhaps my favorite part about the Wallowa country, though, is my favorite beer: Terminal Gravity IPA. The brewery and pub is in Enterprise, just a few miles north of the lake. Every time I visit, I make a pilgrimage there, enjoying a pint or three at one of the picnic tables next to the creek with my doggie at my feet. My buddy from Joseph calls it "God's Country," and if there is such a thing, he's right.

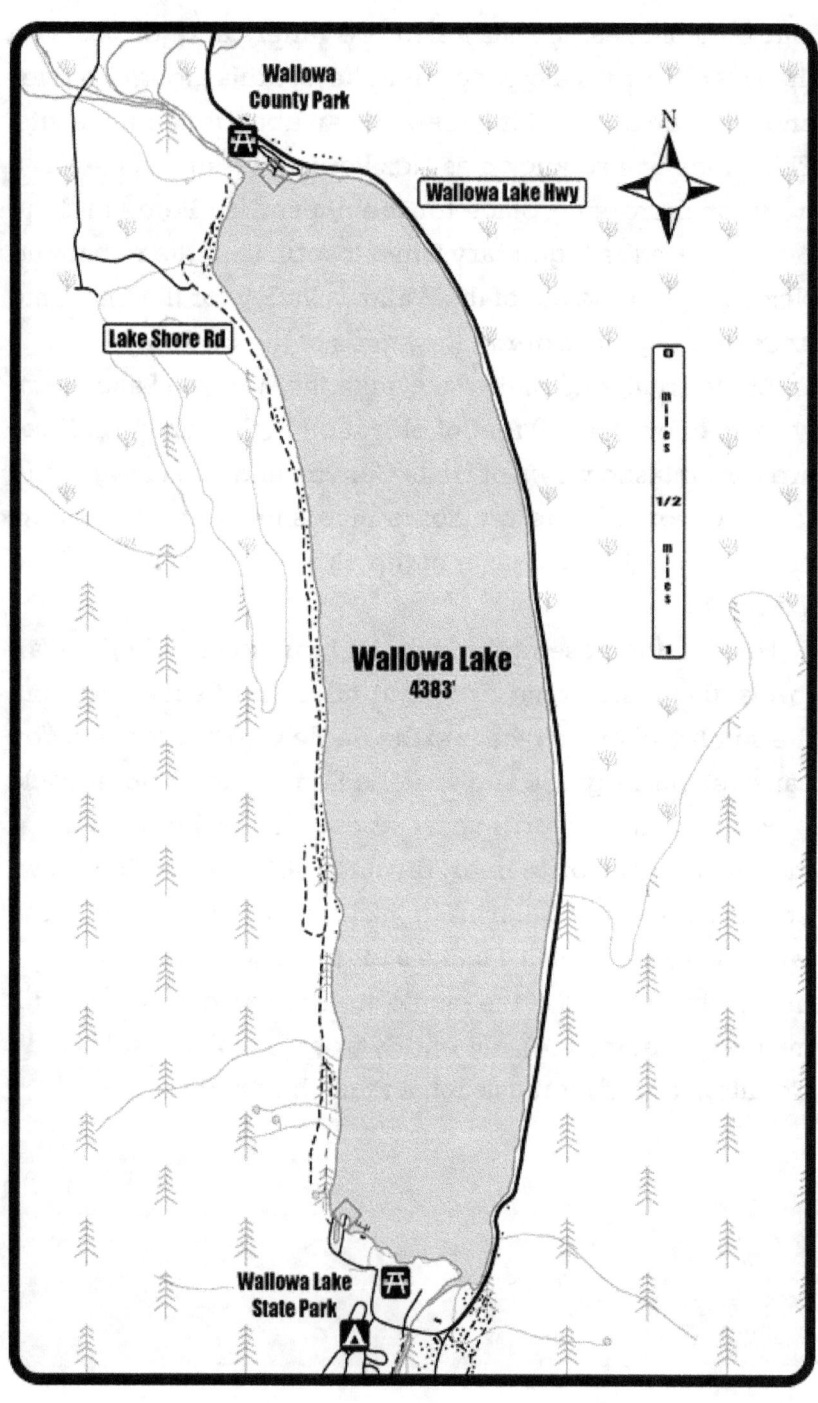

48. Hells Canyon Reservoir – Big Bar:
Paddle through the deepest gorge in North America

Hells Canyon is the deepest gorge in North America. Deeper even than the fabled Grand Canyon, Hells Canyon is nearly 8,000 feet from top to bottom, where the Snake River courses its way to the Columbia. It is extremely steep, rugged country, mostly inaccessible by road, and offers legendary whitewater river runs. It defeated many European explorers trying to cross the continent, and now forms part of the border between Oregon, Washington, and Idaho.

Unfortunately for the Northwest's once-prolific salmon population and other riverine species, the Snake has been dammed in the upper reaches of the canyon. The Brownlee Dam, Oxbow Dam, and Hells Canyon Dam produce lots of electricity, which is "cheap" as long as you don't factor in the true costs of the dams, but they also provide areas for flatwater paddling in the canyon. Between Hells Canyon Dam below and Oxbow Dam above, this stretch of river is essentially a lake (and technically a reservoir).

This paddle is, unique, epically beautiful, and remote. The current is practically nonexistent, river traffic is light (mostly fishers), and the paddling is endless, with lots of coves, side canyons, and islands to explore. There are several riverside campsites, including many in an old orchard, at Big Bar. And the entire adventure takes place surrounded by cliffs and rock spires stretching thousands of feet overhead.

A mini-gold rush started here in the 1860s after nuggets were panned out of several of the area bars. Lots of holes, or "adits," as they're called, were dug in the canyon walls. You can still see many of them today on the drive in. In the 1880s,

Europeans tried to settle in the area, hence the orchard and graveyard at Big Bar, but the area was (rather obviously) not suited to farming or ranching. We explored the remains of an old homestead on the far shore (in Oregon) and saw a flock of wild turkeys making their way in a long line down the hill to drink from the river. Big Bar (the island) looks tempting, but it is very difficult to land upon, and nearly inaccessible.

The downsides to paddling here are poor water quality and excessive heat in the summer. When the water stagnates and heats up behind the dam, the area is prone to algae blooms, which are smelly and can be harmful to humans and deadly to dogs. If the water looks like green soup, do not touch it. Wash immediately if you get any on you. If your dog drinks any contaminated water, head straight for the emergency vet. You can check with the Idaho Department of Environmental Quality on conditions before going, but the best way to avoid algae is to avoid paddling here on the hottest days of the year.

There are two other places to launch/return between Hells Canyon Dam and Oxbow Dam. Eagle Bar, an informal day use area, is 7 miles downriver from Big Bar, and Hells Canyon Campground is 7.5 miles upriver. These access points allow nearly 22 miles of paddling between Copperfield and Oxbow Dam and Hells Canyon Dam. Even though the current is slight, this would be a great place for a downriver float.

I am aware that the launch/return point for this paddle is technically in Idaho. Shhhh!

Difficulty: Easy to advanced, depending on distance.

Distance: 2 to 22 miles. A trip around the Big Bar island is about a mile from the nearest launch/return point at Big Bar.

Directions: From I-5 in Baker City, take Highway 86 west for 67 miles before reaching the Snake River at the town of Copperfield. Turn right to cross the river (into Idaho), then immediately left on Hells Canyon Rd. Follow Hells Canyon Rd through the canyon for 13 miles before reaching Big Bar.

Launch/Return: Big Bar Camping Area. Parking, toilets. No water. No camping or day use fee. Note that there may be lots of rotting fruit on the ground at the northern campsites, depending on the time of year.

Nearby Rental: None.

Nearby Camping: Aside from the Big Bar Camping Area, the Hells Canyon Campground is 7.5 miles back south on Hells Canyon Rd, and Copperfield Park campground at Copperfield.

Nearby Fun: You've come this far down the canyon, so drive another 9 miles until the road ends at the Hells Canyon Dam. The Hells Canyon Creek Visitor Center is located just below the dam, and has interesting information on the river, canyon, and dam. From there you can get an idea of how the river once was, cascading whitewater deserving of the "Mad River" nickname.

The side canyon at Big Bar, home to Allison Creek, has a hike up to a nice overlook you can do right from the campground.

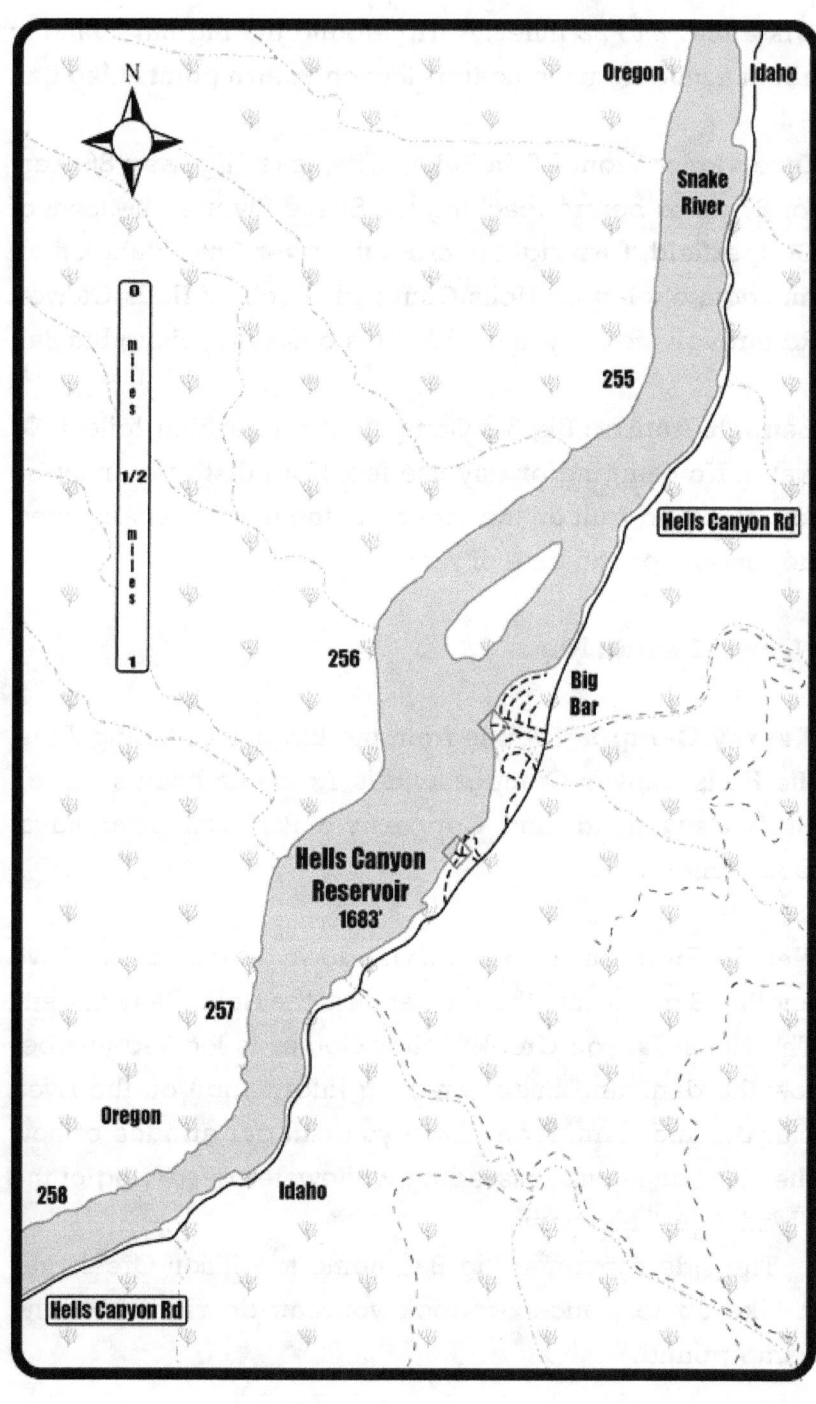

49. Hells Canyon Reservoir – Oxbow Dam: Paddle through the deepest gorge in North America, Part II

Near the top of Hells Canyon, far below the peaks of Idaho's Seven Devils Mountains, the Snake River does two quick one hundred-eighty degree turns through the rocks, making a classic oxbow bend. Idaho Power built one of its dams here in 1961. Between the Oxbow Dam and the small town of Copperfield is a relatively calm, two- to three-mile stretch of river through the sheer cliffs of the canyon.

This is the second paddle in Hells Canyon in this book. If you want to know more about the area, read the previous entry (Hells Canyon Reservoir – Big Bar). This paddle sees little water traffic. There are some small beaches along the route, and usually only fishers for company. Be sure to steer clear of any of the dam structures.

The launch/return point at the Copperfield Boat Launch makes for a more advanced paddle, both because of distance and because of stronger current downriver of the dam powerhouse, where water is released in a torrent from the dam. You should only launch from here if you are an advanced paddler and are looking for a more challenging paddle. From Copperfield Boat Launch, around the bend to the dam and back is 7.4 miles, but of course the return trip is easier because you are going with the current. Round-trip from the unnamed launch/return point across from the powerhouse to the dam is 5 miles, and the round-trip from the unnamed launch/return point on the peninsula to the dam is 2.4 miles.

Yes, two of the recommended launch/return points are technically in Idaho, but if you have to go to Idaho this is a pretty good reason.

Difficulty: Moderate to advanced, depending on the launch/return point (see above).

Distance: 7.4, 5, or 2.4 miles round-trip to the dam from the three launch points shown on the map, respectively.

Directions: From I-5 in Baker City, take Highway 86 west for 67 miles before reaching the Snake River at the town of Copperfield. To reach the Copperfield Boat Launch, continue on the road (the name turns to Homestead Rd here) for another 0.6 miles and find the boat launch on the right. To reach the unnamed launch/return point across from the powerhouse, turn right to cross the river (into Idaho), then immediately right again and go 0.4 miles to find the unnamed pullout on the right. To reach the unnamed launch/return point on the peninsula, turn right at Copperfield to stay on Highway 86. Turn left immediately onto Spillway Rd and go 0.9 miles. Turn left at the unsigned dirt road and go another 0.8 miles along the peninsula to reach the launch/return point.

Launch/Return: See the map and the description above. None of the launch/return points have any facilities.

Nearby Rental: None.

Nearby Camping: Copperfield Park has campsites. There are two campgrounds downriver on the Oregon (west) side.

Westfall Campground is a mile or so downriver of Copperfield, and Ashby Creek is about 8 miles. On the Idaho side, Hells Canyon Campground is 7.5 miles downriver from Copperfield.

Nearby Fun: You can drive through the canyon for another 22 miles downriver from Copperfield on the Idaho side (Hells Canyon Rd). The drive is scenic, there is another paddle to do there (Hells Canyon – Big Bar), and at the road's end is Hells Canyon Dam. The Hells Canyon Creek Visitor Center is located just below the dam, and has interesting information on the river, canyon, and dam. From there you can get an idea of how the river once was, cascading whitewater deserving of the "Mad River" nickname.

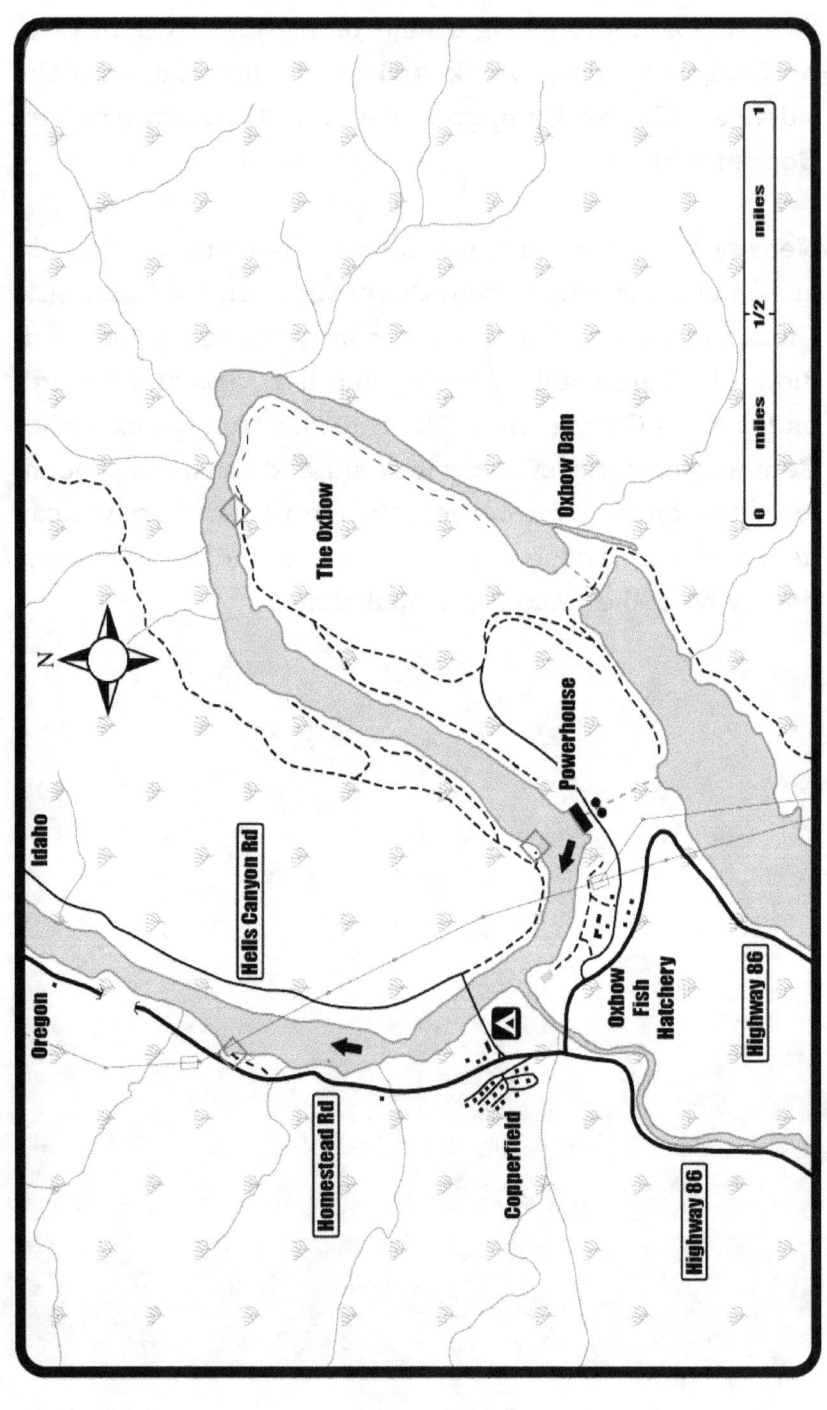

50. Powder River / Brownlee Reservoir: A remote desert canyon at The Crappie Capital of the Northwest

On the south side of the Wallowa Mountains in eastern Oregon, the Powder River flows into the Snake River and into the upper reaches of Hells Canyon. Due to the Brownlee Dam, which is downriver of the Powder-Snake confluence, the rivers back up, forming a nearly current-less riverine reservoir that stretches upriver for some 58 miles.

This paddle lies in the approximately seven-mile stretch of the lower Powder River between Richland and the Snake River. This side-canyon is extremely remote and nearly roadless. The shores of the reservoir are brown-sage hills with a green tint in the spring and the occasional cow wandering around. All of the water traffic are fishers going for trout and crappie (pronounced "crop-ie") here in "The Crappie Capital of the Northwest." Until this book becomes a bestseller, you are likely to be the only recreational paddler when you visit.

Difficulty: Easy to advanced, depending on distance.

Distance: 12.8 miles round-trip from the launch/return point to the confluence of the Powder River and the Snake River.

Directions: From I-5 in Baker City, take Highway 86 west for 39 miles to Richland. At Richland, turn right onto Holcomb Rd, following the signs for Hewitt Park. Bear left after 1.1 miles and the launch/return point is straight ahead.

Launch/Return: Hewitt Park. Parking, toilets, water, shower, wifi. Address is 41132 Robinette Rd, Richland, OR 97870. Day use fee.

Nearby Rental: None.

Nearby Camping: Hewitt Park (see above).

Nearby Fun: The BLM's Oregon Trail Interpretive Site is on the way to this paddle, just outside of Baker City. The Site is located on the actual trail and overlooks the Grande Ronde Valley, allowing visitors to share what would have been a very welcome site for weary pioneers, their first views of the Oregon Country. The site includes restored pioneer wagons circled around a campfire as well as indoor exhibits.

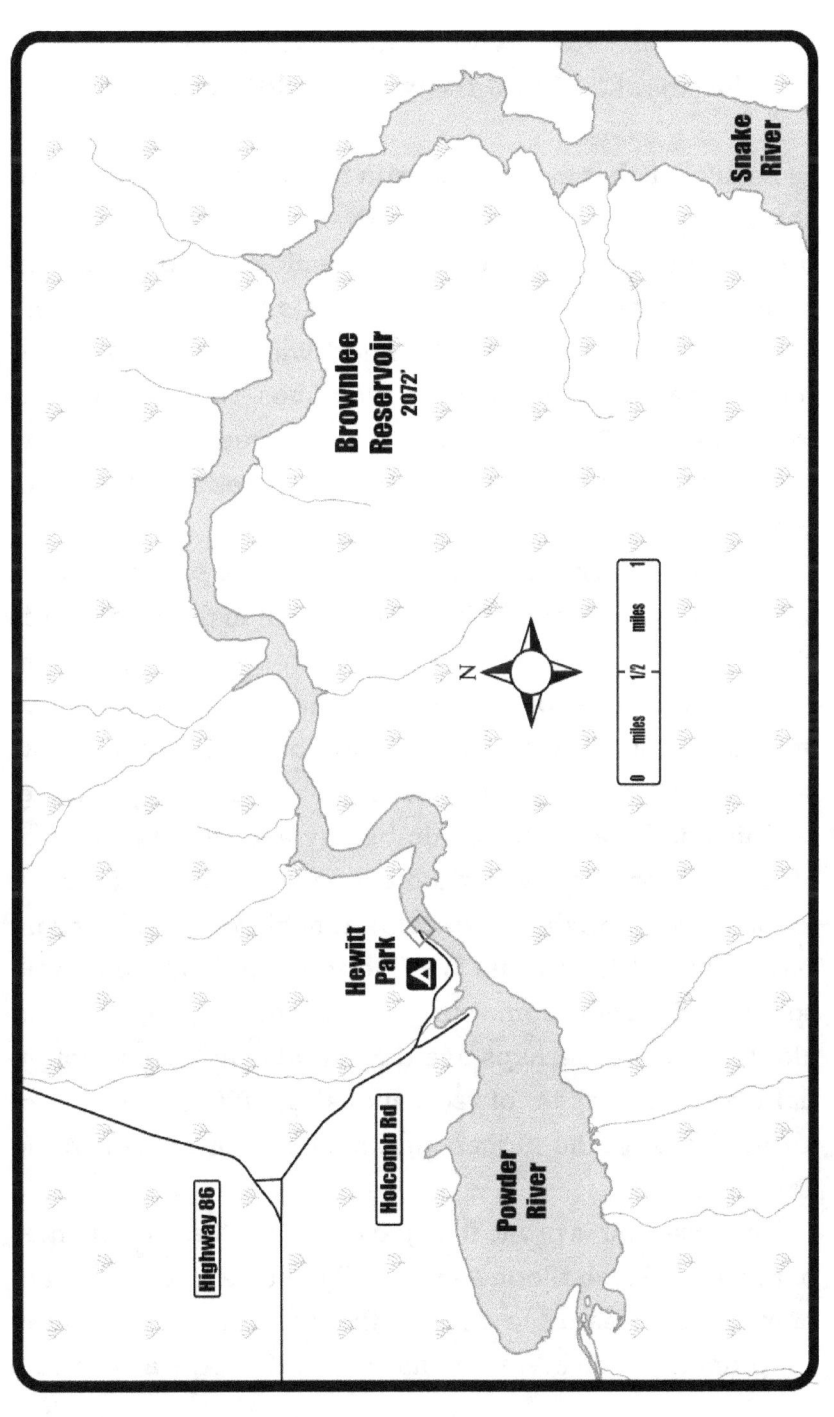

51. Owyhee Reservoir:
The most isolated flatwater paddle in Oregon

Leslie Gulch is a desert canyon filled with towering crimson rock spires that jut strikingly into the sky. The drive down the canyon is dangerously scenic and worth the trip by itself. At the bottom of the canyon is Owyhee Reservoir, another steep desert canyon lined with similarly-striking rock formations in a range of ruddy hues. The reservoir extends for over 30 miles and is very isolated. There are few access points into the canyon and the shores are almost entirely roadless.

Owyhee Reservoir offers nearly limitless paddling in an awe-inspiring desert setting. The current in the reservoir is slack, and the immense rock fins along the lakeshore blunt the winds. The remoteness of the area virtually guarantees you will enjoy considerable solitude on your paddle. I saw only one other party on the river in an entire day of paddling.

This combination of scenic beauty and remoteness creates the potential for a world-class paddle, but water quality tends to be poor, thanks to cattle ranching on the adjacent public lands. This paddle is a "hidden gem," but it could be so much more with some simple regulation of cattle grazing along the shore. Perhaps one day the real and future potential economic impact of recreational paddling will prompt a re-thinking of the highest and best use for areas like the Owyhee.

The reservoir is prone to algae blooms at the hottest times of the year. Algae blooms are smelly and can be harmful to humans and deadly to dogs. If the water looks like green soup, do not touch it. Wash immediately if you get any on you.

If your dog drinks any contaminated water, head straight for the emergency vet. You can check with the Oregon Department of Environmental Quality on conditions before going, but the best way to avoid algae is to avoid paddling here on the hottest days of the year.

Difficulty: Easy to advanced, depending on distance.

Distance: 2 to 20 miles.

Directions: From I-84 in Ontario, go east into Idaho. Take Exit 3 and go south on US Highway 95. In 18 miles, just after the town of Parma, turn right to continue south on Highway 95. Continue south on Highway 95 for another 18.5 miles before turning right again to stay on Highway 95. Go south on Highway 95 for another 21 miles and turn right onto McBride Creek Rd (dirt). Follow the sign for Leslie Gulch. From here, you will cross back into Oregon and go another 24.6 miles before reaching the campground.

Launch/Return: Leslie Gulch Campground. Toilets, parking. No water. No day use fee.

Nearby Rental: None.

Nearby Camping: Leslie Gulch Campground.

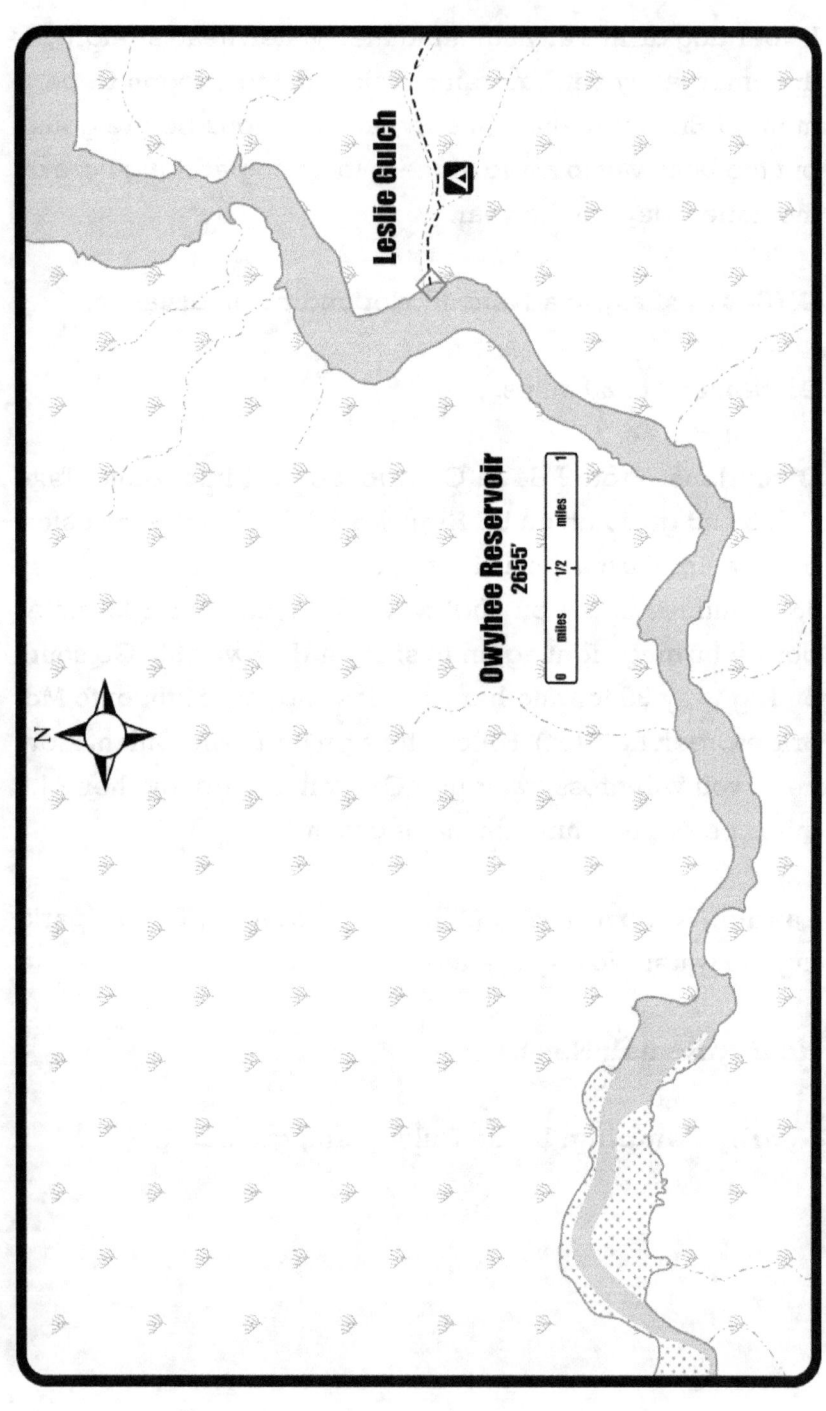

Bibliography

Pertinent information in this book was taken from the following sources:

Engeman, RH. The Oregon Companion: An Historical Gazeteer of the Useful, the Curious, and the Arcane. Portland, OR: Timber Press, Inc. 2009. Print.

Franklin, JF. Gold Lake Bog Research Natural Area. Federal Research Natural Areas in Oregon and Washington: A Guidebook for Scientists and Educators. Portland, OR: Pacific Northwest Forest and Range Experiment Station, Portland, Oregon. 1972. Print.

Giordano, P & the Willamette Kayak and Canoe Club. Soggy Sneakers: A Paddler's Guide to Oregon's Rivers. Seattle: The Mountaineers Books. 2004. Print.

Hanley, M. & Lucia, E. Owyhee Trails: The West's Forgotten Corner. Caldwell, ID: Caxton Press. 2008. Print.

Johnson, DM, Petersen, RR, Lycan, DR, Sweet, JW, Neuhaus, ME, Schaedel, AL. Atlas of Oregon Lakes. Corvallis, OR: Oregon State University Press. 1985. Print.

Landers, R & Hansen, D. Paddle Routes of the Inland Northwest: 50 Flatwater and Whitewater Trips for Canoe & Kayak. Seattle, WA: The Mountaineers. 1998. Print.

Marcus, B. The Art of State Up Paddling: A Complete Guide to SUP on Lakes, Rivers, and Oceans. Guilford, CT: Morris Book Publishing, LLC. 2012. Print.

Palmer, T. Field Guide to Oregon Rivers. Corvallis, OR: Oregon State University Press. 2014. Print.

Thollander, E. Back Roads of Oregon. New York: Clarkson N Potter, Inc. 1979. Print.

Willamette Riverkeeper. Willamette River Water Trail Guide (Vol. 1 & 2). Portland, OR: Willamete Riverkeeper. 2009. Print.

Williams, T. The Willamette River Field Guide: 200 Miles of Adventure from the Cascades to the Columbia. Portland, OR: Timber Press, Inc. 2009. Print.

www.ingramcontent.com/pod-product-compliance
Lightning Source LLC
Chambersburg PA
CBHW070602300426
44113CB00010B/1370